Springfield

Worcester

Boston

Hartford

New Haven

Providence

New York

THE SPREADING CITY

MAP SUPERIMPOSED ON PHOTOGRAPH OF SUBURBAN
DEVELOPMENT BEGINNING IN FARMLAND OF RARITAN
TOWNSHIP, HUNTERDON COUNTY, NEW JERSEY

N

W

E

S

MILES

0   25   5

D0354128

Through the Great City

Books by Anthony Bailey

MAKING PROGRESS

THE MOTHER TONGUE

THE INSIDE PASSAGE

THROUGH THE GREAT CITY

by Anthony Bailey

THE MACMILLAN COMPANY, NEW YORK

Library of Congress Catalog Card Number: 67-13585

First Printing

The Macmillan Company, New York
Collier-Macmillan Canada Ltd., Toronto, Ontario

Printed in the United States of America

In Memoriam:
Roy Bower,
American Consul

Contents

Tight fit is what shapes things definitely; with a loose fit you get no results, and America is redolent of loose fits everywhere.

—*William James*

Let the reader understand that he is invited to travel with an honest growler.

—*Frederick Law Olmstead*

Inextricable lands! the clutch'd together!

—*Walt Whitman*

Through the Great City

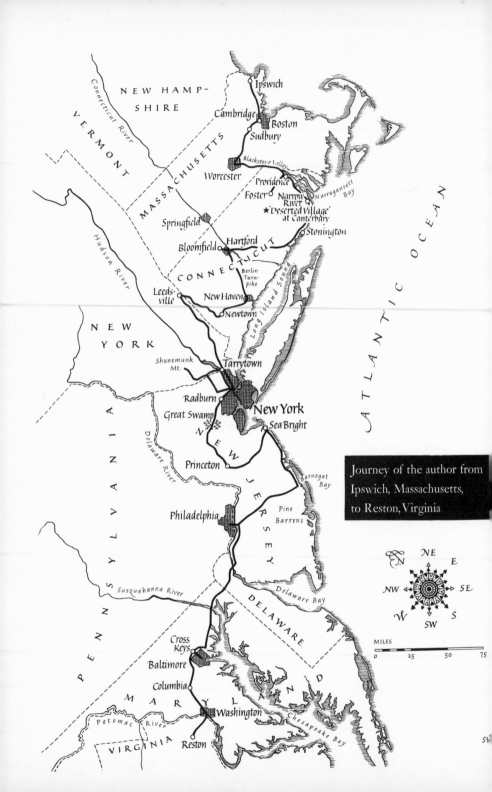

NEW HAMP-SHIRE

VERMONT

MASSACHUSETTS

Connecticut River

Ipswich

Cambridge

Boston

Sudbury

Blackstone Valley

Worcester

Providence

Foster

Narrow River

Narragansett Bay

Deserted Village at Canterbury

Springfield

Hartford

Bloomfield

Stonington

Hudson River

CONNECTICUT

Berlin Turn-pike

Leeds-ville

New Haven

Long Island Sound

NEW YORK

Newtown

Shunemunk Mt.

Tarrytown

ATLANTIC OCEAN

Radburn

New York

Great Swamp

Sea Bright

Delaware River

Princeton

N E W

Barnegat Bay

Philadelphia

Pine Barrens

J E R S E Y

Susquehanna River

Journey of the author from Ipswich, Massachusetts, to Reston, Virginia

Delaware Bay

DELAWARE

P E N N S Y L V A N I A

N
NE
E
NW
SE
W
S
SW

Cross Keys

MILES
0   25   50   75

Baltimore

Columbia

Washington

Chesapeake Bay

M A R Y L A N D

Potomac River

VIRGINIA

Reston

SV

1

Deserted Village

I LIVE in a small town in southeastern Connecticut, a charming, coherent place of a few thousand people. You can walk to the beach, shops, school, and the library; the architecture is tidy and the people fit. But even in such a place I feel now and then the pressure of late twentieth-century crowds and congestion and—perhaps out of the characteristic North American wanderlust—the impulse to move on. There was a particular afternoon early last fall when the houses on either side of my house seemed too close, and I was irritated by the constant presence of people. I reread an advertisement that had appeared in the local paper, the New London *Day*, the day before:

> Canterbury. 189 acres with 20 acre pond.
> Excellent brook. Deserted village. Several
> abandoned town roads through property.
> High, dry land. Secluded. By appointment.

So, by telephone, I talked with Mr. Bill Pearl of the Pearl Agency in Hampton, Connecticut, and Mr. Pearl told me that he would meet me at the Atlantic filling station one mile west of the Canterbury town line at 2 P.M. on the following day. He would be driving a 1963 white Oldsmobile.

I allowed a couple of hours to drive the forty miles to Canterbury. After an early lunch I set out, following the two-lane roads that straggle north into Connecticut from the coast. Fairly soon one has left behind the dense population that depends on the shoreline railroads, interstate highways, factories, and towns. One passes through an amorphous band where factory workers have moved out to the edges of former farming villages, and mobile homes, split-levels, and various concrete block and tarpaper intermediate stages of houses are rising on the subdivided acreage. Then abruptly, from the top of a hill, one has a view of the interior—it is all trees. The trees are still green, though the long drought is making for an early autumn, with a touch of yellow and red here and there. From ground level, occasional dairy and poultry farms become apparent, together with orchards and independent old houses that are fenced against the encroaching forest in the back by half a dozen abandoned cars. The trees, however, are the striking thing. They go on and on as far as one can see, their distant tops forming the northern, eastern, and western horizons. They conceal all roads, telephone wires, and settlements. They create, in fact, a landscape that is closer in appearance than it has been for 250 years to that seen by the first settlers. Francis Parkman wrote:

The exposed frontier of New England was between two and three hundred miles long, and consisted of farms and hamlets loosely scattered through an almost impervious forest. . . . Even in so-called villages the houses were far apart. . . . Such as were able to do so fenced their dwellings with palisades, or built them of solid timber, with loopholes, a projecting upper story like a block house, and sometimes a flanker at one or more of the corners. In the more considerable settlements the largest of these fortified houses was occupied in time of danger by armed men and served as a place of refuge for the neighbors.

The Atlantic filling station with an adjoining general store served as a similar focal point for the scattered houses on the road west of Canterbury. I bought a dollar's worth of regu-

lar from the lady in charge. It was a purchase meant less for the
car than for me; having paid a fee, I felt more confident in my
right to prowl around this territory. I sat at ease and waited for
Mr. Pearl to arrive.

When he did so, it was in a two-year-old blue Comet rather
than the promised Oldsmobile. He was a middle-aged man of
medium height, with a chubby oval face, wearing horn-rimmed
glasses, a brown suit, and a brown silk tie held to a white shirt
by a chrome tiepin. He had the friendly but modest manner
of the sort of real-estate man who knows that most people,
given the right circumstances, will sell something to themselves; they don't need to be pushed into it.

"If you don't mind," he said, "I think we ought to go in your
car instead of mine. Some of those roads on the property have
pretty deep ruts."

He climbed into my somewhat battered Jeep station wagon.
He said, "Turn right out of here," and waved at the filling
station lady, whose return wave suggested that Mr. Pearl ren-
dezvoused there quite frequently on his Canterbury appoint-
ments. I drove north-northeast at his direction for roughly five
miles along sparsely settled Tarmac roads that were hard to tell
apart. We were surrounded by the same anonymous woods that
stretch into Massachusetts and Rhode Island. Mr. Pearl said he'd
had the property listed for three years. It belonged to a Mrs.
Rogers, who was an old lady now, but had lived on it as a child
for a few years before moving to Massachusetts, where she'd
lived ever since. Just after the war she had been offered $25,000
for the property by a shooting club, and her present asking
price of $35,000 was based on that figure, and incorporated the
general rise of prices since then. Mr. Pearl hurried to say (perhaps because of the involuntary hardening of my face muscles
for a moment, which I hoped he didn't recognize for the sign it
was of a pipedream burst), "Thirty-five may be a little unreal-
istic." Although 189 acres was the described size, the property
hadn't been properly surveyed for years, and was probably a

little larger than that. At any rate, the vagueness did not make the place any easier for him to sell. He knew that a few small pieces of the original property had been sold off. The assistant school superintendent from a nearby town was going to build a summer cottage on one plot. A man from Bloomfield had come and looked at the land a few months back. Mr. Pearl hazarded that from various other signs and portents of the real-estate trade Canterbury was beginning to feel the effects of being halfway between Hartford and Providence. People who worked in the cities were beginning to appear out here, looking for houses or land to build on. Canterbury had a brand-new high school. The taxes on the Rogers property were $89 a year.

At a spot where a brook crossed beneath the road we were on, we turned east and followed a lane that went into the woods, paralleling the brook as far as a pond. Mr. Pearl called for a halt. It was too late for me to say that I didn't have anything like $35,000 and was impelled more by curiosity and claustrophobia than genuine land hunger. Mr. Pearl looked at my sneakers and then at his own brown shoes. He said, "Well, we won't need boots anyway—not until we get about a month's worth of rain."

Single file for a quarter of a mile, we followed a path to the edge of the pond. It was much reduced in size by the four-year drought; dark green-gray water rimmed by high black banks, and overshadowed on one side by a prominent hill. Mr. Pearl showed me a slight headland that he'd always thought would make a good building site, and a useful bank of gravel close at hand. The stone dam at the south end was in need of repair. A small flow of water trickled down over the rocks. The pond itself was very flat and still. I looked for bubbles, for signs of life in the dark shallows.

"There used to be bass," said Mr. Pearl. "It wouldn't be hard to stock again."

Boy Scouts had camped at one end of the dam—a ring of blackened stones and charred wood marked the site—and Mr.

Pearl gave his opinion that the best use for the property would be as a summer camp. "People," he said, "are going in for that sort of thing more and more." We followed the scarcely damp bed of the stream downhill until we hit the dirt lane again. It now ran between dry stone walls set thirty feet or so apart; trees had grown up on the roadside of the walls, where a sidewalk might have been, and the lane itself, a bumpy wilderness avenue, lay between them. "This section is what they used to call Wright Mills," said Mr. Pearl, pointing out the foundations of several houses and a griststone lying at the edge of the road. Stone walls that were still in fine condition testified to the work that had gone into clearing the rocky fields. "Those took some wrestling, I bet," he said as we walked beside a stretch of wall formed of rocks as big as bushel baskets.

Flies and mosquitoes buzzed. Nuts littered the rough ground, and squirrels hesitated, hearing us, before darting up the frail trunks of trees. Walking through these woods was a little like swimming just below the surface of water on a coral reef. Up above, the trees branched out thickly to the light, while down below the forest was at once crowded and thin. The trees formed what foresters call pioneer stands, to differentiate them from climax stands that have had a several-centuries-long undisturbed life. "Most of the larger wood here is about seventy-five years old," said Mr. Pearl. "It only takes some twenty years for a field to get covered in. Most of it's oak. There's a little pine, and one or two rough-bark hickories. There are a couple of farms still going in this area of Canterbury. You might be able to rent out some of this ground once you cleared it off."

I did not think Mr. Pearl sounded altogether sure of this, but I asked him what it cost to clear land in this condition. He answered that the hire of a bulldozer generally worked out at $100 an acre, and less per acre for larger areas of land. It wouldn't take long to knock this stuff down. You could push it all into a corner of a field, or pile it into one of the old foundations.

The brook, having gained some water from a hidden source, came to the crest of a little hill and tumbled down through the derelict millrace. Great chunks of squared-off stone had fallen in and the brook flowed over and under them, filtered by the rocks in the same way that the bright sunlight was filtered by countless trees. Near the ruins of the sawmill stood a major group of foundations: barns, outbuildings, and the farmhouse itself. The farmhouse was pre-eminent by reason of a still-standing chimney that, like a diamond blunted at top and bottom, had its greatest girth at mid-height. This rough-faceted former pillar of the house rose from the center of the foundation. Out of a niche in the rocks that formed it, a few feet below the crumbling summit, a slender tree was growing, taking advantage of the old chimney to reach the light and air.

Mr. Pearl suggested that I take him back to his car—he had another appointment that afternoon—but that I then return to look around the property at my leisure. On the way he let me know that Mrs. Rogers might consider taking back a mortgage on the property; it would be difficult to get money out of a bank for this sort of land. And as we shook hands he said that maybe I should consider the asking price more like thirty thousand than thirty-five. The blue Comet accelerated out of the Atlantic station in order to get in front of a school bus that was coming up the winding road, and I turned the Jeep back toward Wright Mills.

It gave the impression of being a recent wilderness. Judging from the remnants of rotten timber lying at the base of that upstanding chimney, the house had still been standing fifty years ago. But for the hamlet as a whole the rot had probably set in earlier than that. This was, in the first place, tough ground to farm. Hinckley gravelly sandy loam, Gloucester fine sandy loam, and a large proportion of miscellaneous stony soils are Canterbury's agriculturally unfortunate lot. The Gloucester loam is generally unsuited to cultivation; grass hay is about the best that can be got from it. Hinckley loam will produce alfalfa and silage corn, which account for the dairy and poultry farming that alone struggles on. When the Erie Canal opened in 1825 many New England farmers got on the move. (Canterbury's population reached a peak in 1820, with 1,984 people. The nadir was 1910, when 868 lived there. It has been going up ever since.) The Erie Canal not only brought in cheap wheat but the idea of the West. Frederick Jackson Turner, the historian, described the time:

All was motion and change. A restlessness was universal. Men moved, in their single life, from Vermont to New York, from New York to Ohio, from Ohio to Wisconsin, from Wisconsin to California, and longed for the Hawaiian Islands. When the bark started from their fence rails, they felt the call to change. They were conscious of the mobility of their society and gloried in it. They broke with the Past and thought to create something finer, more fitting for humanity, more beneficial for the average man than the world had ever seen.

Those who stayed in the East had to compete with western agriculture. Some in Wright Mills undoubtedly made the shorter migration to work in a New England mill town.

I had seen, north of Stonington, abandoned farms before. This was, however, something more, an entire hamlet and its roads gone literally to seed. I sat on one of the smooth-topped stones of a wall near the former farmhouse and considered the mixed emotions Wright Mills aroused. The place was, for a start, a little spooky. There was an immaturity about the second-growth trees, though it was not what Henry James meant when he said of New England, "The very air looks new and young; the light of the sun seems fresh and innocent, as if it knew as yet but few of the secrets of the world and none of the weariness of shining." This spot had some secrets, crude though they may have been; it had a sense of innocence lost without having been exchanged for the knowledge and pleasure achieved in the process of "civilization." There were some fallen-in foundations, some walls held together by inertia. Otherwise in Wright Mills nothing had been gained and held as a result of man's passing. It was, as Mr. Pearl had suggested, a camping ground.

It was also a shock to realize that, although I was in what

most people would call the country, although I was surrounded
by nature resurgent and triumphant, I was not really enjoying
it. I felt uneasy. I kept looking at my old Jeep station wagon,
and finally I climbed back into it. It was curious to think that
this is a kind of "country" we have more and more of. On the
northeastern seaboard, in the area lying in the wide corridor
that runs between the cities of Boston, New York, Philadelphia,
and Washington, the woods are increasing. In 1960, 16.2 million
acres or about 50 percent of the area of that corridor was occupied by woodland. In the French geographer Jean Gottmann's
encyclopediac study of the region, *Megalopolis* (which did a
great deal to popularize that word and many of its more hor-
rendous implications), the following assessment of land use in
the 1950s was made:

> About one-half wooded (including . . . parks outside cities), one-
> third actually used in farming (either tilled or grazed), and about
> 15 percent devoted to special uses (chiefly buildings and roads).
> In recent times the tilled area in Megalopolis, as in surrounding
> areas, has been shrinking in favor of the spread of both woods and
> urban uses. These trends have progressed at different rates in the
> various parts of the region. . . . Whatever the local variation, it must
> be recognized that the major competition for land is between urban
> uses and woodlands, and that *about half of the whole area of
> Megalopolis is green* in a relatively unproductive way.

In Connecticut, Professor Gottmann and his researchers
found, woods took up about one-third of the land area in 1850
and two-thirds in 1950, and the abandonment of tilled land since
the war has been proceeding faster than the rate at which suburbs have eaten into woods on the edges of large towns. He talks
of woodland sprawl, as well as urban sprawl.

I got the Jeep started, and put it into four-wheel drive. Mr.
Pearl had described a route which, climbing up over the hill that
overlooked the pond, would give me a good idea of the extent
of the Rogers property. He hadn't driven over it for several
years, but he had believed it was navigable. I turned left at a
fork in the abandoned road—to the right, a wooden bridge over

the brook had completely collapsed—and motored slowly up the steep face of the hill. I was looking for a view, and I found none; the woods climbed with me. But I also was looking for a way of making a mark, however small, on this spreading, unkempt countryside, and that was allowed me. Every few yards I had to stop to remove a fallen branch from the path. Here and there I had to use a branch to lever out of the way a rock that, perhaps dislodged by ice the previous winter, had fallen from the top of a wall. In one place I had to build up the road surface with branches and small stones in order to get a front wheel over a miniature Matterhorn. On the long, flat summit of the hill saplings were growing in the roadway. One, having been depressed by the front bumper, sprang up again underneath the Jeep, like an arrester hook on an aircraft carrier, and held on. What, however, it held on to—the hand-brake cable—let go and broke. I crawled beneath the vehicle and did some temporary repairs with a piece of twine to keep the cable from dragging along the ground. After another mile or so of track, over which the Jeep bucked like a fishing boat in heavy seas, I was glad to reach a paved road at the border of Mrs. Rogers' property.

Six years before he was killed in France in 1917, T. E. Hulme attended a congress of philosophers in Bologna, Italy. Walking through its streets prompted some observations which he recorded in his notebook, one of which was that at a high point of civilization, country and city were not contradictory forces; they were both artificial, deliberate creations. Of cities, Bologna was a fine example. "You feel always, though you may never see it, the bracing feeling of a disciplinary wall keeping it up to the ideal pitch of town I require, and never allowing it to sprawl into desert."

Stonington, the town in which I live, has in its own simple way a similar quality. Built on a peninsula, it is walled on three sides by the sea and on the fourth by the New Haven Railroad; it can never sprawl. It hasn't arcades and piazzas, but it has a small square with cannons and a larger green common, with the library in the center, flanked by fine New England frame houses. It has streets that meet Hulme's definition of a street as "a place for strolling and talking in, and not a railway." It has the tight fit that shapes thing definitely, the tight fit that William James observed his country was without. Since it is something of an exception, a small stockade on the edge of the wide, formless expanse, Stonington occasionally induces in people lucky enough to live there a feeling that the rest of the country, and the rest of the northeastern seaboard in particular, is going to hell in the most up-to-date version of a handbasket. The sudden prevalence of the term "megalopolis" in books, papers, and magazines bolstered this feeling.

For although the Alexandrian philosopher Philo Judaeus viewed megalopolis as a great city of ideas "that predetermines and commands the material world," the general effect of the facts, graphs, and tables Jean Gottmann assembled in his book *Megalopolis* was to suggest that the material world was very much in command, that the formless expanse was being covered by a huge, formless, and certainly ungreat city. A careful student of the book would have found that the author here and there furnished an argument to support his tone of pedantic cheerfulness. But in general the word "megalopolis" reached the public with the suggestion that, no matter how oppressive the idea of the endless city might strike them as being, it was already too late to do anything about it: megalopolis was here. One had the feeling that even if it were not here, the idea was accepted with such fatalism that it very soon would be.

I had that feeling; but the next time I had the urge to seek the open spaces, I thought I would see if the feeling were grounded in reality. I decided to take the Jeep, still without an effective hand brake, from Boston to Washington. My inquiries were amateur and unplanned. I had glanced at a few of the books on urban design which appear, stiff with jargon and ripe for computers and microfilm, at the rate of three or four a week. I had read H. G. Wells's *Anticipations*, published in London in 1902, in which he foresaw, by the end of this century, old cities dissolving into urban regions, and in which he examined (with the accuracy of genius) present, centrifugal, suburbanizing tendencies—the desire to have a house of one's own, to have a garden, to live in a healthy place for children. He saw that the telephone would be a potent factor in forces making for diffusion. He realized that the general distribution of population was directly dependent on transportation facilities and that as long as people were dependent chiefly on their feet for transportation the radius of a city would be confined to about four miles; with suburban trains the radius would be increased to thirty miles. If he didn't quite foresee Henry Ford and the car, he realized that many businesses—book publishing, for instance—might as well move out into the country. Furthermore, he wrote, "It is not too much to say that the London citizen of the year 2000 A.D. may have a choice of nearly all England and Wales south of Nottingham as his suburb, and that the vast stretch of country from Washington to Albany will be all of it 'available' to the active citizen of New York and Philadelphia before that date."

Since it was available to me, I went to look at it and see how it was being changed and manipulated. I followed my nose, impelled by an appetite for certain aspects of old cities, new towns, and the unsettled countryside. Finally I was interested simply in traveling through this most complex and prosperous portion of the world in early autumn and seeing what it looked like. I made some telephone calls, and wrote a few letters, and set off, leaving Stonington as a touchstone.

2

Into the System

ACCORDING TO geologers, Boston is moving south at the rate of several inches a century. In roughly 800 million years, it will be where New York City is now. For the time being, however, Boston lies 215 miles from New York, which, in turn, is 230 miles from Washington. These are distances that most of the 38 million people in the corridor nowadays cover by road, some by air, and fewer and fewer by rail. (In 1960 the statistics were 60 percent by car, 11.9 percent by bus, 7.5 percent by air, and 20 percent by rail—with rail declining and all the others increasing.) The car gets one at a reasonable speed from one's own door to the door at which one wishes to arrive, but it requires attention, concentration, and parking spaces at either end; it is not particularly efficient, either with one's money or one's time. The plane is speedy, once it's off the ground, but the time spent reaching it and getting to one's ultimate destination from it, makes it little faster (except over the whole 445 mile distance) than the train, which runs to and from the center of cities. And the poor railroad's passenger traffic problems are so tediously familiar that one is liable to forget that even the New Haven

Railroad, in its present bankrupt state, carries passengers to the towns on its tracks as fast as a car. Moreover, despite its extravagantly over- or underheated cars; its dry, overpriced sandwiches; its wet, overpriced omelettes; its dusty, collapsing seats; and thermopane windows turned into seasick-inducing chambers by a rock that had been thrown by a vandal and a railroad-car-washing machine which half filled the window with water—despite all this it sometimes allows one to read, eat, or sleep en route. Nevertheless, for a region that is only one-fiftieth of the total United States land area but contains a fifth of the country's people and produces a quarter of its manufactures, that is, in fact, the most productive industrial region in the world, the state of public transportation is pretty shabby. The last few years have seen some realization of this. At the moment the response is largely in the idea stage, but ideas after all were what Philo Judaeus had in mind, and in this case they have been backed by Congress with a good deal of public money. In order to find out what was being done, after a long period of inaction, to bring Boston and Washington closer together in time, I intended to call on M.I.T., where much of the most radical government-sponsored transportation thinking has been going on, before I set off in slow and relatively haphazard motion toward the capital. I spent the first night of my journey in Ipswich, which is forty miles from Boston, on the northern boundary of the commuters' city.

My friends David and Joan Ernest have lived in Ipswich for eight years. David works for an import-export firm in Boston and is, on Sundays, a lay preacher. Their house is a large, rambling eighteenth-century structure; it used to be two houses, and has several big rooms and many small ones that run into one another. It is a house with many fireplaces, wide-board floors, and—perhaps because of the lack of corridors, which causes one to bump into adults and children all over the place—a very sociable quality. I was surprised to hear from David that they were thinking of moving.

"Eight years is long enough to spend in one place, don't you think?" said David, as he made me a drink. "Anyway, this town is no good for the children. They're not self-reliant enough. They've got too many friends."

As if on cue, a horde of children surged through the living room, apparently on their way from the back door to the front.

"When they haven't got half the street with them, they sit and watch TV. They never read books. Don't you think we ought to move?"

"David was an only child," said Joan, untying her apron as she came in from the kitchen. "He grew up on a New Hampshire farm. In his county there were more cows than children. He'd read *War and Peace* by the time he was twelve."

David grinned.

"But seriously," Joan said, "all our friends are moving. The Mitchells are moving out to a farm near here and the Ginns have bought some land. It seems like the time to go."

Before dinner David drove me out of Ipswich to look at two properties they were considering. The town contains many houses of great age and architectural distinction, but has on the whole a rather scrappy air—as if people had concentrated on their own homes but not on their environment. Many streets lack sidewalks. In time past Ipswich houses were taxed less if the front steps or porch was unfinished, and many seem to remain that way. We drove two miles out of town on a country road and halted at the foot of a drive, from which I glimpsed a large, unprepossessing house, built in the summer-cottage style of the turn of the century, with a shingled tower and many porches. David said we shouldn't drive up, because the owners were still there, and would be till Halloween. The house was unheated; it had twenty rooms, ten acres, a cherry orchard, and a small formal garden. There was a butler's pantry and a partial view of the sea.

The other place was at the other end of town. There was no

house, only a field which, David said, "is sort of for sale. If he likes you and the price you offer, he might say yes." David parked his car in a gateway. The nearest house was half a mile away and the road was devoid of traffic. However, we both felt as if we were trespassing—the reaction took the form of David running up the slope of the hill with long, exaggerated basketball-player strides, while I examined, more minutely than I needed to, the quality of the grass. It was very green, cut short. The field, the shape of a hatchet head, tilted down toward a little creek that ran out with a wood on one side to the tidal marshes. From the top of the rise, the cleared, cared-for field gave a prospect of the woods and the marsh; it was a lovely spot.

"What kind of house shall I build here?" David asked. He spread out his arms and looked, with his long nose and swept-back hair, like a big bird about to take off. "It would have to be a wide, branching house."

"What about a tower? Then you could see the sea."

"From the other place, the summer house, the sea is visible."

We drove back into town, past other fields that were sprouting houses. I said to David, "Wouldn't you like to buy that field and just keep it the way it is?"

"Ah, but I want to live there."

Life is an equation of space and time and people.

David caught his usual early commuter train into Boston next morning. I drove in on the last of the flood tide of commuter traffic and it was an exciting trip. The turnpike was unfamiliar. So was the gambler's spirit of Massachusetts drivers, a spirit apparently encouraged by compulsory third-party insurance. Cars whizzed in at rotaries and intersections from all sides, never slowing down until—in the final second—they were positive the enemy was not going to give way, and sometimes, to judge by the great number of crumpled fenders and dented doors, not even then. It was a general game of chicken. Every man was intent on proving to all his anonymous fellow citizens that he wasn't impressed by them. I *was* impressed. But I took a few seconds now and then as I approached the Mystic River to admire the view—the tall spars of the U.S.S. *Constitution* rising out of Charlestown Navy Yard and the high tower of the new Prudential building climbing above the renovated center of the city. At least the traffic didn't jam. I paid my twenty-five cents toll on the bridge and cartwheeled off toward Cambridge, crossing over to the north bank of the Charles. After wasting twenty minutes in a search for a parking space in the streets, I found a slot marked "visitors" in the M.I.T. faculty parking lot.

M.I.T. is a "linear" university, occupying a good half mile along the Charles River. It is, architecturally, a pleasant enough mixture of collegiate classic and praise-worthy modern, although veterans of the place complain that one of its most famous contemporary structures, designed by the Finnish architect Alvar Aalto, doesn't "work" very successfully as the dormitory building it is supposed to be.

In one respect, my visit was ill-timed. It was registration day, and half of young America, together with representatives of young England, Nigeria, and Japan, appeared to be enrolling. The corridors were packed with students either lined up or moving from line to line. The faculty looked harassed. In another sense, however, the day was well-chosen, for I realized something that nuclear explosions and modern medicine hadn't taught me, since they all could be comprehended as being brought forth by small groups of dedicated scientists. Here, on the contrary, were hordes of youngsters signing up for technology and science and the ever-increasing complication of things. The explosions would not perhaps be as quick and bright, but they would have the revolutionary force of many megatons. As I sat in the office of Dr. William Seifert, assistant dean of engineering, and listened to the thousands of feet moving past in the corridor, it didn't seem surprising that the world of science fiction was so fast becoming the world of fact.

Dean Seifert was a short, bespectacled man in his late forties, with the impatience of one whose job is to try to deliver the future. One aspect of that future with which he was currently concerned was the North-East Corridor Transportation Project, set up by President Kennedy in 1962 with prompting from Senator Pell of Rhode Island and Richardson Dilworth, former mayor of Philadelphia. The Department of Commerce, as a beginning, had sponsored studies into the demands for Corridor transportation until 1980. These studies showed that road transport would continue to satisfy most people's needs till then; that for travel between closely spaced points the car and the limited-access highway would still furnish the best solution; that more airports and better safety procedures would cause air traffic to continue to increase, though the problems of getting to and from airports might remain; and that, finally, given the present rail situation, with declining trade and declining service in a vicious circle, railroads could hope only to compete on short center-of-city to center-of-city hauls, as between New York and Philadelphia.

This was the background against which several meetings were held at the White House in August 1964. Dean Seifert said, "As a result of the meetings, the decision was made that the country should begin to explore the feasibility of a 200 mph or higher rail-like system. A month later, Bob Nelson, who is director of the Department of Commerce's transportation research staff, got hold of us here at M.I.T. and asked if we'd do a short, intensive study of the technical feasibility of an improved Corridor transportation system—a high-speed rail-like system in particular, but we were also to appraise short-haul aircraft and potential highway improvements. We said we would. In fact, within several weeks we had a task force assembled and working.

"What makes all this doubly significant is the low level of effort that's been devoted until now to transportation research and development—R. & D. as it's called these days. In 1966 the federal budget called for $15 billion for R. & D., almost all of it going to defense, space, and atomic energy. R. & D. efforts in defense and space have built up steadily over the last years, and the nation has developed a large body of technical personnel able to move quickly as new needs or areas of interest have arisen. But in transportation—which in all its forms represents about $120 billion or 20 percent of the gross national product every year—there's been none of this. There's been no effective mechanism for adapting the great store of defense and space technology to transportation—particularly ground transportation. There have been no efforts in academic institutions. There has been no supply of bright students eager to make the adaptation.

"Well, we think things are changing. People are becoming interested. Both the faculty and students here are really excited by this Northeast Corridor project. We were given $500,000 to work with by the Department of Commerce. Our effort is multidepartmental—civil, electrical, mechanical, and aeronautical engineers, architects, urban planners, and political scientists. We've given our students the problem as a design project. Anyway, our first action was to establish the broad criteria for the design of a radically new form of high-speed ground transport. Here are the criteria."

Dean Seifert handed me two mimeographed pages, which he suggested I look at while he checked with his secretary a speech he was supposed to deliver in Chicago the following morning. I began with a glance, expecting to be put off by the technical language, but I was soon in deep, although it was somewhat the way it must have been for a sixteenth-century landsman reading one of the navigational guides or mariner's mirrors intended to facilitate a voyage to the new world. Here, instead of soundings and compass courses, were such terms as "dynamic scheduling" and "systems engineering." Since this latter term comprehends a great deal of what M.I.T. is up to these days, and since it anticipates, to use H. G. Wells's word, much of what may happen in the future in our presently rather unsystematized great city, a definition is in order. I can do no better than to borrow one from a book I read later that day, *The Glideway System*, the M.I.T. student design project to which Dean Seifert had referred.

The term "systems engineering" is of relatively recent origin, dating back no further than the days of the Manhattan project (which produced the first atomic weapon). It is used to describe an integrated approach to the synthesis of entire systems designed to perform various tasks in what is expected to be the most efficient possible manner. Thus the term "systems engineering" is used to describe an approach which views an entire system of components as an entity, rather than simply as an assembly of individual parts; i.e., a system in which each component is designed to fit properly with the other components rather than to function by itself.

The systems approach is concerned with many specialities, rather than just one, and the systems engineer needs to have a broad engineering knowledge. Unlike the fabled "Jack-of-all-trades" who was master of none, the systems engineer is required to be master of the over-all system which may involve in its synthesis a whole host of disciplines, which in our recent history were regarded as separate entities reserved for the attending specialists. Today there is a growing demand in industry, in schools, and in government for people whose minds can encompass the so-called over-all picture.

Dean Seifert's list of criteria for a HSGT system (which I have paraphrased here and there) begins:

1. The overriding criterion is that the design should be a *systems design*, where the systems objective is to produce minimum time, door-to-door passenger transport between random points within the Corridor. We did not feel that a system in which access was limited to terminals in just principal cities—Boston, New York, and Washington—would be a satisfactory solution.

2. The High Speed Ground Transport mode of the system must be designed to provide widespread, easy, and rapid access to all locations in the Corridor. This implies that the HSGT mode must have the flexibility to mesh smoothly with local conditions and the design therefore must take cognizance of local plans.

3. The system must provide a level of service in terms of door-to-door travel time, comfort, frequency of service, and fares to attract enough users to make efficient use of the system.

4. The total cost of the system must be acceptable on the basis of services offered and problems solved.

5. The system's accident expectancy must be no greater and preferably less than any present mode of passenger transportation.

6. Must operate in all weathers on schedule.

7. Must be designed so it can be adapted to changes in quantity and pattern of demand, caused by increases or shifts in population, changes in travel habits, access, or land use along the route.

8. Must have at least marginal compatibility with existing feeder arrangements (such as highways) so that parts of the system could be brought into service as soon as they are built.

9. Finally, the system should not generate side- or after-effects that contradict or contravene any stated or implicit social, political, or economic goals of the community, either local or national.

"Have you got to the last point?" Dean Seifert asked, with a slightly sardonic grin. "On that, we know that a HSGT system will make necessary all sorts of adjustments in policies, regulatory practices, and patterns of decision making in the Corridor. The matter of ownership, planning, and financing will be very complex. But we've got over similar hurdles in the past—for instance, with the communications satellite."

I asked what steps followed the drawing-up of criteria.

"We decided that we had to go for something totally new. After all, the automobile didn't come through breeding better horses. We had to arrive at something that has the dynamic scheduling of a car—that leaves when you want it to leave—and that also has the car's psychological advantages. In cars people feel they are their own masters, even when they're stuck in traffic jams. We also wanted our new mode to have the speed of a plane. So we've been examining the components of an entirely new, not just an improved, transportation system. In the past, the arms, legs, brains, and body of our transportation systems have been designed and operated by individual interests. Each has planned his design and made his moves according to what he assumes to be the behavior of the others. If this new venture is to succeed, it has to achieve better coordination with other systems than has been done before."

I was interested in the mechanics of inaugurating this kind of project; I was also intrigued by the Flash Gordon aspect of it. Having read about an express train that worked in an underground vacuum tube, I asked the dean if M.I.T. had something like this in mind.

"Well, that's certainly one thing we're considering. Larry Edwards, from Lockheed Missiles, who's been working on the design for such a system, came and lectured to us here about it. But we're also examining conventional electric traction motors, and motors and turbines in which part of the propulsion unit is on the vehicle and part is mounted on the guideway. We're looking into air-cushion support, many different control systems, and the form the network should take. Should the guideway be located on the surface, on elevated structures, or in deep tunnels—or possibly in all three? We're investigating the varieties of service that should be offered. We'd like to provide aircraftlike speed from main city to main city, but we'd also like to give high-speed service to intermediate cities, such as Providence and Wilmington. We're seeking ways to accelerate vehicles from a local station to mainline speed and connect them to a through vehicle without ever slowing down the through vehicle. Someone who wanted to get off at Providence would move into a Providence car en route, and that car would be disengaged at speed and decelerated for the local stop."

I said, "How soon?"

Dean Seifert smiled. "I have a formal answer I make to that question. It goes like this. If the legislative and financial aspects of this program can be met in a satisfactory manner—and the President has, thank goodness, pushed through $90 million to get it started—then it is not beyond the realm of technical possibility to imagine a system which would initiate service at 300 mph or more, in at least a portion of the Corridor, coincident with the two hundredth anniversary of the signing of the Declaration of Independence."

As I got up to leave, Dean Seifert asked his secretary to sell me a copy of the report the M.I.T. students had made on their HSGT project. I paid $3.00 for a heavy, paperbound, dark-green book. Flicking through it, I came on a sketch labeled "Passenger Modules," showing some long, low, Easter-egglike vehicles. I thought of my Jeep, square and boxlike, sitting in the faculty parking lot. I said, "What about the car? Will it soon be obsolete?"

Dean Seifert gave his head an emphatic, unDelphic shake. "No, it won't. Even in 1980, cars will be running up the greater part of all passenger miles."

The car hands us freedom, which is why we are enslaved by it. I boarded mine, fired up the engine, and—after checking the front-wheel-drive lever to make sure it hadn't slipped into gear, as it sometimes does—directed it into the midday traffic that was swishing inland along the north bank of the Charles. In the Jeep I had a multiple choice of routes which no other form of locomotion, except perhaps foot power, would have given me. There were four or five possible roads in the segment of the compass lying between the south and the west. I chose Route 20, which is the old Upper Post Road, and which runs with the Charles due west through Watertown, Waltham, Weston, and Wayland. It is the old stagecoach route to Worcester.

A book in which I browse every now and then is William Cobbett's *Rural Rides*, a journal of various trips made on horse-back around the English countryside in the 1820s and 1830s. It is a fascinating work, its observations heightened, if anything, by

Cobbett's idiosyncratic fulminations against paper money and his propaganda for the Swedish turnip—which he thought superior to the common English turnip. *Rural Rides*, however, lacks information about one crucial subject, namely Cobbett's horse. If I may self-indulgently imagine someone reading this a century hence, I may perhaps forestall his criticism on a similar count by relating here and now what a 1959 Willys Suburban Jeep Station Wagon is like.

It is by no means a common vehicle, and despite its name, you will see only a couple of them among the several hundred cars left parked by commuters at a suburban station. It is a Percheron rather than a racehorse, with a touch of mulishness, and— shifting animals again—something of a St. Bernard, jowlish and useful. It is also very ugly, and its concessions to "styling" emphasize the fact, like rouge on the face of an old battleax. You climb up into it, as into a London taxi, treading on a sort of running board, a survival which bears the same relation to a real running board that the eustachian tube bears to a gill. (Running boards began to go out with the assassination of King Alexander of Yugoslavia in Marseilles in 1934. where the assassin jumped on the running board of his slowly moving car.) Inside there is room to wear a bowler hat without being in constant contact with the roof, and indeed the Jeep gives one a very dignified, bowler-hat kind of feeling. There are wooden battens fastened to the floor, for supporting various cargoes. All the seats fold forward. There are three gear levers, a strictly utilitarian dashboard, and a six-cylinder engine that is cold-starting but runs well when warmed up. The Jeep was at this time still without an effective hand brake, none of the doors locked, and the windscreen wiper in front of the driver was out of phase with the other wiper. The Jeep had been in use as a beach buggy in East Hampton, Long Island, with the result that salt had rusted away most of the original brake lines, which had been replaced, and most of the tail pipe, which had not. On the Waltham road I became aware of a strong smell of exhaust. I stopped at the first garage, and a mechanic said the exhaust was swirling underneath and coming up through several holes in the floor; it would take two or three days to order a new tail pipe. I stuffed some rags in the visible holes and made the rest of the journey with at least one window always open.

The Boston "urban area" now extends to the factories and developments that, seeking room to stretch and grow, have built on the fields along Route 128, the expressway ringing the city. I cut across 128 and stopped for lunch, halfway to Worcester, at the Wayside Inn, in South Sudbury. This inn has a fair claim to be the oldest operating establishment of its kind in the country. It was built, in pre-stagecoach days of 1686, by the Howe family of Sudbury. A two-story, four-room "ordinary" to begin with, it became Howe's Tavern in 1716 and the Red Horse thereafter. Henry Longfellow, then a Harvard professor, was a guest at the Red Horse in the 1850s, and used the place as the *mise-en-scène* for his *Tales of a Wayside Inn*. Following the publication of that book in 1863, the Red Horse changed its name again. Henry Ford—against whom historians bear a grudge for once saying "I wouldn't give a nickel for all the history in the world"—bought the inn in 1923, and restored it. Unfortunately, one winter night some years later it burned down; only the kitchen was spared. The present building, restored with a Ford Foundation grant in 1958, is therefore just about as authentic as the U.S.S. *Constellation,* of which it is reckoned only eleven feet of the keel comes from the original eighteenth-century ship. However, while the *Constellation* has been modified and restored over several centuries, the Wayside Inn was rebuilt all at once. It has the blandness which is a negative feature of such reproductions. It isn't worn enough. I had beef stroganoff for lunch, which was similarly lacking, being without enough sour cream to give it taste.

The place, however, was busy. A Grayline coach tour had come in, and twenty elderly couples were munching on the sweet rolls and diminutive salads this genteel type of restaurant uses to bolster up the diner while he waits for his main course. The waitress poured me a glass of water, half full, to remind me of the great northeastern drought, now in its fourth year, and I ordered a shot of Newburyport New England rum to get the carbon monoxide out of my blood. Then I turned to *The Glideway System.*

It seemed a marvelously thorough and imaginative investigation of almost every aspect of a HSGT system, imbued with the ideas Dean Seifert had discussed that morning and showing evidence of the hands of other M.I.T. mentors. It furnished, if not a guide to what would happen, a guide to faculty thinking and the student response to it. The students had set up a project organization; detailed the system objectives; and analyzed the network in terms of population, place, and likely demand in order to specify the route of the main line: Washington-Baltimore-Philadelphia-New York-New Haven-Hartford-Providence-Boston, with secondary lines to Wilmington, suburban New Jersey, Long Island, and Springfield. The students had designed in some detail the necessary vehicles. These were streamlined modules, "riding on a cushion of ram air generated by their own forward motion." Propulsion was by means of a linear induction motor, with a fin on the underside of the vehicle and coils in the slotted guideway, which would provide vibrationless, noiseless, smooth power at any speed, as well as most of the braking power. Seventy pages were devoted to vehicle and guideway design, construction, and operation. One chapter, mostly in computer language, dealt with scheduling. The political implications of the Glideway were examined, and the recommendation made that the system ought to be built, operated, and managed through a "mix" of public, governmental, and private-enterprise resources:

A system that makes it seem necessary that the government not only finance it initially but support it throughout its existence is more likely to arouse ideological opposition from those who will see this as "nationalization of the railroads," and is less likely to get through Congress than one which requires governmental participation in the form of managing and operating the system for profit. Furthermore, the system ought to be applicable to other parts of the country; that is, not just to the old, rich and brainy Northeast. Finally, of great importance, it ought to have a bold new image. . . . From a political point of view, the less HSGT looks like the railroad we are familiar with the better it might be. Congress in the past has shown more willingness to put money into a new program . . . than to appropriate money for the upgrading of some program which has been around so long that they are extremely familiar with its "problem" aspects. . . . In addition, a certain governmental tradition exists for dealing with the railroads, and we would probably do well to design a system that cannot be identified with this tradition and, therefore, may receive more favorable governmental treatment.

This sort of sharp, practical thinking permeated the report. It was demonstrated in the discussion of the car and its history-making (and geography-altering) effect on urban growth.

The automobile is a major factor in creating sprawl since large rings of real estate become equi-time-distant from the city center, and hence equally developable. This has the effect of covering land solidly with development, leaving no holes of undeveloped open space. Highways are linear elements providing access at any point along the route. The highway tends to promote the sort of uniformity that planners fear.

The basis of this fear is the monotonous, inefficient, expensive effects of sprawl. Network oriented services, such as water mains and shopping centers, are poorly distributed over a uniform blanket. Schools are far from the student, the post-office is far from the home, and the fire stations have to be in the middle of residential areas. Shopping strings out along the highway, providing aesthetic displeasure and traffic congestion. Industry also clings to the highway, so that trucks and noise invade the suburbs.

The HSGT would promote a different pattern, with circular development spreading from interchanges like ripples from stones thrown into a pond.

After lunch I drove back several miles along Route 20, past shops, stores, lumber yards, banks, and filling stations—all the linear development of the automobile age masquerading under the name of South Sudbury. I turned north for a mile or so to Sudbury proper, where the past was still more evident in the present scene than the future managed to be.

3

The Noyeses of Sudbury

BEFORE THE car, the train. Before the train, the stagecoach. Before that the wagon, and feet, and Indian trails. The Great Trail ran from the present site of Boston to the Connecticut River several miles above the site of Hartford, and having been used by generations of Indians, it was followed by the early settlers, in particular by Hooker and the hundred families who made a second emigration from Massachusetts to Connecticut. In 1638 it was part way traversed by a group of land-hungry residents of Watertown, on the Charles, many of whom had come from the wool-manufacturing town of Sudbury, in Suffolk, England.

Today, the first sense of open space west of Boston comes on Route 27 before it descends a hill to cross the Sudbury River. On both sides of the river the marsh spreads wide, rising at its borders into lush meadows. To the west, Goodman Hill lifts up between Sudbury and South Sudbury. To the northeast stretches a golf course. In the middle of the river valley I stopped the Jeep and got out for a breath of the succulent September air. The southwest wind had a touch of dampness in it, and the sun and the wind played on the tall marsh grass, still green by the river. Every minute or so a car came down the hill and opened up along the straight road across the marsh. Tire rush and wind lash drowned for an instant the genial buzz of crickets and insects. Bank swallows flew.

Thoreau, who used to walk out this way from Concord, complained a hundred years ago: "I listen to a concert in which so many parts are wanting. The whole civilised country is, to some extent, turned into a city. . . . Many of those animal migrations and other phenomena by which the Indians marked the season are no longer to be observed. . . . I wish to know an entire heaven and an entire earth. All the great trees and beasts, fishes and fowl are gone; the streams perchance are somewhat shrunk."

The great expanse of meadow in the Musketaquid Valley, south of Concord, was the land that had been seen and coveted by scouts of the dissatisfied Watertown residents. They had come not only from the Puritan stronghold of Sudbury, Suffolk, but from other places in Wiltshire, Dorset, and Hampshire, and—according to Sumner Chilton Powell, the most recent and most diligent historian of Sudbury, from whose work I have drawn this information—they were bound together by a common background of open-field farming life. They didn't like the Watertown system of freehold grants, fortunate only for those who got there first. They were mostly latecomers. They petitioned the Massachusetts General Court to grant them the meadowland where the Great Trail crossed the Musketaquid, which had the best supply of fodder within ten miles of Watertown and no wilderness to hack through to get there.

Mr. Powell writes: "Just about seven miles west of the far border of Watertown, the trail suddenly dipped down as it left the large groves of oak and chestnut and turned to the southwest. A secondary trail continued into the valley westward, only to disappear in a great broad plain of meadow grass, free from trees, growing as high as a man's waist and in some places as high as his shoulders. The men from Weyhill [Hampshire] had probably never seen such meadows. Their extent, about three thousand acres, was twice the size of the whole Weyhill parish. . . ."

The Musketaquid was full of salmon, alewives, shad, and pickerel; the woods abounded in wildfowl, turkey, bear, and deer. There were no major Indian encampments in the immediate area. In the fall of 1638, the General Court gave the go-ahead to the leaders of the settlers, Peter Noyes, Edmund Brown, and Brian Pendleton, ordering them to go to their plantations and allot their lands—which they did. They founded the town of Sudbury.

The term "new towns" is once again heard in America, but perhaps because of the new towns set up in England, Sweden, and Finland, among other places, since the war, the term seems to have acquired a European overtone. Even among some architects and planners the impression has spread that a new town is not exactly 100 percent American. Such chauvinists ignore their own history, for there is nothing that could be less foreign, more a characteristically American "mix" (to use the contemporary planners' term) of Anglo-Saxon tradition, Puritan sentiment, capitalistic enterprise, pioneer communism, and mutual aid than the settlement of Sudbury. Coming from open-field villages in England, many of the settlers lacked their own agricultural equipment. They were used to sharing tools and labor to work their adjoining strips of land. Twenty years after the first settlement (so Mr. Powell discovered from wills filed at the county court), only one-third of Sudbury men had plowshares and pairs of oxen for plow teams. The village itself was grouped around a common pasture for the oxen. House lots were four acres apiece. A town committee distributed meadowland on a basis of wealth and property brought by a family from England *and* on the number of people in the family. This was a social revolution, because many of the men had been landless laborers and others, like Peter Noyes, had been landholders in a complicated way, with many manorial duties and feudal obligations governing the use and conveyance of land "theirs" in a restricted sense. Those who had been land-rich in England were land-rich here in due proportion. But those who had been landless now had land, even if it was only a small holding. The minister received seventy-five acres. A man called John Loker received one.

Of course, there were also obligations here. Every citizen had to build his share of a fence around the common plowland, otherwise his holding would revert to the town. William Pelham received the fourth largest original land grant in Sudbury, but since he didn't establish a home he was soon dropped from the list of new grants. His brother, Herbert Pelham, a resident of Cambridge, had been a large investor in the emigration fleet, and he received land accordingly. However, since he didn't come to live in Sudbury the town committee refused to allow him to vote. The committee meanwhile kept in hand a section of river meadow, from which grants could be made as population grew. And by the time the population had grown to a point where the land in this "bank account" had run out, part of Sudbury had moved on to found and settle Marlboro, in the same way that the Watertown men had not so long before moved out to Sudbury.

Two years after the first settlement, Sudbury could be considered a town. An order of April 1640 instituted a town treasury, decreeing also that every man who found an unyoked pig should collect ten shillings fine, half for himself for leading it to the pound, half for the town funds. In May of the same year, seventeen citizens passed a law stating the town could pay for the costs of a suit against the treasurer of the Massachusetts Colony, and that the charges would be paid for by a town rate. Sudbury had decided that it could go to law and tax itself. One other important communal step was taken. The town committee appointed Peter Noyes and John Parmenter highway surveyors, and ordered them to see to it that "every inhabitant of this town shall come forth to the mending of the hyways."

I drove into Sudbury, which has a present population of eleven thousand people. I had thought of visiting Whitehall, the estate of the late Ralph Adams Cram, who was an enthusiastic medievalist and architect. Mr. Cram had a big hand in the as-yet-unfinished cathedral of St. John the Divine in New York. (Indeed, some experts believe that Mr. Cram's affection for the Middle Ages may have got the cathedral to a point where it can never be finished.) He once wrote, in the introduction to Henry Adams' *Mont Saint Michel and Chartres*, "To live for a day in a world that built Chartres Cathedral, even if it makes the living in a world that creates the 'Black Country' of England or an Iron City of America less a thing of joy and gladness than before, equally opens up the far prospect of another thirteenth century in the times that are to come and urges to ardent action toward its attainment."

That those stilted words could have been written in Sudbury in 1913 says something about the haphazardness of history and the contrariness of mankind. Whitehall itself may have said more. However, I never found out. As I parked the Jeep outside the white colonial town hall, across from a small cemetery on the slope of a hill, a late-middle-aged man wearing khaki work clothes, glasses with frames at the top only, and a bright red, peaked hunter's cap, came down the steps from the town clerk's office. He had a cheerful face, and as he opened the door of a Pontiac station wagon with an official-looking orange dome light on top, I found myself asking him not for the address of Mr. Cram's Whitehall but for the whereabouts of someone who could tell me about modern Sudbury.

"Well," he said, "there are lots of people. But I guess I'm as good as anyone. My name is Al Noyes—I'm the town's highway superintendent. Tell you what, I'm rebuilding a road, but why don't you come down after me and I'll see what I can tell you on the job."

I followed the station wagon down Route 27 for half a mile. Mr. Noyes pulled up for a moment at a road junction to yell something at three power-company workmen who were replacing a utility pole; then he turned off on a newly oiled side road, swinging the big car between two orange sawhorses bearing placards: DETOUR—ROAD CLOSED. After another half mile he stopped by a pickup truck and got out to talk to a pair of surveyors who were working with transit and measuring pole. While he did so, I walked down the road for a few hundred yards. The dark blue bituminous surface was brand-new and still porous, untamped down by traffic. At each edge was a yard-wide strip of gravel; on one side of the road an embankment rose; on the other it fell away in a slight ditch. On both sides new houses were set back at discreet distances amid the trees. On some of the trunks faded NO TRESPASSING—NO HUNTING signs were posted. The fireplace logs piled by side doors and under carports looked as if they were from the trees that had been cleared for the foundations.

Massachusetts made an early start in road building. The Indian paths widened into tracks with the increase of settlement and trade. In 1639, a year after Sudbury's settlement, the General Court ordered each town in the state to choose men who would cooperate with men from the adjoining town to "lay out highways where they be most convenient, not withstanding any man's property, or any corne ground, so as it occasion not the pulling down of any man's house, or laying open any garden or orchard." This early enforcement of the public's right to move at the expense, if need be, of the individual was backed up with specifications about the width of the right-of-ways, which were to be six or ten rods wide (1 rod = 165 feet) in common grounds. Ordinary road making in those days consisted of clearing away fallen timber, blazing or notching the trees so that the traveler wouldn't lose the track, and laying logs "over all the marshy, swampy, and difficult dirty places."

With a laugh at something Mr. Noyes had told them, the two men in the surveying team had gone back to work. I strolled over and Mr. Noyes gave me a nod of welcome. I asked him if he was descended from Peter Noyes.

"Yes sir. All the way," he said in a deep, country accent. "Though we haven't had any Peters for a couple of generations. My father went with Fred A. Noyes, and my name's the same, but I sign myself F. Alvin. People call me Al. Our family missed the *Mayflower*, so we came on the second boat. I guess this Peter Noyes was quite a character. He's buried up in the cemetery where you met me. We've just been painting the fenced-in area around one of the fancy graves up there. I thought it belonged to one of the nobility, but it turned out to be the grave of Peter's second carpenter."

I asked what, exactly, rebuilding the road entailed.

"Well, I helped build this road in 1924. It was an eighteen-foot road with a thirty-foot take-in, which means that there was six feet cleared on either side of the paved surface. Originally it had a foot of gravel and three coats of asphalt totaling about an inch. Now we're giving it a thirty-foot wide surface within a forty-foot take-in. That's where we have problems, extending the take-in. In one place, a couple of houses back there, we're taking four extra feet on one side and six on the other—you should hear the squawking from the lady we're taking the six feet from! I'm an appointed official now, but until a few years back this was an elected position. I always carried a high vote and got in handily, but no one ever could understand why. People all over town had gripes about me snatching slices of their front yards. Anyway, about this road—it'll still have the old foot of gravel underneath, but we'll top it with three coats of bituminous concrete with a total depth of five and a half inches. Up at the next curve where there's a bit of a swamp, we had to dig down to fourteen feet before we got hard stuff to rest on. That had to be filled. The road we're building will bear a greater weight of traffic. Also, being wider, it'll be safer for children. I want to paint white lines marking off a phantom sidewalk. We haven't got the money for real sidewalks on this sort of road. Over in Wayland they've put them in, but it was five hundred thousand dollars' worth."

A large, red dump truck rolled slowly by, pressed down on its haunches by a full load of gravel. The driver honked at the surveyors and waved at Noyes, who waved back.

"This is what we call a bread-and-butter road. We do it ourselves because it's not big enough to let out for contract to a private firm. But basically we get better construction this way. There's no pilfering. Everyone gives you a full day's work."

Mr. Noyes adjusted his hat. Feeling the warmth of the sun, he moved into the shade furnished by a tree overhanging the station wagon. The wind moved the tops of the pines.

"Talking of pilfering," he said, "Dan, one of those surveyors, was just telling me about a real thorough job that was pulled last week down on Route 20. Cleaned out a whole house—TV, air conditioner, the lot. Sudbury was all right twenty years ago. This sort of thing makes you realize it isn't getting any better."

I asked him if it were really getting any worse.

"Well, maybe not, but we've got growing pains for sure. We're up from thirty-five hundred to eleven thousand in just fifteen years. The men commute from here to those new companies on Route 128 and to Sperry Rand over on 177. A large part is gypsy population—the companies ship men from Michigan to here, and after a year or so from here to Texas. The men make a lot of money—some of them in the twenty thousand bracket—but they don't really belong. They come to the town meeting and complain. The Peter Noyes primary school has been running at double sessions for a good while, but things are beginning to level off. And they phone me up and ask me to have their driveways fixed. Strange enough, it's the ones who are in the deluxe set who really work for Sudbury. The men who run the companies and pay the big taxes. They mingle right in, go to our churches, and don't mind riding in a pickup truck with you."

"You mind moving, Al?" shouted the man with the transit. We were in his line of vision.

Mr. Noyes walked across the road and I walked with him. I said, "Is there any farming still?"

"There's one dairy farm—and dairy farming is what we used to be famous for. I went out as a child picking up milk cans, afternoons after school. I had a set route, and a team. Just the other day I heard an expression that made me think of those days. It was an old Yankee saying, 'John so-and-so, he'll cut his hay three times before he pays up.' We still have some truck farming and of course the greenhouses—Sudbury's known for its carnations. As for the rest, I guess we're growing people faster than we're growing anything else. The developments don't seem to stop. We've got one acre zoning, at least a forty thousand square-foot minimum, with a 180-foot minimum frontage. One developer here is sold out ahead into next year. He's been smart enough to build in a wooded area. Out in the open, sitting in an empty field, houses don't sell. People like trees. We've got an ordinance restricting building to a six percent maximum grade. That's to preserve the hills—and I can tell you the developers would like to get their hands on the hills, put houses on the ridge lines, ruin the views. Then there's the apartment-house trend. I don't quite follow that deal. Maybe it's no taxes to pay. No responsibility for raising a back garden. They'd rather play golf or go boating."

Mr. Noyes paused to nod to the driver who was bringing back the emptied dump truck. A small cloud of dust billowed along behind each of the slowly turning back wheels.

"Anyway, I still have eighty-five acres of the old Noyes property. My son has just built a house there. But my wife doesn't like the family place so I've bought an old house down on the main road. It's a bit more than two hundred years old, and pretty historical. Used to be one of the Underground Railroad stations. The fellow who owned it used to put the runaway blacks in the bottom of his wagon, and cart them up to Leaminster, twenty-odd miles—I guess a day's run there and back.

The wagon had a false bottom and a load of hay on top. From there they'd go on to the Canadian border. Once they left the country they were free.

"It was only a hundred years ago. But then history happens pretty fast, doesn't it? I was just out on Cape Cod last week. Open places where I went as a boy, that became camps and are now towns. Land you could have had for a few thousand a few years ago is now fifteen or twenty thousand. Then you take mortgages. Most of the old-timers around here wouldn't have had anything to do with them. I paid cash for my last car, and the dealer was offended. He was looking for his commission on the interest I ought to have been paying. But who walks these days? I ride around, and I notice the second-car routine. You know, the couple will have one new car. Then he'll drive off to work and she's stranded. But she's got to get to the shopping center down on Route 20. She's got to take the children from here to there. So they get her an old clunker, which pretty soon doesn't run or doesn't suit her. Then there's a new second car. I get a boot out of it."

I said that I thought Henry Ford would too.

"Yes, old Henry was on the ball. He had a big stretch of land here. He was a character, a real down-to-earth type of man. He'd jump over a log or crawl under a wire fence when he was out walking. And he liked restoring things. I remember he got all enthused with an old fellow here who ran square dances. That's my kind of music too. Can't take this Beatles business."

Mr. Noyes smiled. "Have you been out to the Wayside Inn? Henry did that up."

I said that I'd had lunch there.

"If you don't mind paying a bit extra, it's okay. I guess you know they lost most of it in a fire. That was a murderous night. After a wedding party had been there, I think. There was no water. They had to cut a hole through the ice to get to the pond. When you get a real bad one going like that you need hydrant pressure. Only thing left was the taproom. Henry's foundation paid for the rebuilding. They chased all over New Hampshire looking for old men who could hand-hew timbers. I suppose it was worth it. We need to keep a few of the old things around while civilization takes over."

4

Professor Murphy and the Blackstone Valley

WEST FROM Sudbury and through Hudson I drove, before turning south for a few miles on Route 495, a new interstate highway. On the way I thought about Mr. Noyes, the road-builder, at once a pessimistic observer of "civilization" and a not altogether reluctant participant in its march, living in an old house and at the same time making life easier for two-car families. Like the Sudbury road he was strengthening and widening, Route 495 was intended on a larger scale to meet the needs of more people traveling in more cars to more places where more houses are being built, and with more food needing to be carried to them in more trucks from—the local farms having gone—greater distances. Route 495 was also, like 128, a ring road, although built on a thirty-five rather than a five-mile radius from Boston, and a colleague of the circumferential highway systems engineers are planning and building around New York, Baltimore, and Washington. On this afternoon the need seemed to have been prematurely answered. Mine was the only car on the road. I wondered if I'd missed a sign saying that it wasn't officially open yet. Route 495 passed through cuts in hills and onto embankments over valleys, its four concrete lanes ironing out as many difficulties as a railroad track. I turned west again on 9, which runs straight into Worcester—straight, but at 5 P.M. on a weekday evening, not very fast. There seemed to be as many people driving into Worcester as there were driving out of it. There were countless cars turning into and out of the gas stations, supermarkets, discount stores, and donut shops that lined the route.

Worcester is the place where Matthew Arnold, on an American tour, complained of being served cold oysters for lunch—a strange complaint from the poet of Dover Beach. I think he was misheard, and meant *old* oysters. Be that as it may, I eschewed the Luan Lounge of the Holiday Inn Hotel, where I lodged, and after ditching my bags in my room went to sniff out a good restaurant. This problem, common to travelers everywhere, has the advantage of bringing out one's dormant scouting instincts; it also gives you a reason for looking at your surroundings. I walked through central Worcester, which looked like a European city in the late forties. (This impression was one I got in the center of most other cities on my trip.) Here it was urban renewal; there it had been war. Out of desolate, dusty spaces, buildings like the Holiday Inn and a community center were rising. Both decorous examples of low-height, anonymous modern architecture, the inn was marred only by the garish supermarket/movie-theater/bowling-alley type of sign that advertised its presence. I walked around the common, where grass still grew, past the city hall, and down several back streets lined with plumbing supply shops and small furniture stores. The few people around appeared to be waiting for buses to take them home. I stopped in front of a place called Thurstons. Opaque glass prevented me from looking in, so I entered and had my hunch rewarded: gin and tonic (the gin nicely astringent, the durable Schweppes bubbles curiously calming), red snapper soup, grilled mackerel, delmonico potatoes and buttered carrots, and rum cake. I have a taste for Italian or Spanish coffee, and the coffee at Thurstons was the only item I found wanting, but even then it was neither too old nor too cold.

In 1829 Theodore Dwight wrote a small book entitled *Sketches of Scenery and Manners in the United States* in which —in a chapter called "Travelling to Good Purpose"—he gave his advice to the tourist of the time. Having castigated those travelers who lugged around foreign novels and poems, Dwight wrote, "Instead of wishing to see the world through a fancied medium, the rational traveller wishes to view it as it is. He takes with him such books as contain necessary information in a compact and convenient form and, at setting out, endeavours to divest his mind of all prejudice, as well as to prepare his feelings to slide easily over the little trials he must expect, determined neither to fail of the enjoyments which lie before him by extravagant anticipations, nor to diminish them unnecessarily by unfortunate comparisons."

Mr. Dwight was a bit hard, I think, on the foreigners and on the fancied medium. I had a couple of Simenons in my suitcase, together with Yeats's *Collected Poems*, a book by Yale professor George Wilson Pierson entitled *Tocqueville in America*, and the September 1965 issue of *Scientific American* which was all about cities. I did not believe that either the Simenons or the Yeats were any impediment to seeing the world as it is; quite the contrary. Back at the Holiday Inn I put my feet up on the bed and got my after-dinner exercise in Yeats:

> I pace upon the battlements and stare
> On the foundations of a house, or where
> Tree, like a sooty finger, starts from the earth;
> And send imagination forth
> Under the day's declining beam, and call
> Images and memories
> From ruin or from ancient trees,
> For I would ask a question of them all.

I turned to Alexis de Tocqueville next. He came to America in 1831 with his friend Gustave de Beaumont to look at prisons and penitentiaries, was recalled after nine months, and wrote the classic text of the time on *Democracy in America*. I was interested, however, in the feeling he had after having been in the country for a week. It was a feeling of disenchantment that all he saw could be attributed to fate and circumstances rather than to the will of the people—that luck and happenstance were more responsible for America than the positive action of her citizens. It was similar to the impression I had got from reading the work of his successor Jean Gottmann, that the material world was in control, and the idea of America, the vision of the great republic, was in great danger of being swamped down the drain. One had this gloomy feeling, even though one knew that the idea of America persists; that in fact human freedom and human happiness have been realized here to a great extent; that the northeast, in particular, holds as Gottmann says, "the richest, best educated, best housed and best serviced group of similar size in the world"; that it remains a magnet for people from other places in the world at large because it promises health, goods, and opportunity to live well and (except for those for whom the two are contradictory) think well—to ponder, cherish, and extend the original idea.

I was pursuing this train of thought when I ran into one of those "little trials" Mr. Dwight warned travelers they should expect. I was in Room 307. There was a party in 306. I hadn't prepared my mind to slide easily over the amount of laughter, singing, and general racket that came through the flimsy hollowcore partitions that modern building technology has substituted for the solid brick and plaster walls of yore. Jokes you can't hear aren't funny. Furthermore, as the producers of television comedies ought to realize, there is a dissociating factor in the raucous laughter of people one doesn't know and isn't with, and which may be, for all one knows, canned. I tried a Simenon for a while and followed Maigret to one of those small

French provincial inns where he sits, puffing on his pipe and sopping up the local wine and atmosphere, until sooner or later the criminals crumble in the face of his spongelike invulnerability. I envied him. Around 11 P.M., when it sounded as if the people next door not only had their own party going but a party on the television set as well, I seized the phone. The front desk listened politely to my tale and said they would handle it. And so they did. A phone rang next door. The noise diminished, and in a few minutes there was a chastened series of good nights.

At ten next morning I drove to Clark University to see Dr. Raymond Murphy, who had not long before retired from being head of Clark's distinguished geography department. I hoped to get from him, in lieu of Professor Gottmann, a little academic background in the matter of the growing city and perhaps an insight or two into its problems and possibilities. It was another fine day. Since I was early I walked around the Clark campus, which is out toward the western boundary of the city, and seemed to be a useful microcosm of it: at the center, slightly shabby Victorian brick buildings surrounded by contemporary low brick dormitories (to which broad concrete windowsills added the effect of balconies), set amid old residential streets of three-story frame houses, painted drab browns and grays, and with front lawns that generally appeared to be in need of mowing. I recalled one of Gottmann's instructive graphs showing that in the veteran megalopolitan cities older houses like these had lost most of their original value after eighty years, although the increase in the value of the land they were built on may have made up for much of the loss. In these streets, the trees were already beginning to shed their leaves. Autumn seemed appropriately well-advanced.

Professor Murphy was in his office on the third floor of the Clark geography building, a gray-haired, square-headed man with the both bemused and amused look of someone who has spent his life teaching. On the shelves surrounding the office were copies of *Economic Geography*, the quarterly journal that Professor Murphy continues to edit, and on the table in front of him were the galley proofs of his book, since published, called *The American City: An Urban Geography*.

"Most of the books on cities tell you how the city should be planned," he said. "This book of mine, however, is not about the future. It's about the city of today. Of course"—he gave me an appraising grin—"it's technical."

I said, remembering the Glideway authors' plea for Jacks-of-all-trades, that things seemed to be moving in that direction rather fast.

"Well, the modern city is a complicated beast," Professor Murphy said, "and I don't know if there are many generalities about it, understandable by the layman, that are of much value. There are so many factors to consider. For instance, why the city is located where it is; why it has its particular shape; what kind of influence it has and how that can be measured; what its economic base is; what the city's distribution patterns and its functional classes are; who the people are who live or work in it; how the city structure got to be the way it is; how transportation, commerce, manufacturing, residential areas relate to it; and land use for schools, churches, recreation, or such things as cemeteries. Cemeteries are interesting, you know. I've studied them in Chicago. In one chapter in my book I go into their history and development, the reasons for new ones, the profit they make, locational factors, landform settings, extent and rate of use of cemetery land, methods of economizing on space, as well as some broader aspects. It's only a minor urban pattern, but an instructive one for the modern geographer." Professor Murphy took his eyes from a far window and looked at me. He said, "Probably none of this strikes you as the geography you remember from grade school."

I said that was indeed so.

"You aren't alone there. But the increasing complications of life on this planet aren't easily seen, or stated. We're trying to learn how to measure with precision what is going on, what is shifting and changing, and where and why."

"What about megalopolis?" I asked, leaving it to Professor Murphy to decide whether I meant the phenomenon or Gott-mann's book.

He plumped for the latter. "A great mass of useful information. Gottmann has a very individual way of operating. He goes to a city and sits in a hotel room and thinks." Professor Murphy smiled—he was a surveyor and measurer, and not a critic—and that was as far as he was going to be tempted. In any event, I was glad to hear that Jean Gottmann and I had something in common, although I wondered what he would have made of the party in Room 306 at the Holiday Inn. I asked Professor Murphy whether Worcester was a useful place for a geographer to live.

"It's fascinating," he said. "It's full of cultural variety, which the Census Bureau publications, by the way, don't altogether demonstrate. One of my students investigated and produced a map showing how different sections of the city had predominant nationalities—Anglo-Saxons, French-Canadians, Germans, Irish, Finnish, Portuguese, Negroes, Swedes, Italians, and so forth. Worcester is a melting pot which has never truly melted every element down. Another thing—according to the last census Worcester has lost population. Almost every large city in the northeast has done the same. What interests me here is that our neighbor, Springfield, has *gained* population. I haven't investigated yet—it would mean going over there and taking surveys and sitting in hotel rooms—but I have a feeling relief has something to do with it; physical relief, that is. Springfield is fairly flat, while Worcester has a good bit of up and down, which makes building more difficult."

"But despite the loss of population at the heart, aren't the cities spreading out toward one another?"

"Well, yes, in a sense, but it is an inexact use of the term city.

Cities like Worcester and Providence long ago filled up all the land inside their old town boundaries. That's why they are those strange shapes of solid color on any gasoline company road map. They are generally losing population to suburbs, but they can't annex the neighboring towns in which the growing suburbs lie, even though those towns are part of their respective 'urbanized area.' Of course, the neighboring towns have no desire to give up their independent status or their territory.

"This is one of the big problems, for it creates the most serious economic effects for the old, central city. In Massachusetts there is no sales tax; land, and improvements on it, carry a higher tax burden than elsewhere. Consequently, while the central city's costs are rising all the time, the tax base—due to loss of population and the increased use of land for public, tax-exempt purposes—is shrinking. And that's why there is a demand, in New York and elsewhere, to tax the commuters, though at least New York has a sales tax to relieve the pressure, as we don't. There is also the matter of political fragmentation —people work in one place and live in another. There are so many small political units in what is really one urbanized area. All those New Jersey counties and towns and boroughs close to New York are a good example. Toronto has taken a lead in that regard by setting up a metropolitan regional government—but then they may not have quite our tradition of small town democracy to buck against."

Professor Murphy suggested that it was time for a cup of coffee, and I agreed. Outside the geography building he patted, in passing, the trunk of a tall sycamore. We walked down the street to a tiny luncheonette. Dr. Murphy said, "I have a fish sandwich for lunch here every day. They have better coffee than the student union does." We sat at the counter, and a woman brought Dr. Murphy a cup of black coffee and asked me how I wanted mine. "Regular, please," I said, having found that the presence of milk tends to make bad coffee drinkable while it doesn't take away too much of the flavor when—in one or two exceptional places—the coffee is good.

"You asked earlier on if Worcester was a useful place for a geographer to live," Dr. Murphy said. "I meant to say then that I, too, have deserted the central city. I live in Princeton, which is a village eighteen miles north of here. If you study and write about cities, it's important to live in the country—you know the sort of country I mean—where the woods are surrounded by stone walls. Isn't it funny that in New England you can go into the woods almost everywhere? Up around us they aren't posted. I go fishing in all the streams. We live one-eighth of a mile up a lane, and the only places within walking distance are summer houses. The rest of the year it's all our own. Princeton doesn't have town water or town sewerage, and that limits our growth. We're high, and built on rock, and the town would go broke digging drains and ditches. Consequently there's a fair growth of individual homes, but no subdivisions."

Dr. Murphy told me that he'd grown up in the Midwest. He had gone to a public school and mining college and worked in a Kansas zinc and lead mine before taking his doctorate in geography at Wisconsin. He had taught in Hawaii, at Penn State, and at Clark since 1945. He was concerned about the general state of New England secondary education, which was tied to local property taxes; teaching in public schools had become a menial profession; very few of his students came to college able to write proper English—the few exceptions were often Canadian. We had a second cup of coffee, and this time I had it black.

"Where are you going from here?" Dr. Murphy asked.

"Either Providence or Springfield."

"If you're heading for Providence," he said with a grin that admitted his feeling of rivalry with the other Massachusetts city, "you might take a look at the Blackstone River Valley, with all its old mills. That was the economic geography of New England once."

I said that I would do just that.

The Blackstone was named after William Blackstone, who, in 1634, finding the tyranny of the Pilgrim oligarchy as oppressive

as that of the English bishops which had driven him across the
Atlantic, moved into the wilderness north of Narragansett Bay,
built a house called Study Hill, read books, rode a tame bull, and
grew sweet yellow apples that he handed out, in later years, to
the young people who came to hear the original settler of their
region preach. The Blackstone rises in Lake Quinsigamond on
the eastern boundary of the city of Worcester. The river runs
south-southeast for thirty-five miles until, having crossed the
Rhode Island border at Woonsocket, it joins the Seekonk River
at the top of Narragansett Bay. It is a nineteenth-century industrial river now, a junior Merrimack lined with mill villages and
mill towns rather than mill cities. On the Blackstone and tribu-
tary streams are Millville, Milford, Millis, Arnolds Mills, Grants
Mills, Valley Falls, and Central Falls. From Worcester to Providence one is never in open country. There are fields, but there
are houses along the roadside like stepping stones of habitation
between the towns and villages. The Blackstone Valley is a
rather scrappy model of megalopolis.

The day had become hot and humid. I drove out of Worcester and passed through the limbo of scrap dumps and burning garbage that one finds at the edge of cities, as the municipalities fill in swampy land, making territory, perhaps, where
they can no longer annex it. I left Route 146, which runs directly to Providence, bypassing most towns, in favor of 122A
and 122, which run indirectly, swinging from place to place like
the river. Halfway between Millbury and Fisherville I pulled
the Jeep over to the side of the road, shut off the engine, and
had a look around.

The prospect was of an undistinguished, thoroughly average
stretch of two-lane, hard-surfaced, second-class highway. The
roadside was unkempt. Blades of coarse grass thrust up through
rough gravel at the verge, and across the ditch more grass grew
thick and tall. In lieu of a hedge. wild bushes formed a scattered
margin, beginning to turn from dusty green to a dry red. Short
white posts set six feet or so apart marked a patch where the

road bordered marshy ground, and on the left-hand side utility poles marched at regular intervals, creosoted dark brown, their untapered trunks scarred by the crampons of telephone and power company linesmen. In the course of the next mile there were half a dozen buildings: a concrete-block warehouse, belonging to a plumbing supply company; a decayed barn, bearing a rusty yellow placard announcing that the *American Agriculturalist* was taken there; a house down a dirt lane at whose entrance a pickup truck blinked its turning light while its driver napped; a gas station, none too prosperous in appearance, advertising a sale of tires ("Second Tire for 99 Cents!!!"), and a large storage building that, somewhat improbably, proclaimed itself to be a "Discount Meat Center." Beyond it, a fruit and vegetable stand sold pumpkins, sweet cider, apples, and tomatoes, the latter for twelve cents a pound. Houses along the road were generally covered with asphalt, asbestos, or aluminum shingles. One had a notice tacked to the porch railing: "Dolls For Sale." Other manmade alterations to the landscape included a sand and gravel pit, with its tall loading chute, an orchard, in which red apples bobbed on twisted branches, and a little pond, stocked with trout and surrounded with dinky picnic benches for the benefit of a sportsmen's club. In the orchard birds and crickets chirped. In the road a dead skunk lay on its side. Cars passed, and one tailgating another hooted to get by. (The Worcester *Evening Gazette* had editorialized on the subject the night before. Tailgating, it appeared, was the chief cause of Worcester traffic accidents, and the police condoned it. The police said that traffic in the city was by necessity bumper-to-bumper. If they insisted that there be at least one car length interval between cars for every ten mph of speed, then no one in the city would get to their homes in less than an hour. The *Gazette* concluded that what Worcester needed was a whole new set of traffic arteries.)

I drove down the valley, and was surprised to see most of the mills working; the depression and such other causes as cheaper southern labor are usually said to have devastated the New England textile industry. In fact, not all the mills were devoted to their original industry, and for that matter not all of them were devoted to a single task. Part of Fairview Fabrics near Millbury had been rented out to a wheel-pressing firm. Others had given up the production of textiles in order to become furniture outlets or giant discount stores. A handsome mill at Northbridge was manufacturing plastics and chemicals, while the well-maintained mill at the junction of Whitinsville Road and Route 122 was in use as the packing and storage department of the Stylon Ceramic Tile Corporation. In Cumberland a huge mill was now a division of Owens-Corning Fiberglas, and appropriately in the backyards of several mill cottages Fiberglas motorboats could be seen, parked on trailers. The rural mills stood along the banks of the river, faced by water meadows. In the larger towns the mills confronted each other across the Blackstone, and even—in Woonsocket and Pawtucket—sometimes straddled it, as if they wanted to take from it not only water power but light and air as well. Certainly the air changed as one traveled downstream and the fumes of various industrial processes were added to it. The Blackstone itself changed color, from a dull muddy brown to the most unlikely pastel shades of red and blue.

In the nineteenth-century, America changed from a basically rural to a generally urban nation. The industrial revolution brought people in from the farms, where men had steered the plough and women had baked and spun, to the towns and cities, where both men and women worked in factories. In Rhode Island an English emigrant named Samuel Slater set up the first efficient spinning machinery, making it possible to transform a cottage handicraft into a factory-based industry. The cotton mill turned raw cotton into yarn, and since it depended on water power, mills were built by the falls or in places where the river flowed fast. Because such places were often in the country, the mills went out there, as if to meet their new workers halfway; houses for the mill hands had to be built, too. In his excellent book, *Rhode Island Architecture*, Henry Russell Hitchcock writes:

> Houses were built in groups because they were all needed at once when a new mill was started or an old mill enlarged. They were built alike because it was obviously, even with handicraft construction, the most efficient thing to do. They were near the mills because that was also most efficient; and they were frequently built without streets because walking was the only means of transportation available to the operatives. The broad spacing was natural because there was no shortage of land on open country sites; and the houses were well-built and maintained because like the mills they represented a permanent capital investment and also a drawing card in obtaining labor when labor was relatively scarce.

The houses were a special attraction in a time when manufacturing didn't have a snow-white reputation. The stone cottages at Fiskeville or the white frame cottages with trim mansard roofs at Hope demonstrated the difference between conditions in Rhode Island and the textile regions of Great Britain. Although there was no inside plumbing and running water, the rent generally came to no more than 10 percent of the wages of the head of the family, which was a strong inducement for farming people, in places like Canterbury, fed up with the stony New England countryside, or for the large Irish and French-Canadian families the mill owners wanted especially— there were many jobs in a mill that a child could do. And for many of these families, the total wages bought—admittedly with long hours, six days a week, and few holidays—clothes and lamps and other luxuries they'd never had before.

The mill villages were a little like feudal hamlets, clustered around the protecting castle of the lord of the manor, who in this case also owned the company store. Indeed, as long as the industry was run paternalistically, the village thrived. In Massachusetts, mass production set the pattern, and as always quantity made for bigness and impersonality in many aspects of mill life. In Rhode Island on the other hand, the simpler "Arkwright"

spinning process was retained; the Rhode Island mills got a reputation for high-class cloth, and the labor that produced it was
considered highly skilled. The large family–small community
foundation of the industry was reflected in the villages, with the
matching houses grouped in what modern architectural parlance
calls "superblocks," set on cul-de-sacs and pedestrian paths instead of on through streets. Behind their white picket fences
and under the shade of leafy trees, the houses gave the appearance of forming a utopian community. Of course, the houses
were all within earshot of the bell in the mill tower.

Mill workers were too busy to keep memoirs; the second
generation had to write it down. In the early 1940s a lawyer
named A. Archambault wrote a lightly fictionalized account of
his own family's life in a Rhode Island mill village. *Mill Village*
is the title, and the bell rings throughout.

The night watchman was always on his job. He rang seven bells to
tell mothers it was time to put all children to bed. At eight o'clock
he tolled the most weary to slumber; at nine, he summoned all
Christians to bed; at ten, he scolded the villagers for staying up so
late; at eleven, he reminded the sinful that eternity would call them
to account for their derelictions; at twelve, he intoned a tune of
peace and quiet over the sleeping village. His single stroke at one
o'clock was sounded on deaf ears. At two, he played his double
stroke to the glory of mothers warming milk for their infants. Three
bells were heard by the one or two villagers who suffered from
insomnia. At four, his bell began to assume the tone of authority; it
woke up the boss farmer and his two assistants. His five o'clock
clanging of bells was distinctly authoritative. Get up, all of you,
whether rested or tired, mothers, fathers, children. All of you who
have legs you can stand on, get up and slip your clothes on, and
push the kettle to the front of the stove; warm your soup and brew
your tea. . . .

At five fifty-five the mill whistle blew and when the bell chimed
six the village was at work.

Samuel Slater's two mills were giant, frame, barnlike places,
built of wood. After 1810 mills were generally stonewalled,
which was a partial protection against fire, but with timber
beams to carry the floors and machinery. After mid-century,

brick was favored; in the twentieth century, concrete skeleton construction produced more light and less beauty. In Woonsocket the whole series can be seen, though there, as in Pawtucket, the soft red brick of the brick mills has gone black with grime; to appreciate their style and texture the brick mills have to be seen in less built-up places. Not a few look like the main building of Providence's Brown University, which in turn was modeled after Princeton's Nassau Hall. Many have fine Georgian windows set between solid brick piers. Some have castellated towers, and Greek revival belfries.

After the Civil War large boarding houses of the Lowell, Massachusetts, variety made their appearance in Woonsocket, and the utopian middle ages were over. Workers wanted the benefits of larger towns rather than the amenities of the village. They wanted education, electric light, and, in the course of time, cars and movies and the big stores. In the beginning, real estate in the mill villages was untaxed, but when roads, police, and schools had to be paid for, the old tax on the number of spindles in the mills was insufficient. Houses and land were thus taxed, and the mill owners had to meet those costs together with higher wages and fewer hours. Increased rents on the houses merely drove the villagers faster into the towns. In the period between the two world wars, when the whole country was depressed and New England industry was moving south in search of cheap labor, the mill village lost its *raison d'etre*. Although it had been, as Mr. Archambault wrote, "as necessary to the production of cotton cloth as barracks in a military camp are necessary to the maintenance of an army," the mill village had become a decided liability for its owner. If the villages were fortunately close to urban centers where speculative money still existed, or if they contained houses still inhabited by people who were attached to their homes and could afford to buy them, the mill owners managed to sell their villages piecemeal, at auction. Today there are deserted houses set in semideserted villages in many parts of the state.

I had lunch in a diner on the main street of Uxbridge, half-way down the Blackstone Valley. I had a meat loaf sandwich, a glass of milk, a slice of Dutch apple pie, and a cup of coffee for eighty-five cents. Two men at the counter by the door discussed the defects of a Ford truck one of them had just bought for $900.

"Doesn't have the power."

"Nah, I don't trust them if they don't have the power."

A girl of twelve or so on my left was eating pumpkin pie. She told the woman behind the counter, who appeared to be her mother, that she had received an A-minus in English composition that morning. After she had gone off to school I could more easily hear two men sitting at the far end of the diner. One, who wore no jacket over a short-sleeved shirt and a bow tie, was talking about a casino he had visited in Nice, France.

"They had this stripper, see, who came on, boopity boop boop, and—socko!—it was all off, she had nothing on. Boopity boop boop, she was all stripped, no teasing."

He spoke very matter-of-factly; it was hard to say if he was complaining. I was interested that people one encounters in the Blackstone Valley nowadays vacation in the south of France. After paying my bill I drove on toward Providence.

5

Highwaysville

FOR A stranger, the central fact about Providence until a few months ago was the ease with which one got lost driving through it. This fact was the reason so many Northeast Corridor car travelers would commit themselves to the remark, "Providence is a mess," although they had seen very little that could be identified as a city as they drove through, following, say, Route 1 on a tortuous string of temporary roads and bumpy detours through crumbling blocks and huge tracts of redevelopment, with the many twists and turns marked insufficiently by small red numeral 1 signs tacked to fences and telephone poles, which—if one had the usual Providence luck—would suddenly start to sprout the yellow signs marking Route 6. Where, oh where, did one go from there? I intended to spend the following day seeing where Providence itself had got to, after all the upheaval; therefore I reconnoitered part of my route before heading west from the city to Foster, where I planned to spend the night with friends, twenty miles away, which at that latitude is just about the total width of the state.

Rhode Island is not only the smallest but the most densely

populated state. It has the handy size of 1018 square miles of land (plus 290 lakes, ponds, and reservoirs), indented by a 400-mile coastline, and inhabited by 900,000 people. The English nineteenth-century novelist Anthony Trollope, who quickly adjusted to the large American scale, found it difficult to tolerate Rhode Island's eccentric smallness. He wrote: "I should think it would be well for all parties if the whole state could be swallowed up by Massachusetts or by Connecticut, either of which lie conveniently near for the feat." Rhode Island from the beginning was not only small but different. "This colony," wrote the state historian Earl Tanner, "wedged between two strong-minded centers of Puritanism, was a haven of refuge for the otherwise-minded, the non-conformists who did not wish to be governed by anyone beside themselves, and the extremists who did not wish to be governed at all." Rhode Island was the first state to declare its independence of Great Britain, on May 4, 1776, and it was never in any hurry to join the Union.

As for Providence, Roger Williams named the city from "a sense of God's merciful providence," but it was the Revolutionary War that caused it to prosper. Newport, then the leading town in the state, was devastated by the British while Providence was not only never occupied by the enemy but retained its access to the sea; with the return of peace it experienced a boom in shipbuilding and maritime trade. It also became the outlet and market place for the adjoining areas of Connecticut and Massachusetts, and in 1790 Samuel Slater founded a mill in the adjacent town of Pawtucket, launching an industry which was to support Providence for more than a hundred years. The Blackstone, Seekonk, and other streams provided the necessary water power; the port brought in the raw materials; the nearby farms provided labor; coastal ships and then the railroad (after 1847) furnished transportation for the finished goods. In 1807 there were twelve textile mills in the state, in 1812 thirty-eight of them, employing three thousand workers. By 1862 one hundred and twelve factories were producing cotton goods. The industrial expansion encouraged other firms making textile machinery, printing presses, steam engines, wire, machine tools, and costume jewelry. Although Theodore Dwight found the banks of the Pawtucket River "varied and somewhat romantic" in 1826, he also observed that "the influx of strangers, many of them poor and ignorant foreigners, and most of them removed from the wholesome restraints of a better society, has produced unfavorable effects on habits and morals, which is the worst feature of the manufacturing system." Still standing throughout Providence and Pawtucket are the three-decker frame tenements—with a porch on every floor—that housed mill workers, and that were built for the most part around the turn of the century, a time when Rhode Island's population had a higher proportion of foreign-born than any other state. The year 1900 also marked the point when Providence's population formed 41 percent of the state's population. Although this percentage has declined, Rhode Island has remained the most urban state in the Union.

My friend Barney was born in Providence. A painter, he has lived in Chicago, Cannes, New York, and Tangier, and he is not the sort of person you would expect to find living at the end of a potholed dirt lane, two miles from the paved main road, in the desolate outback of Foster, a scattered rural township. Barney, of course, could claim that although he has returned close to his point of origin, he is still fighting the American trend: in a time when everyone is living in or moving into urban and suburban areas, Barney has moved out. Foster and indeed the whole western half of Rhode Island, from the northern border with Massachusetts to the southern Atlantic shore, is scrubby, boondock country, forested with rough pine woods and traversed by lonely roads along which the natives of the region speed in ten-year-old Mercurys, with chrome mufflers, depressed back ends, and fur charms dangling from the radio aerials. There is some development along these roads: a trailer, propped up on concrete blocks that visibly contradict its supposed mobility; a sunken, poured-concrete habitation, set in the ground like a bomb shelter or a potato shed, but which is apparently the basement of a house-to-be and which, with a flat roof, forms the house itself until the superstructure can be afforded; and several unexceptional specimens of contemporary ranch, colonial, and split. Many of the modern homesteaders who live out along these back roads, and who presumably built there because the roads opened up cheap land, work for General Dynamics Electric Boat, the nuclear submarine builder, in Groton, Connecticut, and commute the thirty-five miles each way in car pools. General Dynamics employs more Rhode Islanders than does any Rhode Island firm.

Barney's house is the homestead of another era, an early nineteenth-century farm. The house is built in the so-called Cape Cod style, with a long rectangular first floor and a big stone central chimney, and then two bedrooms up under the dormerless roof. Barney's roof is covered with red-brown chicken coop asphalt shingles, patched here and there with dollops of tar. (The Rhode Island Red, by the way, was developed in these parts.) The house walls are covered with weathered cedar shingles in the traditional Rhode Island manner. The only paint is the white of the window frames, trim, and front door.

Barney and his wife, Miriam, found the house after a long search in which they looked at summer cottages by the shore and abandoned mill houses in inland villages. It was cheap at $4500, and they have put an equal amount into fixing it up. Barney is still a trifle amused to find himself, at the age of forty, living in Rho-Dyland (as he insists it must be pronounced), but he can work well there and make quick trips to the city—by which he means New York—in three hours down the Connecticut Turnpike. He claims that he goes to the Cedar Tavern to meet his painting pals more often now than he did when he lived a few blocks from it; he can, having given up the city, more easily afford it; after a week or so of artistic creation in the mornings and property rehabilitation (building a barn, chopping down poison ivy, etc.) in the afternoons, he gets more enjoyment from the city lights.

The Jeep bucked up the lane to Barney's, and Barney, wearing a tartan shirt, corduroys, and ankle-high boots, met me at the backdoor. "Hey, I thought you were the forest service in that green Jeep. I'm waiting for a visit from them—they're going to show me how to plant Christmas trees. They subsidize you for doing it."

Barney and I went for a walk around his four-acre estate. He showed me where he had cleared land and burnt the poison ivy that had laid him low for two weeks. He, too, had an abandoned town road, dry stonewalls, some foundations of a barn, and a disused well covered with a fine well-stone. Through some thick woods on the slope of the hill behind the house, with the assistance of a colleague, Henry, a sculptor from the Cedar Tavern, he'd made a path.

"The scene here made him nervous," Barney said. "Not enough noise, action, or people. I saw him prowling around with a switchblade knife looking for some woodwork to carve up. So I thought, channel this energy or suffer a chopped-up house. I managed to get a machete, a fortuitous buy, into his hand, and led him out here, pointed him east, and said, 'Go.' Off he went, slashing through the underbrush and trees. I followed behind with a grass whip, smoothing it out. It took us an afternoon. Now we have a path, which makes a circle in the woods and comes back on the far side of the house—the Henry Memorial Path. I'm waiting for Miriam to give me a kid's woodburning outfit for Christmas so I can make a proper sign for it, à la State Park."

The house, spared from Henry's metropolitan aggressions, had been lovingly restored. Barney's paintings hung on rough white plaster walls between the exposed beam ceilings and the wide pine-board floors. Miriam cooked, in the big kitchen-dining room, on a Victorian wood-fired black iron stove. We had true Italian spaghetti, brought from Bleecker Street in Greenwich Village, a sauce whose ingredients had all been bought at the Foster grocery store, and half a gallon of red Fior di California, which Barney with some justice insists is the best transportable cheap wine in the world. It seemed to me that we had, at that moment, most of the benefits of the city with few of its drawbacks. Miriam told me how Barney had located the spot for their new well by dowsing for it with hickory twigs. Barney said they hadn't got a telephone yet because the cost to bring a line in from the mainroad would be $300.

"Miriam uses the phone down at the store on Route 6," Barney said. "The woman there, she remembers that Miriam comes from Scotland, and every time Miriam comes in she looks out from her baggy eyes and says to her 'Get pretty foggy out there where you come from?' We figure that at an average of three hundred and fifty visits a year, in three years time Miriam and the lady storekeeper will be nearing the one thousandth rehearsal of that little speech."

I drove into Providence with the early traffic, glad I had gone over the route on the previous day. The weather had the promise of again being hot and muggy. I parked in the lot behind the Sheraton Hotel, in central Providence, reserved a room for that night, and then walked around Kennedy Plaza (which used to be Exchange Place) to the offices of the Rhode Island Statewide Planning Program, where I had an 8:30 A.M. appointment with Richard Bouchard, the program director. Bouchard was in his shirt-sleeves, a big man in his early thirties who looked more like a professional football player than a planner. It is a common complaint that planners don't give enough consideration to "people," but even more common, I believe, is a failure to understand that planners are people too, who get held up in traffic jams, enjoy watching a game of ice hockey, and want to improve the way in which they live. In fact, in the course of my random sampling, I found city planners exceptional primarily in that most of them seemed to live on farms and held the belief that the great age of the city was imminent, if only "people" could be got to realize it.

"I'll tell you as simply as I can what we're up to," Bouchard said. "We've been in business just a year. Rhode Island is a vital link in the Boston-Washington corridor of population, trade, and finance, and it's got a good chance to prosper. But right now the tempo is fast—we're really rushed, because the advance is simultaneous on so many fronts: more people, more jobs, more houses, more roads, more recreation, more utilities. All these big changes make demands on natural and financial resources. The need for land and the use of land is being altered. There are many conflicts, and there are going to be many more. To avoid those conflicts and make the most of our resources requires careful statewide planning. That's what we're doing. Here in New England, only Connecticut is doing it too. Of course, we're a 'city-state'—the Providence metropolitan area contains three-quarters of the state's population—and to get federal funds these days you have to plan on a metropolitan basis as well. In our case that means planning for Attleboro, which is in Massachusetts. One of the first things I did in this job was bring the Connecticut, Massachusetts, and Rhode Island highway departments together, and now they meet once a month to discuss improvements that affect each other, and I keep track of what they're doing. As long as we can keep up with the road builders I'm fairly happy."

Mr. Bouchard went on to say that it was, as I might not know, National Highway Week and that, assuming I was interested in highways and their effect on a city like Providence, he had put my name down for a bus tour with state officials that was leaving the capitol in half an hour to view the new sections of Interstate Route 95 being built through the city. One effect of new highways, of course, is to facilitate car travel which, in turn, injures public transport systems. The major Providence bus company has been increasing fares and discontinuing services for a number of years. Mr. Bouchard pointed out to me, a few seats ahead of us in the chartered bus we boarded by the capitol, the director of the new State Transit Authority, a banker who was working out how to take over the financially pressed metropolitan bus lines and make a go of them. (He was also planning the inauguration of a hydrofoil commuter ferry service on Narragansett Bay in 1966. Boston, which has a retired army general running its combined transit system from an office at M.I.T., and New York, where Mayor Lindsay is trying to bring transportation order out of chaos, have yet to take to the water.) Also aboard our bus were members of the local press, radio, and TV, a representative of Keep America Beautiful, Inc., Chamber of Commerce officials of Providence, Pawtucket, and the Blackstone Valley, and men from the governor's office. The Governor would join us for lunch. Our conductor was Angelo Marcello, Director of Public Works, a smartly dressed, energetic man who won the sympathies of the passengers soon after the start by announcing, as he looked out through a window to tell us what was going on in a particular area of road building, "Wait a moment. Right now I'm lost."

One thing Interstate 95 will do is make it impossible for the through traveler who stays on it ever again to get lost in Providence. It runs in a clear, sinuous river of concrete from one end of the city to the other. On this day some sections were open, some were about to be opened, some were still only roughly graded earth, and in one place on the south edge of the city there were still fields, visible from a country road, where the expressway would soon plough its course. We traveled through regions of the old city where factories were going to move out of the way of the new road. We passed the railroad yards that divide the city, and were shown the New Haven roundhouse that also had to get out of the way. The New Haven—the interstate of yesteryear—has been slow, Mr. Marcello said, to give him the facts and figures on the relocation of the roundhouse, so in the meantime a maze of detours wound around it, marked with the notorious Providence route signs and arrows. We saw a place where the highway was depressed, though it could have been built at street level; the houses up above had been helped in terms of both their view and their drainage and, since there is no altruism in highway building, the earth excavated from the depression had been used in the next section where earth was needed to fill in swampy ground. We visited a place where an interchange was going to be located, and Sears, Roebuck—quick to gain so valuable a site—had already begun to build a shopping center. Marcello pointed out to us two particular problem areas, one a cemetery where forty-four hundred bodies had had to be shifted after every living relative of those interred there had been contacted and given his permission for the move. (We live in polite times. When Captain Marryat, author of *Midshipman Easy*, visited Providence in 1837, he was upset because the railroad passed over an old cemetery. The British officer exclaimed about the Yankees, "Here do they grind down the bones of their ancestors for the sake of gain!") The other place that had given the road builders trouble was a suburb called, of all things, Friendly Community. There, Marcello said, the opposition to an interchange had been extremely vociferous. At hostile protest meetings people asked, "How can they possibly do this to a middle-income neighborhood?"

Rhode Island, Mr. Bouchard told me, got a late start in the federal interstate highway building age, which may be roughly dated 1955–70, and to which much planning here and elsewhere is a direct short-term reaction. In Rhode Island there had been little desire for new roads and hence little federal money. In 1960, Angelo Marcello had started things moving and kept things moving to an extent where the state was now ahead of the rest of the country in getting its share of the interstate highway program finished. We stopped at one place on the tour where it was possible to sense some of the energy and excitement that Marcello had aroused. The stop was for a coffee break, but the coffee and doughnuts were served at a spot on the road, neatly chosen, where construction work was in progress. Graders and bulldozers rumbled past, and clouds of dust rose in the bright sun. Big yellow Mack trucks carrying dry-batch concrete dumped it into the hoppers of two huge mixing machines, after which water wagons rolled up to fill the mixers, which then proceeded to release the manufactured concrete in front of a machine known as a Rex slip-form paver, but which just about could be called a road-making machine.

I would have liked to have Al Noyes's comments on this juggernaut of the megalopolitan age. The machine was twenty-two feet long and twenty-five feet wide, weighed thirty-two thousand pounds, and looked like a careless mixture of parts from a giant sled, a bulldozer, a tractor, a concrete mixer, a plough, and several dozen lawn mowers. The Rex company's operating pamphlet says proudly,

Leading wing wall plates keep the concrete within the paving lines. . . . The tracks of the slip-form paver travel in the same trenches as the sub-grade planer. Uniform consistency of the batch is important since variation in moisture content will result in differential settlement and shrinkage of the concrete. The adjustable strike-off screed controlled by hydraulic cylinders advances and retracts. The screed is set about one inch above the height of the finished surface and spreads the concrete the full width of the pavement. By levelling the concrete to the compacting equipment a low head is maintained at the final strike-off. . . . Behind the strike-off, two pan vibrators and two tamping bars consolidate and puddle the mix to push the coarse aggregate slightly below the surface. This operation leaves the concrete ready for the finishing operation. . . . Squeeze! . . . As the paver moves forward the concrete is pressed down and squeezed out behind the plate under the load of the 32,000 pound machine. . . . Slip-forms added to the full 22 ft length of the machine trail in individual sections 16 ft long behind the machine . . . These forms hold the concrete for 8 to 12 minutes, depending on the forward speed. . . . A burlap drag attached to the end of the last of the series of forms gives the final finish.

I watched this leviathan inching forward, and the smooth concrete roadway being pressed out behind. One man was operating the machine from a position on a sort of bridge-deck. A number of other workmen, who looked as if they might have been put out of work by it, were standing in awe alongside. The Rex Company indeed claims that its machine eliminates four to ten thousand feet of steel forms, one form-handling truck, one pin-driving rig, two form setters, nine to eleven form-setter helpers and tampers, one compressor operator on the form-setting gang, one truck driver and one helper on the same gang, one jack hammer operator, one spreader operator, one transverse finisher operator, one longitudinal float finisher operator, and two belting and burlap-drag equipment handlers. In paving costs the company claims the machine saves five thousand to eight thousand dollars per lane per mile. (This particular section of I-95 was one and a third miles long, six lanes wide, and—partly because of the drainage problem—had the high cost of $6.5 million.) Behind the slip-form paver came a curing machine. After that, once the concrete had set, workmen with circular saws would cut joints several inches deep, to prevent the concrete from cracking. Then a final three-inch wearing course of bituminous concrete would be placed on top, although the concrete itself was smooth enough to drive on.

We had lunch at the spanking-new Providence airport, which gave the embarrassed impression of having provided facilities in advance of the demand for them. Perhaps it, too, was suffering from the competition of the highways. Governor Chafee, a lean and handsome young Republican, who won his job by 398 votes in 1962, and kept it by more than 80,000 votes in 1964 and 1966 (this in a state with a Democratic legislature and two Democrat senators), had several bites of a steak sandwich, praised Angelo Marcello and the U.S. Highway Department representative, thanked the press for helping get public support for a bond issue for new roads and the airport, and then dashed off. Governor Chafee had, I thought, beneath the look of charm and vigor a touch of bafflement which a man ahead of his times, or held from promotion by two equally liberal senators in the other party, might be justified in possessing. Bouchard said, "He's great. He eats breakfast most days at the luncheonette near our office. He sits at the counter. One advantage of Rhode Island is that if you have a problem about something it isn't hard to run into the Governor somewhere and ask him about it."

After lunch I had expected to go back into the city, but Bouchard introduced me to Ned Friday, chief of the Planning Division of the Rhode Island Development Council, Bouchard's parent outfit, who said, "How about taking a ride to get the whole picture?"

The ride was a flight. Friday led me out to a runway where we boarded a small helicopter and wedged ourselves, next to a pilot in shirt-sleeves, on the bank of seats under the plexiglass bubble canopy. We rose with less sensation of lift than one gets in an elevator—the ground simply diminished between our feet, and the racket of the noisy motor drowned any popping that might have taken place in our ears. We flew in a great circle south of the city at a height of fifteen hundred feet, observing parks, islands in Narragansett Bay dotted with summer houses, fields along a river, housing developments, shopping centers, a school, and some shipyards; we flew for a while over the Blackstone and its mills, and then over big patches of three-decker frame houses and the smaller area of historic rehabili- tated red brick buildings around Brown University. We flew on the fringe of some woods and finally we returned along the length of Interstate 95 that passes through the city.

We hadn't managed to talk much in the helicopter because of the engine noise, but going back into town Friday said, "What our present problem boils down to is this: we have a fixed amount of land and an increasing number of people. We also have the car, which has been bringing about a rapid change in urban structure. Cars and highways open up hitherto distant places—large areas of cheap land all around the city suddenly become ripe for industrial or residential development. People move out, particularly the young people and the wealthy people, leaving behind the poor and the elderly and the unproductive. Hartford lost 7.5 percent of her center city population in the 1950–60 period, Worcester lost 8.3 percent, and Providence lost 16.6 percent—which is a whopping figure. So you get suburban sprawl and an increasingly dilapidated city. In regard to the land that's opened up by roads like I-95, we have a study underway now to see what the state can do to buy or control land alongside new highways, so that it can prevent ribbon development or block the wrong use of land at valuable interchanges. Because highways like this alter time relationships, we're pushing our park system desperately, planning boat-launching areas, camping sites, and hiking trails, while we have the chance.

"Of course, the new roads are part of a centralizing process, too. In Rhode Island we've brought all our public health services into one spot. Furthermore, we're closer than ever to Connecticut and Massachusetts. We have quarterly joint meetings of New England state planners. We are beginning to talk in terms of regional instead of state education. We are asking questions such as 'Why have a woman's reformatory in Rhode Island for only twelve inmates—how about one for all New England?' And one other thing that people often forget: these new highways not only make it easier to get through or out of Providence—they also make it easier to get into it."

What will they do when they get there? I went for a stroll around the city before dinner and found in the pleasures of that excursion a partial answer: they will come in and walk. Walking in a city can be as great a pleasure as walking in the country; it is walking in the suburbs, along strict, unpopulated sidewalks, with people staring suspiciously from cars, that is impossible. Providence had one of the earliest nineteenth-century shopping arcades, which facilitated moving under cover from shop to shop; and nearby the city has now sponsored, following the example of Fresno, Toledo, Pomona, Ottawa, and Kalamazoo, a twentieth-century version of the arcade—a pedestrian mall. Five blocks of Westminster Street have been permanently closed to traffic, the street has been paved over from building wall to building wall with yellow-topped concrete, and birch trees, shrubs, lamposts, and benches have been set here and there along it. Several of the side streets have joined the movement and become extensions of the mall. Where a crosstown bus route traverses the main pedestrian way, warning lights flash, as at a railroad crossing, and buses pause before going through. At the southwest end of the mall several parking garages sit ready to scoop in the cars that can go no farther.

When I visited it, the mall had been open for only a month, but it already looked well-used. People were walking, sitting on the benches chatting, or window-shopping as if these were not novel things to do, but a pleasant, habitual way of spending an hour or so. The shops in the mall appeared improved and dignified by their new ambiance, and by the lack of noise, exhaust, and traffic, even when in many cases they still possessed the same sleazy glass and chromium shopfronts that could be found in other, unmade-over streets. In some instances a shopfront below had been improved, while the upper floors of the same building showed signs of long negligence and disuse. A number of the buildings were—especially in their upper levels—architecturally interesting, and one was grateful to the mall for making it possible to stand (or sit) and stare at them without feeling one was blocking a flow of pedestrian traffic or was in danger of being knocked into the path of a car. I went into a bookstore, and a young assistant told me that the mall seemed to be good for business, although monthly returns had not yet been compared. (In June 1966, some merchants said their business had gone up at least 20 percent.) The fact that all of the shops in the mall were open and in business (which wasn't the case in the surrounding, still-trafficked streets) seemed to be significant of the mall's attractions. It also had a cumulative effect of making the mall a brighter, more populous boulevard, in which someone visiting one shop tended to go on and visit a few more in the same area. Two of the larger department stores on the mall were apparently about to make use of this fact and channel a little of the trade by building a small plaza at second-floor level across the mall so that shoppers could walk undistracted from one store to the other. Walking was what the mall restored to the city person or the city visitor, and walking in such an environment without worrying about parking or the dangers of being killed at every corner is exercise without tension—it gives renewed meaning to the word promenade. On the way back to the Sheraton I passed two young women who were discussing which way they should take to the bus stop. It was a dispute settled quickly when one said, "Let's go through the mall," and her friend agreed.

At the Sheraton I had dinner—an overpriced, overcooked but nicely served meal. I sent back the Brussels sprouts. People who —on the basis of restaurant meals—condemn the British for their cooking of vegetables should order Brussels sprouts in half a dozen American public dining rooms. I know, of course, that it is supposedly either great poverty or great wealth that encourages great cooking; the Sheraton was intended to accommodate neither.

Having called the hotel operator and asked to be awakened at six the next morning, I turned in and read part of Sarah Kemble Knight's *Journals*. Madam Knight journeyed between Boston and New York in the years 1704–5. As one of her later editors noted, 1704 was "the year in which Peregrine White, the first child born in the Plymouth Colony, died, the same year as the publication of the first newspaper on the continent, two years before the birth of Benjamin Franklin, and twenty-eight years before George Washington was born." If this doesn't serve to place Mrs. Knight or give one an idea of the condition of the country, it may help to add that her trip, made to settle an estate in New Haven, took place over unmapped roads, through untouched forests, with many rivers to be forded and few places where she could be sure of a comfortable night's rest along the way. She set off in early October. Guides had to be hired here and there on her route. She—a woman traveling alone on horseback—was much marveled at, and deservedly so, for she put up with fatigue, swamps, ferry rides in canoes across dark, rushing rivers, and drunken locals at some of her stops for the night. At one place in this Narragansett country Mrs. Knight was kept up, as I was in Worcester, and composed her resentments thus:

> I ask thy aid, O potent rum!
> To charm these wrangling topers dumb.
> Thou hast their giddy brains possest—
> The man confounded with the beast—
> And I, poor I, can get no rest.
> Intoxicate them with thy fumes:
> O still their tongues till morning comes!

Mrs. Knight made me feel that I had been pretty lucky in my own easily surmounted misfortunes to date. At the stage post just before reaching Providence she called for something to eat. There were no Brussels sprouts to exchange for a salad. "The woman brought in a twisted thing like a cable, but something whiter; and, laying it on the board, tugged for life to bring it into a capacity to spread; which having with great pains accomplished, she served in a dish of pork and cabbage. . . . I, being hungry, got a little down; but my stomach was soon cloyed, and what cabbage I swallowed served me for a cud the whole day after."

6

Wetland

IPSWICH HAS some of the finest coastal marshes in the Northeast, and because Massachusetts has passed pioneering legislation to preserve those and other marshes in the state, David Ernest will find that if he builds a house with a view of them his view will last. I had been told that Rhode Island—behind Massachusetts but ahead of Connecticut in this respect—was now trying urgently to save her own marshes from the devastating forces of the highway age. Being someone who from childhood has continued to associate happiness with mud and water, I rose with alacrity at an early hour and drove southward out of Providence and down the western shore of Narragansett Bay to Saunderstown, in order to meet Dr. Nelson Marshall, professor of oceanography at the University of Rhode Island, who was conducting a survey of the state's marshes.

Dr. Marshall was a burly man, with tanned face and a sailor's wrinkles around his eyes, wearing a plaid shirt and an old tweed sports jacket. He sat behind a desk crowded with papers, books, and a microscope in the low, modern oceanography building set (several miles from the main campus in South Kingston) on the

73

slope of a hill facing Narragansett Bay. He said, "The situation is this. A marsh takes a good thousand years to be created. It can be destroyed in a day. It takes, I should say, a hundred years to make just one foot of salt-marsh peat, and it can't be restored the way a forest can. For the last two hundred years we've been filling in marshes without thought of the consequences and for the last twenty years we've been doing it fast. In Rhode Island we've just awakened to the fact that if we want to save what we've got left—which is about four thousand acres of coastal wetland—we've got to act now."

The marsh-destroying forces that have been and are still at work are agricultural drainage, flood control projects, dumping, pollution by industrial and human effluents, and the construction of roads, houses, factories, and marinas. Many of these have gone unchecked for so long, in the first place, because many people still think of marshes as murky bogs infested by ghouls and mosquitoes or, in the second place, because of the mistaken notion that a marsh, as a place of mud, birds, and seashells, has little more than aesthetic value. Few people were defending marshes for their great economic value. In fact, as Dr. Marshall pointed out, marshes are food factories that directly or indirectly nourish plants, fish, and birds, and provide shelter for young ocean fish. A salt marsh produces organic matter equivalent to an Iowa cornfield of equal size. A study of a tidal estuary in Connecticut, surrounded by salt marsh, demonstrated that one acre of it produced three hundred pounds of edible scallops every year, which is more than the beef yield from an acre of good grassland. During their first year of life such commercial fish as winter flounder and bluefish find food and shelter in marsh areas. Striped bass, menhaden, shad, and alewives spend part of their time feeding in marsh-lined estuaries and rivers. Furthermore, marshes act as spongy bulwarks against coastal erosion and flood, which million-dollar man-made defenses could never replace. To this end New Jersey began a coastal land acquisition program in 1932 and now has nearly a hundred thousand acres of protected land, much of it marshes.

Following various unsatisfactory court battles to protect Rhode Island marshes, Dr. Marshall and ten colleagues got together in 1965 to ask the state for a two-year moratorium on marsh development and destruction. They didn't get it. So, with Governor Chafee's help, they made another attack, and this succeeded. Rhode Island's state government acquired power to purchase marshland with funds from the federal "Green Acres" program, and legislation in the state assembly provided for the zoning of salt marshes. Under this bill, the director of the Department of Natural Resources was empowered to issue a written order, to be filed in each town hall, designating the situation and dimensions of "coastal wetlands or parts thereof, the ecology of which shall not be disturbed and the use of which shall be restricted to those uses compatible with the public policy of this state."

Therefore it was necessary to find out what constituted the present ecology of the marshes. It was a job that would have taken many years if done by a scientific team working methodically. Dr. Marshall and his associates decided that a marsh inventory was needed as soon as possible in order to give the legislation substance, and so they recruited a corps of volunteers, twenty-five strong—underwater engineers, zoology students, housewives, doctors, oceanographers, botanists, biologists, and such professional men as the manager of the Block Island Light & Power Company. Dr. Marshall then conducted a one-day workshop session at a marsh in Galilee, near the small fishing town of Point Judith, to teach the volunteers what to look for, and everyone waded around and got nicely wet and dirty. The state was carved up into working areas, and teams appointed to cover specific marshes or, since a marsh could run from one to several hundred acres, parts of marshes.

"How do you feel about a walk?" Dr. Marshall said.

I replied that when I wasn't driving a Jeep around the Northeast, I was inclined to move by sailing or walking. I had brought with me both boots and sneakers.

"Two of our graduate students were supposed to go out and

make a marsh inventory yesterday, but they're going this morning instead. They'd be glad to have you along."

Dr. Marshall introduced me, in the next office, to Jay Moore and John Tietjen, of the oceanographic school. Moore was six foot one and was wearing boots. Tietjen was six foot four and was wearing sneakers. We got into Tietjen's VW sedan, drove up the hill, and then turned south for several miles on what the road signs called Scenic 1A. Moore, a native of Washington, D.C., told me that after leaving college, where he'd studied marine biology, he had worked five years for an advertising agency in Manhattan. Finally he had tired of the carrot he felt was always dangling just in front of his nose. He felt fed up with sundry metropolitan pressures. He decided to return to marine biology. When word got around the agency of what he was doing, many of his co-workers expressed their envy, and said they'd be doing the same thing if it weren't for the mortgage or the kids or the wife. Moore wasn't sure how genuinely they meant this, but he knew that for himself the decision had been wise. He was now investigating the scallops of Niantic Bay. The day before he'd lost a half-week's work as a result of leaving an electric pump running the night of the new moon; there had been an abnormally low tide and the pump had gone dry and burned out. He didn't look particularly unhappy about this loss. In fact, he looked happy that this was the sort of calamity he had to face in his new career.

The hero of *Parade's End*, Ford Madox Ford's series of novels about a man he puts forward as the last English Tory, is called Christopher Tietjens. John Tietjen had never read Ford, but he had, like that author, not only a German father, born in Bremerhaven, but a mother born in Bavaria. Tietjen was studying for a doctorate with a thesis on an obscure marine algae called Remetodis.

"Here we are," he said, as we drove off Route 1A and across a small river. "This is Middlebridge. The river is the Pettaquamscutt, also known as the Narrow River."

The scenery had improved away from Scenic 1A. The river, a hundred feet wide (or narrow) at this point, flowed southward through margins of gray-green and brown-green marsh which on each side was bounded by low, slightly wooded ridges, with a house set here and there amid the trees, at the most one every half mile. A hundred yards downstream a man stood in a dilapidated dark gray skiff raking for quahogs. Two more skiffs were moored to stakes set in the mud beneath the abutment of the bridge we had driven over. From the stains on the abutments, I could tell that it was low tide; I donned my sneakers rather than my boots and followed Tietjen and Moore onto the marsh.

We walked springily. The ground was firm yet receptive underfoot, and the smell of marsh was strong. It was the smell of decay, of a million microscopic things living and dying and piling up on one another, plankton, algae, and small plants, all adding to make peat and building up land until larger plants and even trees could take root in it. It is a process that would in the course of time turn all salt ponds into marsh and then into salt-free land if it weren't for the fact that the sea has been rising some three or four inches every century as the glaciers melt; in New England the building of the sea has more than kept up with the building of marsh land. At any rate, the smell of the marsh by no means diminished the taste of the air on this clear and sunny morning. We walked along a small track of bare mud that led onto the plateau of marsh grass stretching between the river and the trees marking the solid shore.

"If you look closely," Tietjen said, "you can see that this marsh ground slopes slightly upward as it goes toward the trees. You can see how the zones change—how there are different kinds of marsh vegetation according to the elevation or distance from salt water. A difference of a few inches altitude is enough to change the type of cover. The salt in the soil is the controlling factor."

I asked him to identify some of the vegetation for me. I suffer from the common desire to know the names of growing things and the equally common failure to remember what they are called.

"Most of this light green zone closest to the water is *Spartina alterniflora*," Tietjen said, "also known as salt-marsh cord grass. There is a certain amount of *Spartina patens* or salt-meadow cord grass mixed in with it; *Spartina patens* is slightly finer than the *alterniflora*. The sharp stuff here and there is *Distichlis spikata;* on the edge of the brownish zone that begins about two-thirds of the way to the trees is *Juncus Gerandi*, or black rush. The purple plant in bloom is sea lavender—*Limonium carolinianum*—and then there's the seaside goldenrod—*Solidago sempervirens*—which roughly marks the limit of the salt marsh. You can see the cattails growing where the fresh water begins to seep in. The small trees behind, which are oak, locust, and crabapple, wouldn't grow if there were any salt in the soil."

While he talked, Tietjen had been numbering these zones of vegetation on his inventory sheet, which was held on a clipboard. He numbered them from the lowest elevation by the river to the highest by the trees. He estimated the percentage of marsh each zone comprised and the density of the zone. The inventory form gave him a choice of densities—rare, sparse, common, or abundant. It had also required him to identify the marsh and its location on the master inventory map. Later sections to be filled were for details on the substratum, birds, mammals, major marine fauna, conditions affecting the salinity of bordering tidal waters, indications of man-made abuse of natural marsh features, and indications that existing or projected modifications to the marsh or surrounding areas were altering or would alter the marsh. A final "general subjective evaluation" had to be made on the importance of conserving the tract under study as a natural resource area, and the volunteer was asked to include pertinent comments on the urgency of the particular situation.

We ambled along, sometimes following the river edge of the marsh, sometimes tracking across it toward the salt-free land.

Jay Moore had appointed himself the wildlife observer—a copy of Peterson's *Field Guide to Eastern Birds* poked from his windbreaker pocket—and the first he brought to our attention with a shouted "Look!" was a great blue heron—despite its name a rather gray bird, with yellowy green legs and whitish head and neck, but certainly "great" enough, with the wing-spread of an eagle and a height of four feet when standing. This heron flew slowly and silently down river. Moore, quoting Peterson, said its call was *"frahnk, frahnk, frawnk."*

On the river edge of the marsh we came to what Tietjen described as "an extensive mat"—a slimy coating of blue-green grass rimming the little foot-high cliff of bare mud. The river itself was clear; one could see scallop shells and eel grass on the bottom. During high spring tides this edge of the marsh would be covered and would swarm with tiny fish. Farther in, small islands of salt-free soil had formed in places where the peat substratum had buckled upward and risen sufficiently above the tide line to allow terrestial vegetation to take hold. Poking his foot at the eel grass, Moore said, "Some of the people at the lab think this stuff—it's called *zostera*—may be useful. They're looking for an antibiotic and this may fit the bill. Of course, it's also useful in the marsh cycle, the food chain of light, water, bacteria, plants, fish, and animals. Trophic dynamics is the name of the process."

A large brown area between two marsh hammocks turned out, at a close look, to be a pond covered with sludge. The sludge was mosquito larvae, thousands of minute wriggling things. (For some time I had been discreetly smacking my hands, neck, and face, a process designed to knock off a few of the mosquitoes that were strolling around on me looking for likely spots for exploitation.) Tietjen explained that, although other parts of this marsh had been ditched to drain ponds like these, this part had not. Ditching was to be preferred as a form of mosquito control to the use of many pesticides that annihilated other forms of marsh life. The oceanographic school had studied ditching, which to be effective had to be done correctly; the school had drawn up specifications for proper ditches. They should be no more than forty inches wide and fifteen inches deep. They should lead toward the seaway and allow the tide to move freely in and out. They should be redug not more than once every five years. The invasion of marsh plants into the ditches was a good thing, because it provided protection for young fish, and the ditches by introducing seawater discouraged land plants from growing in the marsh. All in all, the ditches encouraged the exchange of substances that produced marsh life. One ditch I examined seemed to be covered with patches of white bacteria and populated with mud snails feeding on the *zostera* along its banks. Under the bacteria, squadrons of minnows slipped through the eel grass.

Jay Moore had his binoculars out again, and was panning the stretch of marsh across the river. "Herons," he said, "four, five, six, eight, nine, good grief, a lot of them. Black duck too. Half a dozen."

In the course of the walk we also saw a kingfisher, tree swallows, bank swallows, gulls, loons, sandpipers, two crows, a green heron (a small bird with a chestnut-colored neck that would soon be flying down to Florida), and a pair of swans cruising upstream. Where the Narrow River, joined by a branch stream coming from Wakefield, dipped under Scenic 1A and out through a gap in the dunes to the sea, there was a bare spot of hard marsh mud denuded of vegetation. Presumably the tide and current were fiercest here. The only items of interest were a dead gull, some driftwood, a shell of a horseshoe crab, and such human debris as a light bulb, two beer cans, and several expended shotgun shells. Beyond the bare patch was an area which in contrast looked like expensive carpet.

"*Spartina patens*," said Tietjen.

I asked why it looked unlike the *Spartina patens* we'd seen before.

"It's very thin—it can't support its own weight—and therefore it's lying down."

Moore wriggled his boots in it. "Terrific stuff," he said.

We came to the remnants of a fence; old posts with rusty eyebolts, meant for now long-vanished wire, stood at various angles of heel, in a row that led toward the trees. A house was just visible beyond the ridge. Tietjen said, "This is someone's property, which is another of the factors we're up against. Most marsh in Rhode Island is privately owned. In colonial times the marshes were the most valued assets of a coastal town—people prized the right to own part of a marsh and harvest the hay. Even today, although the title deeds are generally pretty foggy by now, some people will say you're trespassing for walking through their marsh."

Moore said, "We're supposed to write it in the inventory if we're run off any place."

"A couple of years ago," Tietjen went on, "conservation interests here fought several court cases to try to prove that land below the mean high-water mark was state land, and therefore couldn't be dredged out or dumped on by individuals. These proceedings, however, only confused the matter. In one case, the man who drove the dump truck was the defendant, and he didn't know nuttin'. It was a real tangle—it was hard, for instance, to get anyone to agree where the high-water mark was. That was the point at which Dr. Marshall and others went to the governor and got things started. Now the state has the responsibility to preserve the marshes, but the state is still under a lot of pressure.

"Take this river as it winds north of here. Up at the head of it, at Saunderstown, is Gilbert Stuart's house—it was made a National Landmark recently. For locals another landmark is Bill Lacey's house by the bridge where Route 138 crosses the river. Lacey is an old recluse who used to rent out skiffs to fishermen, but he says no one rents them now that the river's so polluted; so murky you can't see the bottom in four feet of water the way you could a few years ago. Well, between Lacey's tumble-down cottage and Gilbert Stuart's house there's a lot of development, riverfront subdivisions, and consequently more boating and the need for a marina and all that. The Mettatuxet Betterment Association, which is mainly summer people, wants the state to dredge the river. There's no doubt it's silting up, but no one has yet looked to see where the silt is coming from—maybe it's coming from those cleared areas where there are now houses and yards instead of trees. And the problem is to stop them from dredging before they've investigated what the side effects may be. Dredging to one depth might be good for the marsh, especially if there's pollution coming downstream. Dredging to another depth might be terrible."

I had lunch in the seaside town of Narragansett Pier. This was a nineteenth-century watering place that had gone to seed; that had, more precisely, been burnt down and blown away. The pier itself went in the great 1938 hurricane, which is the natural phenomenon people still talk about all along the northeast coast—a fact that makes one realize how rarely people are aware of nature until it kicks them, hard. The pier-head buildings, designed by McKim, Mead and White rather late in their heyday, were partially burnt down several years ago. I had a pork cutlet, mashed potatoes, and peas in one of the few lunching establishments still open nearly a month after the end of the season, and then a brief walk around the town. Narragansett Pier seemed to be the sort of place that prosperity enables to show a decent face, powdered and painted; in bad times the commonness and grime would show through. Although there are some big, well-kept houses along this shore, the Pier, as it is called, sets the tone that is matched by hundreds of summer shacks, built of tarpaper, asbestos shingles, and concrete blocks. Architects who—thinking of Saarinen's TWA building and Maillart's bridges—call this the age of concrete may be right. But what is a great freedom at the top, allowing buildings to escape some of the strictness of steel and stone, may be rather a sloppy freedom at the bottom. Or so it seemed to me as I drove along Route 1A around Point Judith Pond and cast a gloomy eye on the concrete blocks that everywhere seemed to support old cars and mobile homes, and were serving as the unfinished walls of ranch house foundations and quarter-acre estates. Route 1A joins Route 1 and heads west along the coast, behind Matinuck, Charlestown, Quonochontaug, Weekapaug, and Misquamicut. Dunes and summer houses occupied the beach, and ribbon development strung out along the ill-paved road. A new Route 1 was under construction, and trucks were lumbering along it with loads of gravel; but there was no slip-form paver working and the general pace seemed slower, perhaps because it was not a federal project but a fifty-fifty one, done with the state matching federal funds.

At Haversham the road turns inland slightly to negotiate the river that divides Connecticut and Rhode Island—the Westerly River, as the inhabitants of Pawcatuck, Connecticut, on the western bank seem to favor calling it; or the Pawcatuck River, which is what they call it in Westerly, Rhode Island. Mrs. Sarah Kemble Knight had tribulations at this spot, first seeing the river in flood at high tide. But having forded it, she was very glad to reach Stonington, where—after all her hardships—she was "very well accommodated both as to victuals and lodging." As indeed I was.

7

Moving Out

I STAYED at home for the night. At dinner my wife brought me up to date with the week's news: Bonnie Davis had had a baby; the Hoaglands had finally found an apartment that suited them; the Merryweather house had been sold for sixty thousand, which was twice as much as Lynn Brush had paid for it ten months ago; the Ribieras had a new car and had a big fight out in the street with Mr. Nilson, who had been accustomed to parking his car in front of their house; two teen-agers had been arrested for rifling the change machine at the village laundromat; and, biggest news of all, a great squabble was going on about a new factory that someone wanted to set up over on Quiambaug Cove—allegedly the last piece of unpolluted water between Stonington and New York. She didn't say triumphantly at the end of this (as she might well have done), "You see—it's all happening here."

I asked her to tell me about the factory, since it was a kind of factory-in-the-country that I was going to see the next day.

The account was this. A Stamford company specializing in factory construction had bought a tract of land on Quiambaug

Cove for another firm, whose name and product the Stamford outfit refused to make known. The land around the cove was still mainly either residential or open fields, although one factory which made wire clips for industrial purposes had a low, well-designed plant on the shores of the cove's inlet, between Route 1 and the New Haven Railroad tracks; on the other side of the inlet, closer to Route 1, the Connecticut Light and Power Company had set up a district office and service facility. At a meeting of the zoning board, officials of the Stamford company assured zoning commission members that the factory would not violate any of Stonington's strict ordinances. They continued, however, to refuse, for (they said) competitive reasons, to reveal what the factory would make. The zoning board agreed to rezone the factory site from residential to industrial.

Thus the row began, with the "mystery company" on one side, backed by various supporters, and all sorts of people who were highly vocal on the other. As do most towns, Stonington has numbers of people who are all for bringing to the town new industry, which has the reputation of paying large taxes, boosting employment, increasing local business and local income, and sending no children to overburdened public schools in the way a new subdivision does. Many people claimed with justice that a modern factory—like the Kellems wire clip plant, already on the cove—was far better looking than either a collection of ranch houses or colonial-style apartment houses, one of which had, a year before, been spoken of as a possibility for this same site. Moreover, the town selectmen seemed to have committed themselves to the new factory as a good thing.

Despite the opposition—which claimed that the plant didn't fit the recommendations of a planning consultant the town had hired to draw up a plan of development four years before—the factory would probably have been a shoo-in if it hadn't been for the geography of the situation. The prevailing wind is from the southwest. The proposed factory lay directly southwest, over the brow of a hill, from Montauk Avenue, Stonington's so-called Gold Coast, where fifty- to one-hundred-thousand-dollar houses are strung along a bleak road that runs across the hilltop. The houses have a fine view of the village and the sea beyond—in fact, on a clear day a view that extends to Montauk, Long Island. Having good connections, some of the owners of these houses managed to find out that the proposed factory was to extract magnesium from sea water; chlorine gas and hydrochloric acid were said to be involved in the process. An additional danger was seen in the lime dust from settling basins which could blow over the countryside and kill vegetation. What is more, the factory allegedly would dump 360,000 gallons of fresh water daily into the tidal cove, presumably upsetting the natural balance of the place, and disturbing the shellfish, fish, ducks, and swans that live there.

At a public meeting most of those attending voted against the plant. One hundred and seventy-five people registered with the clerk of the meeting their disapproval, while eight people spoke in favor of it, several of them spokesmen for the Stamford outfit. Since the zoning board refused to reverse its 5–0 decision, saying they trusted the company's promise to abide by Stonington ordinances against contamination and other nuisances, the opponents of the company went to court, intending to prove that the Planning and Zoning Commission failed to abide by the town plan of development, approved a "spot" zoning change, and denied the neighboring property owners due process of law at the public hearing by refusing to divulge significant information about those requesting the zone change. The opponents hired excellent counsel, including the mayor of New London and an attorney from a law firm that specialized in zoning cases—a firm that happened to be in Stamford. Some 350 Stonington residents were prepared to act as plaintiffs in the action and were ready to fight the case for two or three years, if necessary, not only to keep out the purported magnesium plant but to reverse the change in zoning. Having the right and—what makes the right feasible much of the time—the money to do this, the opponents expected the company to look elsewhere for a plant location.

Meanwhile, certain questions remain unresolved. Has Stonington lost a good thing? Why was the company acting so mysterious if it weren't feeling guilty about its process? Is it generally true that companies flout ordinances once they are established in a town and paying useful taxes? Assuming the opponents of the plant are right in their defense of the cove and its delicate ecology, should they win their fight through such weapons as procrastination and wealth?

Elsewhere, if not on Quiambaug Cove, factories are appearing. Next to the Stonington high school on the road to Westerly a large modern plant has been built in the last year, with plenty of parking and loading space, with bright architecture and well-landscaped grounds; while in the center of Mystic Village five miles away sits the empty three-story brick mill-type building the company vacated. Dr. Murphy, at Worcester, said he'd found that in investigating what made good sites for factories, he was also investigating good sites for subdivisions. Indeed, in parts of New Jersey competition was fierce between them. In *The New York Times'* "Annual Review of Business" (January, 1966), the Lehigh Valley Development Council, seeking new factories, trumpeted itself as "Center of Megalopolis, USA," while on another page Woodbridge, New Jersey, proudly displayed a map crisscrossed with railroads, superhighways, and connecting roads together with a long list of Woodbridge companies. The unanswered question was where do the people of Woodbridge live, and do they like it? All over the Northeast—as H. G. Wells foresaw sixty years ago—businesses are tending to move out of the older cities, like middle-class families seeking cheaper and healthier places to live.

To make such a move, people generally go on Sunday afternoon drives, glancing at various communities; they see where friends have moved, and ask their advice; they end up visiting a real-estate agent who takes them round to look at houses. For restless companies there are plant location specialists who undertake all these tasks. In New York, before making my trip, I made a call on the Fantus Company, one of the leading firms in this contemporary business of advising companies what site to select and of advising towns what companies to seek. Fantus has "relocated" some 2500 companies employing more than a million workers. Most companies have the same desires: they are looking for lower labor costs, lower taxes, improved access to raw material, more skilled labor, and lots of room for expansion.

Older cities fall down in most of these respects. New York, as the biggest city, seems to fall hardest. In 1942 New York housed forty-two firms with more than a thousand workers apiece, and in 1962 it was down to nineteen. Leonard Yaseen, chairman of Fantus, told me that the one-story plant, which came into vogue as a more efficient building at the end of the depression, had been a big factor in the need for room. Moreover, moving across the river to New Jersey had cut many companies' power costs by one-third. Notable had been Sperry Gyroscope's move to Lake Success, Long Island, from Brooklyn in 1942, taking thirty-five hundred workers out to Nassau County and spurring that county's growth. An instructive move was that of Richelieu Pearls, which a few years ago moved fifty-five miles from Brooklyn to Holbrook, in Suffolk County, Long Island, although this added an hour to the transportation time required to get their simulated pearls to Manhattan customers. Offsetting this, they found in Holbrook reduced taxes, lower insurance rates, cheaper labor, and more efficient production. In Brooklyn they had had an old building and wouldn't have been able to afford the construction of a new building like the one they owned in Holbrook. Furthermore, they had clean air. In the city the pearl company had been rejecting 10 percent of its production because of dull appearance—the grimy metropolitan air affected the plastic coating of the artificial pearls. In Suffolk County the rejection rate fell below 2 percent.

These days Fantus is especially interested in office-firm relocation. In the course of interviewing all of the major firms in uptown New York, Fantus had found what Mr. Yaseen called "an alarming consistency of response." What such big companies as banks and insurance firms were particularly upset about was the calibre of their clerical employees. The executives felt that at least half their staffs didn't know how to dress properly, how to enter an office, or how to be anything but apathetic about their jobs. There was a shortage of operators of office machines. Most city kids—the company executives felt—were trained either to go to college or to be unemployable; they certainly weren't cut out to be clerical.

While many factories were moving to small towns and rural areas, most of the office-firms were going to the suburbs in the way IBM and General Foods had gone to Westchester. There the "right kind of worker" was easier to come by, particularly from what Fantus calls the re-entry group, women who are married and have children in school, have limited working ambitions but are willing to do a good job for a decent wage. Some companies were moving to sites between Washington and Baltimore, Baltimore and Philadelphia, or Philadelphia and New York, where they could take advantage of people commuting *out* from the suburbs of two cities to the firm between. (The Long Island Railroad carries 10 percent more workers outward from New York City than it did six years ago. Public Service Bus Lines, serving New Jersey suburbia, has also announced a big increase in reverse commuting. An interesting case is presented by Princeton, New Jersey, which sends an equal amount of commuters to Philadelphia and New York; however, a greater amount of people are now commuting in from elsewhere to the new factories and offices around Princeton.) Altogether this trend indicates one of the most potent forces working toward a suburban city along the whole length of the Northeast Corridor.

The suburban company that I stopped to see moved nine years ago, and it moved not out of New York but out of Hartford, Connecticut, to a site most unlike those to be found among the New Jersey subdivisions or along a circumferential road such as Boston's Route 128. The Connecticut General Life Insurance Company moved five miles from the center of Hartford to some lush, rolling fields in the still unbuilt-up countryside near Bloomfield. I drove up from Stonington in the early morning, along the coast to New London and then striking inland, along Route 85 and Route 2, through such small towns as Salem, Colchester, and Marlboro. The hills were wooded, the valleys full of mist and the road empty. Hartford itself seemed busy. Tall new buildings rose into the sky from what appeared to be a large concrete tray twenty feet above road level—a project called Constitution Plaza, which is considered to be one of the best small-scale redevelopments of a run-down central city area. The Travellers Insurance Company (insurance is *the* business in Hartford) put up $35 million for the development of the land and to back the building of five new office buildings and a hotel grouped around a pedestrian plaza. Phoenix Mutual Life Insurance, which had been thinking of moving out to suburban West Hartford, stayed and built its own green glass oval-shaped building connected by a bridge to the plaza. G. Fox, a department store, constructed a twelve million dollar annex and E. J. Korvette moved into some adjacent premises.

This glimpse I had of Hartford, the walk I had taken in Providence's Westminster Mall, and a more detailed look I had later on at Philadelphia, combined to suggest that there is no need to despair for the central city so long as initiative and imagination are used to make it a place of convenience, interest, and character. And for those who retain a prejudice in favor of cities, another reason for optimism is that few exiting companies have shown anything like the imagination displayed by Connecticut General in its move out of Hartford to Bloomfield in 1957.

In one sense, Connecticut General was in the tradition of the mills that went out to the meadows along the Blackstone Valley to be near the natural and human resources they needed. In another sense, Connecticut General was like an eighteenth-century English nobleman making sure that the country house he was building and the park that surrounded it were as distinguished and truly life-enhancing as could be. From the road, one drove in through open gates, formed from two single I-beam steel girders, and then beneath an immaculately clipped hedge, following signs that led along a Tarmac drive through a green field. Shortly, over a low rise, appeared a long, three-story glass and steel structure, looking a little like Manhattan's Lever Brothers Building lying flat on its side, and giving, indeed, the immediate impression that it would look as well two hundred years from now as it does today. It is an unassertive building that doesn't yell "stare at me!" the way some modern buildings do; it was designed by Gordon Bunshaft of Skidmore, Owings, and Merrill, who designed Lever House. Four interior courtyards, arranged by the sculptor Noguchi, bring a miniature countryside within. The building itself is set amid three hundred acres of grass and trees, and on looking around from the top of the rise it seemed to me the sort of countryside one sees in Constable landscapes or in the background of Gainsborough portraits, with stately oaks, formal meadows, and the ridges of the wooded hills rising green from the misty valleys. A great pond lies before the building, while a family group sculptured by Noguchi has been placed on a conspicuous knoll. In that classic, Anglo-American circumstance those abstract red granite figures seemed at first a little out of place; but they were perhaps no more so than a gazebo or a Grecian summerhouse might have been beside a country house.

I toured the building with a young lady from the public relations department. Her name was Andrea Calabreze, and she was handsome in a suitably classical way. She was about to go back to the central city as a reporter for the Hartford *Times*, but she seemed to have a very real enthusiasm for the building as she pointed out the absolutely up-to-date Mies van der Röhe chairs in a reception lounge (chairs first seen in the 1924 Barcelona exhibition) and the Knoll desks in executive offices. She named the materials used in the interior: teak, walnut, cherrywood, travertine marble, glass, and steel. She dispensed such illuminating facts as that—Connecticut General being interested not in short-term speculation but sound long-haul maintenance—a very good floor tile had been rejected in favor of one that cost 4 percent more. We looked at large bright spaces full of desks and young women behind them. The floors of these areas were almost entirely open, with no posts, columns, or permanent walls. The company is thus able to enlarge or reduce departments as business varies; insurance policies can be processed in a horizontal, assembly line operation, which is the most efficient. We looked at auditoriums, lounges, shops, the cafeteria, the executive offices, data processing rooms, libraries, and the courtyards, in one of which there had been a string quartet recital the night before. Nearly a quarter of the interior is given over to employee nonworking activities; but the whole building gave the impression of taking the people who work within it into account.

As an entity, the building seems solid and secure in the way that an insurance company's headquarters must; it is flooded with daylight yet firm on the ground. The firmness is partly an effect of the quality of the parts. Although the office partitions are movable, they look permanent (first designed for Connecticut General, they have since been put into wide production); for example, where the partitions butt against an exterior plate glass window, a filler strip designed for the job gives the joint a precise and perfect finish. Anyone who has ever done house carpentry or built even a bookcase out of pine boards would appreciate the Connecticut General building. It makes clear that when people complain that craftsmanship is dead, that you can't get a workman to do a thing right anymore, they are thinking on the wrong scale: craftsmanship is possible when you are making a Gemini spacecraft or a building such as this. It is craftsmanship with no flamboyant signature scrawled across it. *Architectural Forum* wrote soon after it was finished, "The entire building is *designed*, and there are no cracks showing between the approach to the overall plan and the corners of the wood panelling. It is pervasively complete; the patterns of rectangles—everything is rectangles—range from the minute to the mammoth, but they are all so subtly related that the architect renders himself almost invisible. When you look to find him, or his mark, in one particular spot, you find instead a view of the countryside, neatly framed. . . ." The building's excellence was indeed pervasive. So much so that my only doubt was whether in the long run it would be a good thing to work inside a masterpiece.

Connecticut General moved out of town for many good reasons. A study in 1947 had shown that the company had ten years before it grew too big for its downtown Hartford offices. In 1950 the company bought three hundred acres near Bloomfield. Two years later, having conducted studies into the horizontal type of operation, the company concluded that it would work for insurance as it had for other industries, and so they decided to build anew. Frazar Wilde, who was then president and is now chairman, sent out teams of executives to canvass architectural schools and firms across the country, with the result that the Manhattan firm of Skidmore, Owings, and Merrill was named designers; the Turner Construction Company— which had built many New York City structures—became the builders; and Dr. Walter Voss of M.I.T.—which seems to pop up everywhere in northeast cities where bright things are going on—was appointed consultant in materials. The building was planned and designed in a cooperative effort, with a number of teams threshing out aspects of the overall problem. A two-story mock-up costing $100,000 made easier the working-out of such features as ceiling construction and lighting; a good part of this

cost was recovered in the open ceiling, with baffles over flores-
cent lights and a sprinkler system, which was installed in the
actual building. The teams had one big battle. This was fought
over the eight-story tower that Skidmore, Owings, and Merrill
wanted to house executive and nonexpandable offices and—
aesthetically—to furnish contrast with the low main building.
Mr. Wilde and his colleagues were worried that this tower
might be considered a symbol of executive snootiness; that, as a
Connecticut General memo of the time put it, it would maxi-
mize intracompany distances and minimize intracompany proximity. An influential and less long-winded Philadelphia client
said simply that he thought the tower was undemocratic. In
the end, the tower was reduced to three stories and a penthouse
—a judicious and effective compromise. Mr. Wilde's office in
the penthouse had to do without the fireplace the chairman
wanted, but it does have a rather snooty antique Georgian desk
and chair.

The building and grounds cost twenty-three million dollars,
which is a great deal more than most companies would spend
for a similar amount of office space. I had lunch in the cafeteria
with Henry Dawes, director of personnel, who said it had been
easily worth that figure. "The building has paid for itself in just
the lower turnover of employees," said Mr. Dawes, a charming
gray-haired man in late middle-age. "The insurance business
needs girls and women for clerical jobs, and we used to have a
very high turnover rate in Hartford—over 26 percent in 1956.
We expected to lose 10 percent in a single month as a result of
moving, but we lost less than 2 percent. Since the move the rate
has been 19 percent a year. Our absence periods for both men
and women are the lowest in the industry. Our business is growing faster than that of other companies, but so is our produc-
tivity per worker. We've only added 5 percent to our clerical
force while other large companies have added 15 percent."

There are various problems attached to having women as
nearly three-quarters of a total staff of twenty-five hundred.

They get married and pregnant and have husbands who move to distant places. They like to go shopping during their lunch hours, buy strange sandwiches in delicatessens, and take courses in German language or Spanish literature. Mr. Dawes was worried about how they would take to spending all day among the fields of Bloomfield. Connecticut General decided to provide many of the services of a city: library, theater, gym, beauty salon, and soda fountain. There is a large dress and novelty shop, interestingly stocked with cosmetics, childrens' clothes, good china, etc., and always full at lunch hour. This latter-day version of the mill village company store makes a profit. Connecticut General sent the girl who runs it to a store management course at New York University; like many other companies of comparable size, it will sponsor the further-education of any of its employees, paying 70 percent of tuition costs after the successful completion of a course.

The building itself may have an educational effect. Mr. Dawes was impressed by the case of a young Negro girl who came to work for Connecticut General with much against her: poor looks, unhappy family, and no ambition. "Now the girl is articulate," said Mr. Dawes. "It's a delight to walk around the building with her. She sees things that other people don't." Miss Calabreze thought the building imposed its own discipline, making one feel that one's desk should be tidy at night. She also suggested that some people took a little while to get used to the fact that they were part of the Connecticut General "family" (which is what the company calls its staff) all day, with food provided at low cost and the number of calories indicated, and with such services as income-tax preparation assistance and free battery charging for cars that won't start. As I wandered around, I had a momentary feeling—brought on, perhaps, by the Mondrian-like colored partitions—that I'd once had in Holland; a feeling of wanting to throw things around and make everything a little less clean and tidy. Could the building possibly be too pervasive? Mr. Dawes said he was surprised that no sociologists had yet turned up to study the Connecticut General workers; he thought, however, that a tendency to get inbred was counter-acted by the turnover of employees; there were surprisingly few intercompany marriages, and the presence of so many women had the effect of keeping the men extraordinarily polite.

There is no doubt that the building demands respect and is treated with it. There has never been any vandalism. The build-ing was made of expensive materials, and Mr. Benjamin, who is in charge of the maintenance of house and grounds, has found that the first class construction, the absolutely finest materials, and the rural setting have all paid off handsomely. The company believed that painting would have to be done every five years—after nine years, no painting has yet been necessary. Because of the natural surroundings of grass and trees, with little dust and no smog, the air-conditioning costs less to operate—filters are changed twice instead of four times a year. Windows are washed once every two months instead of every one. There are no overshadowing buildings and the vast amount of daylight has meant lower electricity bills. In fact, the costs of operating the building and grounds are lower now than they were in 1957. The 230 acres of green landscape are looked after by eleven men using a great deal of large, efficient machinery (Mr. Ben-jamin is proud that Connecticut General operates its grounds more cheaply than the West Hartford Parks Department oper-ates its parks). The artificial three-and-a-half acre pond not only serves an aesthetic purpose but also forms the cooling reser-voir for the air-conditioning system, the water supply for irri-gating the grounds, and the source for water to quench any fire. Connecticut General carries its own fire insurance through one of its subsidiary agencies, but because Bloomfield still has a volunteer fire department, the premium is a little higher than the thrifty Mr. Benjamin thinks it might be.

As a new, large taxpayer, Connecticut General has helped Bloomfield build a new school. Of course, it has also caused people, some with children, to move to Bloomfield and other nearby towns. Although originally thirteen buses ran daily to bring the workers to work, only five are needed now because people have moved nearer or have shifted to their own cars, making necessary a second parking lot—1619 cars was the daily count in the two lots when last taken. There is room for more parking areas and more cars, but despite the fact that the areas were designed as an essential part of the building and the landscape, they don't quite fit. In one lobby there is an interesting model of the buildings and grounds, including trees and cars to scale, made in 1957. The cars look awkwardly old-fashioned; the building does not.

What the building reflects most of all is the landscape: the grass, trees, clouds, and sky. Unlike Lever House, it has not been surrounded with poor parodies of itself. The landscape improves the building and is itself improved by the reflections encased on the glass and cast back. One can see how Gordon Bunshaft could remark recently, without boasting, "It looks better all the time." As I walked around the grounds, I admired the tall old oak that stands on a neck-shaped peninsula jutting into a pond. There used to be six swans on this pond, including a pair of rare black Australian swans, but they became a nuisance for the Connecticut General gardeners, and have been replaced by tidier ducks. The grounds are planted with tulips, daffodils, roses, azaleas, alyssum, rhododendron, begonias, and narcissi. Among the trees are pin oak, sweet gum, honey locust, sugar maple, Chinese scholar, ginko, Japanese silverbell, golden rain-tree, flowering crabapple, and the American hornbeam, all of which Connecticut General was delighted to see mentioned in a list of twelve nearly perfect trees published by Rutgers' department of ornamental horticulture. A brook leads into the west side of the pond, at which point it is crossed by a footbridge. Alongside the brook a path leads into a small copse, where there are birdhouses in the trees. At one point big stepping stones allow one to cross the brook. The whole landscape is man-made or man-altered—and altered well. Unless he was looking for them, a stroller in the grounds would not be forced to take much notice of the more specifically recreational areas set aside for picnicking, horseshoe pitching, croquet, softball, shuffleboard, and tennis.

At the moment, the grounds belong entirely to Connecticut General and there has been no pressure on the surrounding acreage. There are some houses up the road a way, but not many of them. There is still a fine view of Avon Mountain, which in most parts of the world outside Connecticut would be called a hill. I got the impression, however, that if the right company needed the space, Connecticut General wouldn't be loath to sell some of its rural acreage. After all, they are in business to make a profit, and, although their headquarters has been selected by the American Institute of Architects as one of the ten "Buildings in America's Future," there is no doubt that three hundred acres will be a great deal of space for one company to occupy not far from now in America's future. For some reason, out there in the Bloomfield meadows, one felt the threat of congestion more acutely than one did in the already-dense city. Perhaps because I intended to call on Mrs. Richard Griswold, a staunch advocate of birth control, at my next stop, in New Haven, I had brought up the subject at lunch with Mr. Dawes. It struck me that a company—especially an insurance company—would probably be pleased to exist in a world with more people, in which they would sell more and more insurance.

"Not at all," he said firmly. "It's an exploded theory that you need a continued rise in population for continued prosperity. All the signs in the world point to Malthus being right. We'll probably achieve or at least maintain a high standard of living if we control our population. It's the higher standard of living that causes people to buy more insurance. Mr. Frazar Wilde thinks the population explosion is the world's most serious problem, and so do I. I go around lecturing on the subject, though I'm not such an effective speaker as Mrs. Griswold. Over in Glastonbury they have a new school. It was crowded the year it opened. Those children will not get the education they might have received. No, I'd say as a company we're thinking about the future—our being out here in this shape and form is part of that thinking. And so are some of the projects we're involved in, like the symposiums we've conducted on air transportation, and superhighway impact on cities, or the investments we're making in such experiments as the new city of Columbia, in Maryland."

I told Mr. Dawes that I also had Columbia on my ramshackle itinerary.

"I'm not surprised, but our interests aren't just coincidental. An insurance company is naturally interested in security and progress, both of which only can be obtained, we believe, with planning and imagination. I'd say that in Mr. Rouse, who's pushing Columbia, and Mrs. Griswold, who's pushing birth control, you've found two of the foremost examples of people who are doing their damnedest to make this so-called megalopolis a truly great city."

8

More and More People

ON THE way to New Haven I felt both the growing pressure of people and the oppressive impact of a highway: in fact, they were combined in the Berlin Turnpike, which formed the connecting link between Hartford and the Wilbur Cross and Merritt Parkways. I was forced to take the Berlin Turnpike, otherwise known as "The Strip" or "Death Alley," because the final section of a new six-lane expressway, Interstate 91, was still two weeks from opening. In any event, it was instructive to see one of the most notorious examples of nonplanned ribbon development in the Northeast. The network of roads around Newark and Union, New Jersey, compose a greater conglomeration of the species, but for the most single-minded expression of the principle—a democratic principle taken to its absurd and logical conclusion—that everyone has the right to build a gas station on his own land if he wants to, the Berlin Turnpike has no competitor. Of course, it isn't simply the fifty gas stations. There are, as well, in that miserable twelve-mile strip, some forty motels, motor lodges, motor inns, and even motor hotels, to grade them roughly in their self-styled order of swank. There are sixty "eating places," including snack bars, custard shops, donut outlets, hotdog stands, diners, bars and grills, restaurants, delicatessens, and country taverns. There are miniature golf courses, bowling alleys, drive-in theaters, and outdoor furniture shops. One place, Outdoor Glamor, was selling plaster religious statuettes in various shades of blue, while nearby establishments specialized in such items as "LBJ Hats" and "Certified Dormers." Most of the buildings were in architectural masquerade and perhaps reflected their owners' desires to be backwoodsmen, ranchers, or knights of the Alhambra. Plastic pennons fluttered noisily over the courtyards of gas stations. Neon signs sizzled meretriciously in the warm sunlight. The roadside was edged with ragged grass and the inferior Tarmac of turn-ins and parking lots, while between one place and the next there was rarely evidence of the neighborliness that decides on hedges or a painted fence or even a joint strip of well-kept tar or lawn. Each place was independent and at war. Many were also ready to sell out, for signs were displayed all along the strip, "For Inspection Call . . ." or "High Gross—Inspect and See."

The Berlin Turnpike is part of one of the oldest highways in Connecticut. In 1799 a stagecoach route was opened between Hartford and New Haven, which were co-capitals of the state until 1875, when Hartford got the job alone (and, as a result of waiting, a splendidly Victorian state capitol). The original turnpike, built at a cost of $2000 a mile, departed from the usual eighteenth-century practice of following trails and riverbeds; it was laid in a straight line, revering nothing that stood in its path, and in at least one instance preferred to pay damages to a householder (he collected $57 from the turnpike corporation) rather than avoid going through a frontyard. The turnpike corporation made a net profit of $3000 a year from tolls.

In recent years the turnpike, now a free road, boomed because it was the one connecting link between the end of the Wilbur Cross and the Massachusetts Turnpike near Springfield, on the route generally taken by people driving between Boston and

New York. The road was used by some forty thousand cars a day. Moreover, because the strip happened to be roughly half-way between Boston and New York, many drivers stopped there to refuel their cars and themselves. With unlimited access to bars, and unlimited return access to the turnpike, accidents were common—seventy occured in 1964, and two resulted in deaths. To the two towns through which the road runs—Berlin and Newington—all the cars and their passengers signified revenue; as income to the merchants in the first place, and as income for the municipalities that taxed the merchants in the second. If one had to pick one word to explain the development of the strip to near saturation point, one might pick "greed," which can kill a place, and people, just as it can kill an individual. Zoning is an expression of moderation; and in places that are liable to the municipal equivalent of obesity, it is as essential as counting calories.

The Turnpike itself was not about to drop dead simply because of the opening of Interstate 91. The merchants association was in the process of setting up billboards in Hartford and Meriden to tempt drivers onto the old road. The going may be rough for a while, but as more and more cars appear on the roads and the present interstate system becomes obsolete (the graphmakers say this is likely within twenty-five years, but they don't allow for such innovations as the HSGT system), the present slack on the strip will presumably be taken up. *Fasten Seat Belts.*

I had never been in New Haven before. The view from the train is negligible, and when I drive down to New York from Stonington I take the Connecticut Turnpike, which swoops over the city in such a way that one's prospect of the place is of rooftops, advertising signs, clocks, temperature gauges, and sundry notices for exiting and merging traffic. It seems very little different from one's view of Norwalk, Bridge-port, or Stamford. With luck in New Haven one is granted a moment, when negotiating the high, cambered bend above the oil storage tanks, to snatch a glance at the harbor, where an Esso tanker may be docking. Otherwise there is nothing to suggest the town's particular character.

Having booked into the Taft Hotel, a hostelry of faded splendor, I had the evening before me in which to try to catch that character. Since I also wanted to catch some dinner, and had a yearning for veal with peppers and mushrooms, and a side dish of spaghetti, the search for an Italian restaurant was the thread on which my twilight impressions were hung. I first of all circumambulated the village green, which was established as such in 1638, and is bounded on the west and north by Yale University's nineteenth century versions of building-art in the middle ages. Building-art in 1965 was manifest south of the green where new construction stood in all stages of steel and concrete skeletal development—several office buildings, a sky-scraper for the Knights of Columbus, and a new hotel. Behind these projects squatted a brand-new Macy's department store, windowless above but with windows for window-shoppers below (I paused by an attractive display of wine bottles, and decided that Valpolicella would go nicely with the veal). Across the street was a striking concrete zigzag lattice work structure that turned out to be a parking garage. I watched a car drive in, get hoisted by a traveling gantry lift, and deposited in an open slot fifty feet above the ground. I had half a mind to retrieve the Jeep from the little open lot down the street from the Taft and bring it here, just for the thrill. But I also had less than a half-full stomach, and plunged on.

I passed a pizza place that was closed. I passed more new stores and a half-finished concrete tower looking like a multi-sided filing cabinet with drawers pulled slightly out. This was the Dwight Housing Project for the Aged, designed by Paul Rudolph, former dean of the Yale school of architecture, and at this stage of construction it appeared to be a good deal less sexy than the concrete parking garage, which was also his work. In other streets whose essential features were wide roadways, trees along the sidewalks, and three-story houses set back behind high stoops, I found municipal projects and numerous buildings being privately spruced up. New Haven is a small city of 152,-000 people, of whom nearly a quarter are Negro and Puerto Rican poor. In the last ten years the city has made a successful effort to get rid of its once ubiquitous slums. The mayor, Richard Lee, and the city planner, Edward Logue (who is now planning for Boston and consulting for New York City) saw to it that the city was first in line for federal grants—in fact, despite its small size, it received more for urban renewal than any other city except New York, Chicago, and Philadelphia. Mayor Lee went to Washington the very day the law was passed implementing the federal rent subsidy program for low-income families. In New Haven this will enable two hundred poor families to move into private housing, and thus make unnecessary the building of another "project," entirely full of poor, which tends to become quite quickly another slum. New Haven's policy, which is being adopted elsewhere, has been *not* to move low-income families into low-income projects, but to scatter them in more prosperous areas. In renewal sections middle-income co-ops have been built. So far five thousand two hundred families have shifted homes, and some of the problems uncovered by such moves have been sorted out with the help of the Ford Foundation. A community program has been started to provide legal aid, youth job services, and nursery schools. Many businesses have been relocated within the city, and new factories have gone up in new industrial parks. One view to be had from the Connecticut Turnpike is of the Long Wharf section on the edge of the harbor. There, in an industrial park, the advertising power of architectural excellence is made evident by a long, low, black glass-fronted factory building. Having found the name on a nearby sign—Sargeant Hardware—one remembers it.

New Haven, of course, has its bomb sites and the sense of a long blitz that one finds in most of these two-hundred-year-old cities; it also has a hopeful feeling, perhaps because it is a university town with many young people in it, of things being on the upgrade. What it didn't have on my meandering route that evening was an open Italian restaurant. By the time I got round to asking the proprietor of a newspaper shop where one might be found, I was at the other end of town from the restaurant he recommended. So I accommodated my plans to my hunger and descended into the Heidleburg Cellar. The bratwurst was soggy, but at the next table two men were discussing how best they could promote the attractions of a motel they owned out of town. They compared the advantages of mailing lists, phone campaigns, and billboard advertising. What they most wanted was a slice of the wedding party and businessmens' convention trade, and I thought it a good augury for New Haven that they had come into the city for their conversation.

That night in my eighth floor bedroom at the Taft, overlooking the green, I read two items in *Scientific American*'s special issue on cities which seemed to me relevant to my meeting the following morning with Mrs. Griswold. The first was the remarks of urban affairs expert Charles Abrams, who believed that, at a density of fifty persons per acre, "the entire population of the United States could be accommodated on the West Coast, with nearly everyone having a view of the Pacific. About 70 percent of the US population is now concentrated in urban and suburban communities occupying in total only a little more than 1 percent of the nation's land area, and the greatly increased population expected by the year 2000 will still take up only a little more than 2 percent of the land." (Mr. Abrams' optimism about the amount of habitable space in this country would be more convincing if he acknowledged the existence of waterless deserts, inaccessible mountain ranges, floodable cotton fields, and arid prairie as part of the total land area. Furthermore, he might show signs of recognizing that there might be some difficulties in situating some two hundred million people on a coast geologically liable to earthquake, volcanic explosion, mud slides, and fracture, whose water supply problems are considerable, and whose natural life, whether in the form of redwoods or condors, is fast disappearing under the impact of roughly one-tenth of that number of people.) The second item was a description by the Californian sociologist, Kingsley Davis, of those increasingly urban communities we live in: "The large and dense agglomerations comprising the urban population involve a degree of human contact and social complexity never before known. They exceed in size the communities of any other large animal; they suggest the behaviour of communal insects rather than of animals."

This brings to mind a drawing that appeared in the 1965 year-end issue of *Life*—an illustration of the plan of some Princeton University thinkers for a linear city in the near future. It showed an open, indeed almost desolate countryside (some of Mr. Abrams' unoccupied 98 percent of the land), reminiscent of the scrubwoods of northeastern Connecticut or the Pine Barrens of southern New Jersey. Across this expanse ran the linear city. At first, it struck me as merely a gigantic continuous building, snaking over the contours of the land; then it seemed to resemble a mammoth articulated freight train, whose freight was every facility and activity of the city; finally I saw that it was a huge and infinite chicken run.

The basic cause of the spreading city is more people. It is the cause least discussed in the professional, semi-technical writings about megalopolis that I have come across. And yet it has for certain people a frightening reality.

The Planned Parenthood League of Connecticut has its offices on a street of shabby, massively porched Victorian houses, next door—the juxtaposition is a trifle sensationalist—to the New Haven Girl's Recreation League. My visit took place four days after P.P.L. had opened a family planning center in its offices, to give medical advice and assistance in birth control. It was roughly five years after P.P.L.'s previous clinic had been closed by the New Haven police, acting in the wake of protests that they enforce Connecticut's rarely enforced law, section 53-32 of the General Statutes as revised in 1958, "Use of drugs or instruments to prevent conception. Any person who uses any drug, medicinal article, or instrument for the purpose of preventing conception shall be fined not less than fifty dollars or imprisoned not less than sixty days nor more than one year or be both fined and imprisoned." The accessories statute states that anyone "who assists, abets, counsels, causes, hires or commands another to commit any offence may be prosecuted and punished as if he were the principal offender." The man who actually brought the charges against the Connecticut P.P.L. was James G. Morris, a Roman Catholic father of five, who worked as the night manager of a car rental agency. Mr. Morris said, "I think that a Planned Parenthood Center is like a house of prostitution. It is against the natural law." The codefendants were Mrs. Griswold, executive director of the center, and Dr. C. Lee Buxton, chief of the obstetrics department and the infertility clinic of Yale University. They welcomed their conviction under Connecticut law because it enabled them to appeal the case to the Supreme Court. Early in 1965 the Supreme Court spoke on the subject, and as a result, contraception is at last legal in Connecticut, and birth control advice, assistance, and counsel may be given.

Mr. Morris' description of a Planned Parenthood Center was not well matched by what I saw. In a downstairs room—floor painted gray, walls white—three women accompanied by some small children were waiting their turn to see the doctor. A woman in a white smock directed me up a narrow staircase into a small office which also seemed to serve as a storeroom. Cardboard boxes were stacked up behind a desk. Piles of pamphlets held open a closet door. On the walls there were a map of the world, some graphs, and a poster which said simply "Four Babies Every Second." In order to sit down I had to remove from a chair an open box of bumper stickers printed with the words "Trouble Parking? Support Planned Parenthood."

I was looking at this when Mrs. Griswold came in, wearing a well-tailored pearl-gray linen suit, a string of pearls, and with her white-gray hair swept back, looking ten years younger than her age of sixty-five. "A poster we ought to have pinned up is the Maytag advertisement," she said. "Do you know the one I mean? It shows a woman with sixteen children, and she's happy because she has a Maytag washing machine. Well, if you start with sixteen children as your factor, the way things are going, in a few generations you get umpteen billion people. We're getting to be like the fruit fly."

Estelle Griswold was born and brought up in France. She had ambitions to be a concert singer but gave them up to become a medical technician. During the war she was an assistant instructor of pathology at George Washington University. After it she worked as a resettlement officer with the displaced persons program in Europe. For thirty-nine years she has been married to Richard Griswold, who has now retired from business; they have no children, a fact, she says, that can be as traumatic as having too many. "We spent a lot of money trying to have a child, but in those days not much was known about infertility. I felt vulnerable taking on this job because I had no children. In fact, I refused to take it, but everyone insisted, and it certainly concerned me, so here I am."

Of all the industrialized nations, Mrs. Griswold told me, America has the highest rate of unemployment, the highest rate of public dependency, and the highest rate of population growth. Big families have been an American tradition, a frontier necessity for farming new land and ensuring sufficient survivors of the various perils of pioneer life. Indeed, with the close of the frontier and a great decrease in infant mortality, family size shrunk. During the depression, the population of the country actually began to decline. But with the end of World War II babies boomed again. More Americans got married than any other Western people (nearly 95 percent of adult Americans marry at some time in their lives); they married earlier, at an average age of twenty-three for men, and just over twenty for women; and they had their children earlier. Consequently American growth rates zoomed, and a slight decline in the birth rate since 1957 hasn't affected the long-term trend. There has been no decline in the total number of children expected by the average American family. The population of 193 million in 1965 is likely to be 270 million in 1985 and more than 350 million by the end of the century.

Clearly that number of people puts a demand on space and on the basic fabric of human society which a simple equation of people per square mile does not begin to reckon with. The demand is most visible in suburban sprawl and city traffic jams (a motor truck averages six mph in New York today; a horse-drawn truck averaged eleven mph in 1910), and a little less obviously in the cost of highways, schools, and sewage systems, and in the waste of many hours spent getting to and from work. Yet perhaps the greatest burden springs from the fact that it is the poor, and the poorly educated, who are having the most children, setting in motion a vicious circle of poverty, large family, unwanted children, poor schooling, early marriage, unemployment, and yet more poverty. It is a situation which is grim for the people concerned, and creates a heavy load for the rest of the community. In this county, the load is presently increasing: the recipients of Federal Aid to Dependent Children funds, which generally go to mothers and children with no father in their house, numbered 4.4 *million* in January 1966.

"What frightens me most of all," said Mrs. Griswold, "is the shortsightedness of the average middle-class American. He's doing all right. He's got a well-paying job, a house in the suburbs, the kids in school, the taxes are high but still they could be worse. He doesn't realize how much worse they're going to get unless he wakes up. We are a *have* nation. We think we always will be.

"The only way to get these things across to men is with statistics. They're not interested in the overburdened mother and the unwanted child. I lecture to the Kiwanis and the Elks, and I put it in terms of tax increases and future controls that may be needed on, say, job movements and the sale of land. There won't be any more two-acre plots. Every club and estate on the shore of Connecticut will be requisitioned in the next twenty-five years for use in state-provided services. Then there's foreign aid, which everyone from Senator Fulbright on admits is going down the drain. It isn't keeping up with the population growth in most Asian and South American countries —it may even be encouraging that growth. We can't say 'control your population' until we control our own—and that's essential. The world is finite. We aren't—as some religious leaders have hinted—going to find an easy way out by sending our surplus population to another planet. Read this."

Mrs. Griswold handed me a serious-looking periodical, entitled *The Journal of Heredity*, March-April 1959. It was bent back to expose an article by Garrett Hardin, of the University of California—"Interstellar Migration and the Population Problem." Mr. Hardin wrote that the nearest star with possible planets for colonization was Alpha Centauri, 4.3 light years away. A rocket traveling at the speed of one of our present moon rockets (19,000 mph) would take 129,000 years to reach Alpha Centauri. In several centuries, using nuclear energy, it might be possible to make the trip at seven million mph, which would cut the trip time to 350 years or roughly the length of time between the arrival of Captain John Smith in Virginia and the inauguration of President Eisenhower. Furthermore, "since the present annual rate of growth of the world's population is 1.7 percent [and assuming that the passengers continued to pursue the course that had driven them to interstellar migration] by the time the first ship arrived at its destination, the whole fleet of spaceships enroute would enclose a total population six times as large as that still present on earth."

Having, with a smile, disposed of that exit, Mrs. Griswold went on to say that Connecticut had at the moment 2.8 million people and the third highest per capita income in the United States. It had also 9 percent of its people in some need of public assistance; 280,000 earning below $3000 were, certainly from a medical point of view, indigent. These were the people who were generally having large families, which in many instances they do not want. Many of them are Negro, which increases the problem. They generally live in crowded places in crowded cities, which in turn makes the cities a lot less attractive for other more fortunate folk. They lack contraceptive help, and that increases the number of illegitimate births—the average rate of such births is twenty-two per thousand unmarried women of childbearing age, and the rate among the poor is nearly seven times as great. This raises the costs of public assistance: Aid to Dependent Children recipients will get more than one and a half billion dollars in 1965. As Malthus pointed out, the gross national product tends to increase arithmetically, while the population rate—and consequent costs of services to people—soars geometrically.

"What we're trying to do here is reach these people," said Mrs. Griswold. "We're trying to make our service not only available but accessible. We hope to make this service part of regular hospital postpartum programs. Bridgeport, Norwalk, Stamford, and New London hospitals are either doing this or planning to do so. A lot of women we have to seek out. After they've had a baby many of them never get back to the hospital for a postpartum checkup—they're already pregnant again. We're sending out questionnaires to local doctors to find out which of them will take patients if we refer them. We're hoping the state will issue a declaration of policy that will allow the public health officers to pitch in and help us. We need local groups to transport indigent women in to see us if they can't get doctors to advise them. A woman with five children finds it difficult to move at all, and if she can't come to see us, we'll have to try to get to her. It's urgent."

The budget of Connecticut Planned Parenthood is $125,000 this year, made up of contributions from some four thousand five hundred people. Mrs. Griswold is unhappy because there are at least six thousand people in Connecticut with annual incomes over $50,000—she would like them to cough up, and she would also like broad-based support from people who could afford to give ten or twenty dollars a year. "We need a lot of money in order to set up satellite centers near low-cost housing. We need to expand our trained staff. Right now our services comprise the fitting of approved contraceptive devices—including the new interuterine coil—and instruction in child-spacing. We consult with and refer to specialists childless couples who wish to have children. We provide premarital education, and educational material for schools and groups. We don't want to compete with private physicians, so we confine ourselves to patients who can't afford private medical help or who can't get it. Anyway, we need the private doctors, because we can't do the job alone. We also need new laws to allow for therapeutic abortion in case of incest or rape, and to allow voluntary sterilization. We need so much."

I thought I detected a slightly weary note in Mrs. Griswold's voice, and I asked her what hope she had.

"Oh, hope—there's hope," she said. "There has to be. People have to be able to revere life. They have to be people, not numbers. They have to have time and space so they can love. Anyway, I've never lost a battle yet. It was 1923 when Margaret Sanger introduced this subject to a large crowd at the Parsons Theatre in Hartford, and even though it's taken us forty-three years to get this far, it took just about as long to get votes for women. We'll make it. It's a twenty-four-hour-a-day job for me. I speak to five large meetings every month, and I'm trying to train volunteers to speak at the meetings I can't get to. I wish I had time to get round to all the hospitals and take the doctors and knock their heads together. I'm a roughie. I don't think doctors are sacrosanct. They're dedicated, but most of them can't see further than their noses. Another thing, we just can't move in on a community. We need a base of intelligent support to get the message across. For what this is all about is *control*. It's a much better word than planning—family planning was always a puritanical way around the subject of sex, for when that's involved people got all choked up. I think we're learning how to talk about it, which is a start. Control is the power of direction, and if we're really human we should be able to direct our lives. At the moment the situation is almost out of control, and we're running hard just to stand still. We haven't got so much as a breathing space."

9

Friends in Newtown

IN TIME past, one's friends lived nearby and could be called on by taking a walk through the village or a ride uptown. If they moved away, one wrote letters for a while, but they had moved —and really gone—for good. Now, although one has friends generally where one lives, in the course of a lifetime a number go to live elsewhere and yet remain friends; in my own case, when I number twelve people who meet the test of being able to take up with me more or less as they left a few months or a year before, I find two are in Europe, one is in Canada, one is in California, and the rest are scattered the length and breadth of the Northeast Corridor. We seem to be in the process of forming a new sense of community, made possible and then inevitable by the car, the telephone, and our own mobility. On this particular afternoon I drove west out of New Haven bound for the cottage, in Newtown, Connecticut, of my friends the Duchamps, who had invited me to stay. I drove west-northwest on Route 34 to Derby, on the Housatonic, and then followed the river inland for seven miles, crossing it on the top of a dam just below the village of Stevenson. The river itself is beautiful, but its banks are defaced by hundreds of shacks and cottages and converted railroad cars. It is a nice demonstration of a paradox, common in the urban age, that everyone has built there for the fine view and the view has been devastated by everyone being there.

Following Gerard Duchamp's complicated directions, I turned on to Route 25 in the village of Sandy Hook, veered right at the junction by the flagpole in the village of Newtown, stopped briefly at a drugstore to buy a copy of the weekly Newtown *Bee* ("Best Advertising Medium in Western Connecticut"), and then buzzed on, past the road to Brookfield, past the Cancellation Shoe Store (the final landmark), and took, as directed, the next left, the Old Bethel Road, up which I drove for a few hundred yards before turning off on a private lane that ran up the hill.

This is hilly country, a mere ten miles from the border of New York State and fifty-five miles from midtown Manhattan. The hills are closer together than those in eastern Connecticut and the land gives the impression of having been ruffled up in short, sharp ridges, which are wooded now, but not long ago were uncovered. The Duchamps have an eggman in his early sixties who recalls when the hillside on which their cottage stands was all fields. By the time the local sculptor built the place, fifteen years ago, trees had to be cleared to make room for the foundations. And now Gerry—who works for an airline in Manhattan—chops timber every spring and fall, not just to provide exercise for himself and fuel for the Franklin stove, but to keep the advancing forest from closing in.

It was, however, easier going than in the woods near Canterbury. The Duchamps' Peugeot had made fairly well-worn tire tracks up the lane on weekend visits, and Gerry had filled in some of the deeper ruts and holes. An occasional branch was knocked aside by the windshield, and scratched noisily along the tall flanks of the Jeep, and when I drove off the lane to park in a small cove of saplings, the car fitted perfectly into the landscape, so well camouflaged I doubted if it could have been seen from the air. The cottage sat off to one side of the lane, which went on up the hill to a spring at the summit. I had arrived before my hosts, who were driving out from the city for the weekend; away from the roads, with the noise of the Jeep's engine gone, the feeling of isolation was sudden and strong. Like Thoreau, the owner of this place could undoubtedly say with a sense of truth, "There are square miles in my vicinity which have no inhabitant." At that moment a plane flew overhead. (A few months later two airliners collided over this area and one crash-landed in the woods of Danbury not far away. I wondered then what Gerry had thought at being so forcefully shown that his rural retreat from airlines and the city was within an ever more crowded air-traffic holding pattern.)

Gerry had told me under which stone they kept the key, and small spurts of rain began to fall as I let myself in. Deprived of a walk in the woods, I settled down to read the Newtown *Bee*. It was a large, almost square newspaper, with a foggily printed antique look. It had four sections of thirty-two pages, nine columns to the page, and cost fifteen cents. The front page photograph was of a new factory that had just opened in town. This was wedged in by announcements of wedding anniversaries, a Republican family outing, a fireman's ball, taxpayer property listings, school fund appropriations, the historical society program for the month, and the opening of the fund drive for the visiting nurse association. The front page also had a story—rather confusing to anyone who expects from all newspapers the background ("this is the story up till this installment") generally given by *The New York Times*—about some goings-on in nearby Southbury. The new reader was very much *in medias res*, but he managed to gather that at the Southbury polls, the previous Saturday, the local electors had thrown out planning and zoning by 783 votes to 619, thus enabling construction to begin on a retirement community, called Heritage Village, which apparently hadn't fitted in with the former planning and zoning laws. One hundred and sixty-three nonresident property owners voted in the referendum. On the same day, a stormy town meeting passed modified planning ordinances which town officials hoped would hold Southbury together until the dust settled. Southbury appeared to be suffering growing pains. I was interested to see on a page of area school news that the school system was larger this year by 261 students. The Newtown school superintendent John Sommi was quoted as saying, "In our dynamic society, constant pressure is felt by the schools to keep abreast of new developments. In a world confronted by an explosion of knowledge, the schools must continuously reappraise aims, methods, and organization to equip students for life in the world of tomorrow. . . ."

It was a bit of a relief to turn to the classified ad pages of the *Bee*. The *Bee* office was taking orders for no trespass signs, 12" x 12", printed on waterproof cloth with "special" ink at twenty cents apiece. Someone wanted to swap "Seasoned lumber 2 x 6's, 2 x 4's, siding, etc., from 20 x 60 shed, for taking down and removing shed." A 1954 1100-gallon septic tanktruck was for sale for $2800, and if that didn't interest you, there was a "Used Jamesway Barn Cleaner, 3 yrs. old in good cond.," no price mentioned, and "Large Amount well rotted horse manure, reasonable. Will deliver." There seemed to be the reverse of an unemployment problem in the Newtown area; jobs were open for carpenters, auto mechanics, dairymen, milk deliverymen, well drillers, machinists, swimming pool construction workers, tree men, laboratory instrument assemblers at the new factory, and, not least, a chef. Many barn, garage, and attic sales were listed, for this is antiquing country. I noted but hesitated to draw any definite sociological conclusion from the statement that Brookfield Country Players were casting for their next production, Leonard Bernstein's urban musical "West Side Story."

It rained at dinnertime. Gerry, his wife, Ann, and I sat at the table and listened to the downpour, scarcely able to talk for the tropical noise it made on the thin roof of the cottage. Like the coming of a monsoon it seemed to mark the change of season, the end of the dry summer. Gerry was excited by the rain because his well had gone dry and he had been drawing water from the spring at the top of the hill. The general Northeast drought was at this point in its fourth year and was something that finally seemed to have been apprehended by town and country dweller alike as the danger it was—though for a weekend countryman like Gerry, having a well go dry was more emphatic than being denied a lunchtime glass of water in a city restaurant.

When the rain eased, we talked about the places in which we lived. We had a large bottle of Chianti to finish. Thunder roared in the distance and lightning flickered through the now fortunately dampened trees. Gerry and Ann had been thinking about moving out to Westchester or Fairfield County, but they now thought they would sit tight for a while. Gerry said commuting was a painful waste of time. They had a choice of places to be since they had an apartment and the cottage. Moreover, they felt they still *needed* the city.

"How so?" I asked.

"Oh, a number of things," said Gerry. "Ann's mother lives there. We have the apartment, which took some finding, and it's swell—the building's swell. We have friends who live in it or nearby. There are children the same age as George, and then there's the park, two blocks away—the park is great. Ann has her part-time job at the museum, and she'd miss that. Once a week I play poker. Every other day I walk home fifty blocks up Fifth, or Madison, or Park. Of course, the city's a mess, everyone can see that, but for us it's still marvelous. For the time being I think we'll stay."

In the morning, the Jeep was plastered with wet leaves. Before I left, Gerry and I found that there was water in the well, and walking to the brook that ran in the gully beneath the hill, we saw that it was no longer dry.

10

A View of the Mishmash

SOMEONE WHO is a little less enchanted with the city than Gerry Duchamp is Lewis Mumford, a man who has probably been the most powerful educative force in this century in architectural and civic studies; a writer, teacher, and journalist whose concern for the American past and the American earth has opened gates to and cleared paths through new fields; a self-termed "generalist," of whom Philo Judaeus would probably have approved, who has generally maintained a keen sense of particular, revealing facts. As a generalist, or a Jack-of-all-trades, Mr. Mumford is a little out of favor with the specialists of the new professions whose birth he has overseen. The sociologists tend to distrust the "creative writer," and some second-generation immigrants have an understandable nostalgia for the crude chaos of the gridiron which makes them intolerant of a scholar whose idea of a civilized city has more in common with T. E. Hulme's Bologna. Urban experts obsessed with social problems and racial strife find Mr. Mumford's concern with the physical form of communities a distraction. Nathan Glazer, in a recent piece in the Sunday *New York Times Magazine*, actually seemed to blame the continued existence of an urban Negro problem on Mumford's interest in new towns and Jane Jacobs' interest in creating small and varied neighborhood blocks. This was hardly sporting since, until the last year or so, few people have shown any desire to put those ideas into practice. It isn't hard to throw over ideas a damp blanket of "things as they are" or even "what people really want," though it might be considered amazing that the complementary phenomenon of Detroit-produced cars and mass suburbia can be regarded with respect on a continent where people once "really wanted" to slaughter all the buffalo (result: no buffalo) and own African slaves (result: the urban Negro problem). Lewis Mumford's approach is unfashionably organic. He questions—as Joseph Wood Krutch described the similar interrogation by Thoreau—"the ultimate human worth of mechanical invention and the uses to which it is put." I had read such books of his as *Sticks and Stones, The Brown Decades,* and *The City in History,* and I thought that, on a trip of this kind, to call on Mr. Mumford was about as natural a thing to do as to drive on a superhighway or see a factory among the fields.

I drove north from Newtown. The rain had vanished, and it was a fine, chill morning—the first that one could truly say was autumn. Squirrels scampered off the lane. Leaves fell silently in the wet woods. I admired the countryside on this part of the Connecticut–New York State border, which was like a relief model I'd seen in Dr. Murphy's office in Worcester, used in geography classes to make obvious distinctive topographical features—broad valleys lined with prominent ranges of hills and rivers running more or less north-south. The hills become steep and clustered around Amenia, New York. I stopped to orient myself at a circa 1950 roadside tavern called The Log Cabin, where I also had a ham sandwich and a glass of beer, while listening to a conversation between the woman behind the counter and several regular patrons of the place who gave the impression of unbudging attachment to the locality. They were talking about a kid who had been arrested for drunkenness; the police said he'd been drinking at The Log Cabin. Our hostess said, no, she'd just served him fried chicken. "That's right," they all said, looking at me.

On the telephone, Mr. Mumford had told me what turning to take off the highway from Sharon, Connecticut, in order to reach Leedsville, a small hamlet of a dozen houses scattered along a country road. His was the seventh house, opposite a yellow mailbox. It had been built, I knew from his writings, in the 1830s, "just when carpenters were beginning to lose their sense of fine proportions . . ."; a simple, white frame clapboard house, whose materials perhaps pleased its owner more than the proportions—"That is the best part of wooden architecture, it is always unfinished, always inviting reconstruction. It contracts or expands, rots or recovers, with the life it encloses." A large tree shaded one end of the house, and a porch shaded the lower story. Sitting in a tall chair on the porch was Mr. Mumford, rather like the solitary figure in a painting by Edward Hopper; he was prepared to flag me down, for visitors unused to the scale of Leedsville often drove straight by.

Lewis Mumford did not look to be seventy-one years old; with a gray, military moustache, he reminded me of a British army general I had once served under in West Africa, although this impression was, at second glance, countered by his gray-brown wool shirt, red wool tie, and shaggy brown tweed jacket, cut with pleats and half-belt at the back in the Norfolk fashion, popular between the wars and associated, in my mind, not with generals but with people like George Bernard Shaw and the Fabians. Mr. Mumford's accent had an English touch to it; he reads *Punch* weekly and quotes Osbert Sitwell and Matthew Arnold as familiarly as Emerson and Thoreau, but his hospitable manner struck me as essentially American. We sat in a small living room whose effect was of densely packed bookshelves and handloomed rugs; in a dark leather case a scroll from the

University of Edinburgh lay on the mantlepiece. I asked how long he had lived in Leedsville.

"We moved here in 1926—there was a sort of exodus of our friends from the city. Henry Wright moved out, and Clarence Stein—you know, I've never seen Clarence's place in Ossining—and we came up here. It's one of the loveliest valleys for miles around. We knew the Spingarns, who bought Troutbeck, the estate that had belonged to the naturalist Myron Benton, and they sold us this house on the edge of it. We live here most of the year. It's not a patrician village. The man across the way is an attendant at a school for the feeble-minded, and our other neighbors are a mailman and a carpenter. It is an excellent place for writing, but in the winters I am generally in residence at a university. I'm going to be up at Harvard for the next three months, and I look forward to that."

I asked if the city was reaching out to Leedsville.

"In some ways," he said. "We have three new houses along the road, and there hasn't been growth like that for a hundred years here. There's also a new fertilizer packing plant, and a sand and gravel works that's an absolute curse. In a minute you will hear a roar and then the house will begin to shake. It will be one of their trucks going by—great diesel monsters. They seem to use this road more and more frequently. Of course in some ways we are further from the city than we used to be. The railroad has cut back to two trains a day now—one down the valley to New York and one back. It takes two hours and twenty minutes by train and about the same time by car. The fact that everyone drives is naturally what ruined the train. I was one of the earliest advocates of expressways, but I'm afraid I didn't see how they would be built, making many of the mistakes the railroads had made such as cutting cities in half, and in the end subsidized to such an extent that railroad passenger business is being made extinct. A good transportation system doesn't boost one form of travel in order to destroy another form. The car is inefficient for commuting, and it was a means to great freedom only as long as the minority had it—but that's a paradox about most of the things we owe to technology. Did you read about the tests they've been making in San Francisco? It seems one's blood pressure rises considerably when driving on a crowded turnpike."

I said that, having looked again at *Sticks and Stones,* and *The Brown Decades,* I had been impressed by the author's optimism —by a feeling that he might have had hopes for the ultimate perfectability of North American man.

Mr. Mumford smiled a calm smile. "I think those books expressed the mood of their time. When you reach *The Culture of Cities,* which was written in the mid-thirties, you find a change. There's a chapter in that book called "A Brief Outline of Hell" in which the Second World War and the total destruction of cities by air attack were anticipated. And nowadays anything one writes is undoubtedly affected by the fact that in the last fifty years we've lived through two great wars, in which absolute evil has been manifest on a worldwide scale, and in which the lives of sixty million people have been cut short. Our civilization shows few signs of stability. In fact, the present unchecked growth of the city is evidence of its inherent instability."

I breathed the word "megalopolis."

Mr. Mumford gave me a rather testy look. "Yes, megalopolis. These days the word is generally used by urban experts who are trying to convince other experts that it's some new kind of city, instead of the urbanoid mishmash it actually is. The real megalopolis in ancient Greece was still residually an entity; but this present thing. . . . Well, I prefer Patrick Geddes' word for it. In 1915 he termed it a 'conurbation.' "

Mr. Mumford got up and found a book—*Cities in Evolution* —on a shelf. On the way back to his chair he poured two glasses of dry sherry, and after he had handed one to me and taken a sip of his own, he began to read. " 'The present Greater New York, now linked up, on both sides, by colossal systems of communications above and below its dividing waters, is also rapidly increasing its links with Philadelphia—itself no mean city—and with minor ones without number in every direction. . . . The expectation is not absurd that the not very distant future will see practically one vast city-line along the Atlantic Coast for five hundred miles.'

"There you are—that was written fifty years ago, and in another fifty this city-line may stretch continuously from Maine to Florida. But to suggest that this megalopolis or conurbation represents a new scale of settlement to which we have to adapt our institutions and our personal needs masks historical reality. I think it allows apparently automatic forces to become a substitute for human purposes. I agree with one thing: megalopolis is fast becoming a universal form. Our dominant economy is metropolitan, with no enterprise really effective unless it is closely tied to the big city, which in turn is becoming dehumanized, an overgrown container. And as the city gets larger, the giantism leads to mammoth shortages, like the current water shortage, and breakdowns [this was a few months before the northeast power failure and the crippling New York transit strike]. Fairly soon a stage is reached where no one understands the whole situation. Moreover, much of the present thought about the development of cities proceeds from fashionable ideological assumptions about the nature and destiny of man, and from a deep contempt for organic processes. The trouble, the true trouble, is that such assumptions tend to be self-proving. The more widely they are believed, the better they work. The more swiftly they work, the sooner they come to a dire climax."

I said that I took this to mean the very notion of megalopolis, disseminated widely enough, would help produce megalopolis in fact.

"Precisely."

"Then what's to be done?"

"The first thing needed is a deeper insight into the processes of history. This would be a first step towards discipline and control, a knowledge of self that would allow for normal growth—and that growth would best take place in smaller units, with organic limitations."

The words discipline and control reminded me of Mrs. Griswold's remarks, and I asked Mr. Mumford what relation the population explosion bore to the feeling of things being out of control and overgrown.

"To someone my age things are undoubtedly too crowded," he said. "You notice it on Regent Street in London or on Fifth Avenue in New York. I go down to visit my daughter in Brooklyn now and then, but I don't enjoy the city anymore. The one consoling factor, as viewed from Leedsville, is that the overcrowding so far is taking place in the already crowded places. Among the poor, ignorance and lack of medical help is a cause of the high birth rate, but I believe that with more prosperous people an unconscious anxiety about war has a lot to do with it. At any rate, when a situation of this kind reaches the point that the graphs all show it is rapidly reaching, then the situation tends to be self-corrective, by one means or another."

"The bomb may fall?"

"The bomb or, more likely, a breakdown of society—a psychological breakdown—if the present processes go unchecked. Take, for an example, the amount of stuff written on this subject of the city. Books and papers flow into this house every day. It's too much for one man to cope with, and so I throw a lot of it away. That is a form of breakdown—ignorance as a result of too much specialized knowledge. I'm now writing a big book on technology and the nature of man. I go back into the early history of the human race because, from the beginning, we have shown signs of irrationality in our handling of technology. I'm uncertain about the future. It may be that we'll have to go back to a lower point in order to begin again. I am writing in the assumption that we should save the best things in our civilization, so that after the breakdown we'll be able to get started in a better way."

It is sobering to listen to a man whose wisdom one admires, and whose ability as a prophet is demonstrably high, deliver a verdict that the human race might be about to go off its head.

Mr. Mumford smiled trenchantly. He said, "Of course, much of this depends on whether you believe that man and his future should be judged on the basis of the last fifty years. If not, we may have some leeway. There's always the possibility with a tumor that it may destroy the organism at whose expense it has gotten so swollen. It's also possible that nature may redress the balance and get rid of the tumor. I would be more optimistic if the response to the situation were stronger. Yet the response may be rising—I've found in teaching that the most recent generation of students is not prepared to take things lying down. In the fifties, the classes I taught were all bored with my talk of nuclear perils; they were only interested in good safe jobs and pensions. I think that may have changed."

I asked if there were equally hopeful signs for cities themselves.

"There are some. The New York State Office of Regional Development came out with a plan in March 1965 which, instead of resting content with the continued, interminable growth of New York City, stresses regional development. It suggests the division of New York State into ten regions, each with its own center of gravity; in fact, ten regional cities that are gatherings of cities, towns, villages, hamlets, farms, and parks. What the report didn't emphasize were the things needed to make such a regional policy work: regional councils, land control, as in the Ruhr, where embargoes can be put on uses of land which don't conform with public policy, and new towns. Furthermore, the report kept the spirit of the times by treating the technological forces and institutional practices now in operation as if they were immortal."

Mr. Mumford looked into the small pool of golden light in his sherry glass. "So few people bear in mind the human values. Only machines will be able to prosper in the mechanical environment we're creating. No doubt it is crucial, in one respect, that people be got back into the center of cities, but you can't expect them to go back to live in mile-high apartment projects or in oases scattered thinly among car parks and expressways. The centers of cities are valuable because they bring people together. Fortunately, there has been some recognition of this, and some good things have been done in Philadelphia and the southwest section of Washington, D.C. A sound way of coping with the urban dispersal is through new towns, and a number of these are now being built. What Henry Wright and Clarence Stein tried to do at Radburn in the twenties may finally be paying off, although for a single developer the problems of constructing one are still enormous. But sometimes it's the fate of a really brilliant piece of planning to go ignored and un-copied altogether, like Stein's Chatham Village in Pittsburgh. Chatham Village has returned 6 percent since it was built in 1932. It is two hundred row houses on an interestingly uneven site, surrounded by a greenbelt, and it's always fully rented—in fact, there's always a waiting list to get in."

When I got up to make my farewell, Mr. Mumford said, "Come out by the back way and see the garden."

We went out through the kitchen door, and strolled over a formal patch of grass to a hedge at the bottom where one could look out across a field. The field rose and then fell to a line of distant trees. Beyond were the Berkshire foothills and a high knoll Mr. Mumford identified as Oblong Mountain. The garden ran parallel to the road, from which it was masked by trees, and in a small grove a clearing had been made, with a group of unpainted wooden chairs gathered as if waiting for someone to sit in them. "This was my son Geddes' favorite spot," Mr. Mumford said. "He was killed in the second war. We've kept it the way it was." Beyond the grove was a vegetable patch, where the Mumfords grew their own asparagus. The cultivation of the garden was not intense; parts were wild and straggly, and other parts were neatly ordered; and as we wandered along the path Mr. Mumford pointed out to me the red currant bush his wife had planted, or an unexpected wild flower.

I drove toward Manhattan in the late afternoon, down the Harlem Valley, and alongside the Croton Reservoir. Route 22 became the Saw Mill River Parkway, and the dense city, beginning in the upper reaches of Westchester County around Bedford Village and Katonah, was concealed for a while by the pleasant landscaping of the sinuous parkway, with green sward running to the river's edge, and great drooping willow trees. However, the traffic soon thickened and curdled. An old lady in an old Buick ploughed resolutely along in the middle of the two lanes, and no one honked at her, although now and then a driver would summon up sufficient courage or foolhardiness to squeeze by. One woman, trying this, lost her nerve, twitched her wheel, and braking, went into a momentary spin. I was grateful for the recently installed steel fender that divided the opposing lanes of traffic.

11

The Center of Things

AS ONE comes down the Henry Hudson Parkway along the river in the blue dusk, the enticing city shimmers and glows. The tall buildings above the park are sillhouetted against a lavender sky and brought alive by the haphazard lights of apartment windows. On the river, tugs tow a covey of late barges to the Jersey shore. The bend of the elevated highway frames the funnels and spotlit white superstructures of large ships. A thousand cars—the fragile containers of so many private emotions and destinies—move at leisurely intervals toward the beckoning lights, the beacons of a place that is now more than ever full of promises. The city at this hour is never real; it is always fabulous. One may be pardoned for falling momentarily into a giddy dream of fame and wealth and love, in which these lights never fail and the music never ceases, for the dream presumably is common; without its sustaining power these onrushing cars, and the city itself, would disappear.

Beyond the veil, it took me twenty minutes to find a parking place. The Hetheringtons, with whom I was going to stay, had an apartment on West End Avenue in the nineties, in one of those massive between-the-wars brick apartment buildings that stand in dour solidity—their benefits, their breeding, their endurance all turned inward and not nervously flaunted in the manner of their flimsier postwar descendants. Most of the side-streets are lined with four-story brownstones, with tall stoops and bay windows, which are interspersed by the occasional small apartment building or residential hotel. In these, the weekly rents are often paid with city welfare checks and the teen-age tenants collect their pocket money from possessions citizens may have carelessly left on the seats of parked cars. Since the Jeep couldn't be locked, I took the unsettled nature of the neighborhood into account. I unloaded my bags and left them in the lobby of the Hetheringtons' building, across from if not actually under the eyes of the doorman, who was sitting reading *El Diario*. Then I circumnavigated that block and the blocks adjacent to it. Not only were there no parking places, but the streets were narrowed by cars double-parked, through which traffic weaved its way as on a slalom course. In one block a man was attempting either to get in or get out of a parking space a car and a U-Haul trailer, which had jackknifed against the curb. I sat for several minutes while five taxis hooted behind me and the driver worked out which way to turn his steering wheel to make the car go one way and the trailer go the other. Once past this impediment, I soon realized that other cars were prowling the same streets looking for parking room. They traveled at a looking speed, close to the side of the street on which, through prior knowledge of the parking signs, they knew it was most convenient to park. There seemed to be a rough protocol about it (or perhaps it was only common sense), but if two or three cars found themselves dogging each other along the same street, on reaching the end of the block they would all turn off in different directions. It may have been that they simply wished to avoid the embarrassment of one of those urban confrontations in which the stern of one's own car meets the bows of another, trying to dart into the same space. After a while, I began to feel that there was something shameful about this sin-

gle, excessive preoccupation that had us all in its grip. I drove
faster than was practical for scouting the car-crowded blocks.
Finally, after twenty minutes of getting farther and farther
away from the Hetheringtons, I took a run back along West
End Avenue. What joy! There, smack in front of their building, a huge car was pulling out, its power steering system
whining peevishly. I claimed the place by double-parking in
front of it with my right turn-signal light flashing. Then, when
the spot had been vacated, I backed in, with a mixture of luck
and judgment, parking in one movement, which gave me the
only satisfaction to be had in the whole miserable process.

In the elevator there was a hand-printed notice taped to the
wall:

TO ALL TENANTS
Call Mr. Hermann, the building owner, in Scarsdale at [the number
was given]. Tell him you are withholding rent until essential services, including proper number of doormen, are restored. A meeting
of tenants will be held later this week. Your section organizer is J.
Garrick, Apt. 12b.

Alec Hetherington met me at the door of 15a; he teaches
political science at a New Jersey college and commutes out
from the city. I asked him about the notice—was the revolution
about to begin?

"Come on in," he said, with a smile. "I'll tell you about it at
dinner."

I want to describe the Hetheringtons' apartment. It isn't the
sort of suite one imagines Hollywood stars to have on Central
Park South, with a view of the park one way and the midtown
lights the other, with white wall-to-wall carpeting and a couple
of white grand pianos. Nor is it a crummy old-law tenement
of the kind in which a million of the city's inhabitants live, like
the railroad flat I saw one day in East Harlem (in a building
whose owner was unknown and which was being kept going by
the rather threadbare communal spirit stirred up by a city health
inspector). There, garbage thrown down from higher apartments was piled high outside the kitchen window and old pieces

of linoleum were tacked over the ratholes in the room where the baby slept. The Hetheringtons' apartment is of a type rarely described, and yet it is what makes thousands of middle-class people like the Hetheringtons (or the Duchamps, who have a slightly smaller version on the East Side, in the nineties) call New York City home. Unless they have lived in it for a long time, it probably costs them a little more than they can afford; but—like the city itself—most of the time it seems worth it.

One enters by way of a foyer; at the Hetheringtons' there is a narrow hall table, with a mirror over it. Nearby, two spacious closets contain lights that go on when one opens the door to hang up a coat. There is wall space against which to stand a grandfather clock, hang up a barometer, and display some eighteenth century maps of the Island of Mull, in the Inner Hebrides, which is where Alec's grandfather came from. In one direction the foyer opens out into a large living room—and large in this case means about twenty-five by fifteen, a good deal larger than one would find in most suburban houses. At the far end a long window overlooks West End Avenue. On one wall is a fireplace which works, and the facing wall is covered with bookcases. Two couches, several arm chairs, and a piano do not make the room seem crowded. The three bookless walls support half a dozen paintings of the Hudson River School which Judy Hetherington inherited from an aunt.

The Hudson itself is just visible down a crosstown street onto which the windows of the master bedroom look. The row of three bedrooms is dependent on a corridor that runs from the foyer parallel to the length of the living room. There are two bathrooms, one of which can be reached only through the master bedroom, the other at the end of the hallway for the use of all. These bathrooms reveal a good measure of the apartment's quality. They are all white tile to shoulder height, and white plaster above—the plaster generally has deep cracks running through it, for the paint is renewed by the landlord every three years, and is now relatively as thick as the layers of Troy. There is a built-in tub of generous size. By depressing a plunger on the spout, the water is forced upward to the shower nozzle. The porcelain sink is of the pedestal variety, with a wide rim around the basin to cope with the domestic clutter of shaving objects, combs, and lotions. Over the sink a cabinet is inset behind a mirrored door, with four or five narrow glass shelves holding razor blades, shaving soap, Band-Aids, talcum powder, and boxes and bottles of unguents, laxatives, antilaxatives, capsules, cough medicine, eye drops, nasal sprays, and various shaped canisters with prescription labels on them, which are half-empty and cost so much that—though they have probably lost all their power and will never be used again—they can't be thrown away. Between the sink and the toilet a four-inch-diameter pipe rises from floor to ceiling; this is the only bad feature. In winter one has to be careful not to brush against it, because it is often red-hot.

The third doorway from the foyer leads to a pantry, a maid's room and small bathroom, and the kitchen. This is not an up-to-date feeding station with wall-oven, center counter, and formica work flats. The sink, stove, and refrigerator are all separate, prominent, and bulky, and although they are in good condition, they don't seem quite properly placed. The sink is next to the window, and one has to turn through three-quarters of a circle to find a space on a side shelf to put down a wet dish. Anyone pulling out a chair to sit at the tiny kitchen table effectively blocks all other motion in the room. There is no built-in washing machine (there are some in the basement of the building) and no live-in maid. A woman comes three days a week to help clean. Alec uses the maid's room as a study.

The apartment was well built. The floors are oak parquet, sanded, varnished, and waxed. There are numerous electric outlets. The walls are thick, and the ceilings fairly high; steel beams, boxed-in, make the ceilings in some rooms narrower than the floors, but the effect is reassuring rather than disconcerting: one knows the beams are there. The doors are heavy, and the windows open easily, a point for which one is particularly grateful in winter when the valves of the radiators jam, and can't be shut off. Being high up, the apartment receives quite a lot of light. Because the Hetheringtons have three children and use as a bedroom what might be the dining room, the dining table is placed at the end of the living room closest to the kitchen.

There were two other guests at dinner, Harold and Marcy Swann, who lived in the west seventies, close to the park. As we ate, Alec told us about the problems of the building. The owner, Mr. Hermann, had recently cut down the service staff from seven men to two. For a few days there had been a complete breakdown of maintenance. There had been no heat, no hot water, no doorman, and the garbage—uncollected from outside the kitchen doors—had overflowed down the back stairs. None of this was what the tenants felt should be expected in this kind of apartment house. There had been a protest meeting in the synagogue across the street, at which the tenants adopted a policy of applying to the rent commission for rent reductions and of making calls to Mr. Hermann at his Scarsdale home at all hours of day and night. Thereafter, one doorman turned up, although he was on duty only at certain hours. The heat, hot water, and garbage collections were restored. According to leaders of the tenant opposition, Mr. Hermann was trying to force out with this diminished service some of the older tenants in rent controlled apartments, who had been in them for many years and were paying extremely low rents. Mr. Hermann, according to the impassioned speech he made to several callers before he had his telephone disconnected, was in dire financial trouble because he had been swindled on his mortgage. In fact, Alec said, few of the tenants were applying for rent reductions, most because of apathy and some from an unbased fear that if they did so Mr. Hermann would have them evicted. At any rate most people were finding that the situation was endurable; the fabric of existence hadn't quite collapsed. In some ways the landlord-tenant struggle was proving to be an effective social cement, for people were actually talking to one another in the elevator. Alec himself felt that Mr. Hermann might be telling the truth about his mortgage problems, and that the building, like the city, might truly be hard to run with an aging population, low revenue, obsolete equipment, and so many employees needed to keep the place going. But this was an unfashionable point of view—Hermann was the popular villain. Alec thought it likely that Hermann would lose control of the building and that a bank or investment firm would take over behind a new tough management; they would jack up the rents and make the building pay. People would groan but would put up with it.

"The columnist Murray Kempton says we New Yorkers are the frontline troops of the urban catastrophe," said Harold Swann.

"I read that piece," his wife said. "He had a great epigraph for it from *The Entertainer*—'Don't clap too loud, it's a very old building.' "

"It was in *The New Republic*," said Swann.

"I like Kempton but he overwrites," said Judy Hetherington.

"Why is *The New Republic* good and *The Reporter* dull?" asked Alec at large, and the conversation broadened into one of those wide metropolitan tracks in which everything alluded to has the tinge of gossip and the pleasures of being knowing and inquisitive and groupy. City folks' chatter.

Late in the evening we discussed plans for the morrow—Sunday. Having waded through the papers, the Hetheringtons were going up to the Cloisters.

"We have a two-hour limit on the papers," Judy said.

"I take the "News of the Week in Review" and the sports section in the bus to Fort Tryon," said Alec.

I would have liked to go with them, but I had commitments for the day. Sunday in the city is a day that, when we lived there, always made sense, had a raison d'etre, that Sundays elsewhere seem to lack. Perhaps it was the park, or the museums, or simply the liberty to wander around, bumping into acquaintances one hasn't seen for a long time, but who, that day, have chosen the same route through the Natural History Museum to the weather station in Central Park and around, via the model yacht pond, to the cafeteria at the zoo. Once in a while we would go to the Cloisters and lap up the whole marvelously contrived atmosphere: sculpture, stonework, herb gardens, the view of the Hudson and the Palisades, and the recorded medieval music, all joining to remind us that we were part of history and occasionally in charge of it. It seemed to be one of the best things in the city—an essential element of what for us the city was.

"I'd offer to give you a ride to Fort Tryon," Harold Swann said as he and his wife were leaving, "but I'm afraid I'm no longer a car owner."

"So you finally wised up," said Alec, who believes it doesn't pay to keep a car in the city.

"We were wised up," Marcy Swann said flatly.

"What happened?"

"You remember my old Mercedes?" Swann said. "Not a fancy car, but a good one. When I parked it, I always left it in neutral, with the hand brake lightly on, because otherwise when people start pushing you you're liable to have your transmission wrecked."

"They actually push you—to make a space?"

"You bet," said Swann. "It's warfare. Listen to this—I think it's what happened—someone pushed my car back against someone else's. Trouble was, the other guy was also squeezed in at the rear, already enough to make it hard to get out. Well, this sort of thing happens all the time, but this was one of the real nuts, one of those you only have to touch off ever so slightly, and *boom*, they're berserk."

"What happened?"

"Just that: *Boom!* He set my car on fire. At 2 A.M. Poured

gasoline all over it and then threw on a book of matches. I guess he managed to get his own car out by bashing my car first of all. There were some witnesses, but they didn't get a close look."

"The police?"

"Oh, you know the police. They said they'd investigate. They poked around for a couple of days. They had the honesty to tell me they were quitting—my insurance would pay off, because it was malicious damage. They had two murders in the precinct to worry about."

"Isn't there anything . . . ?" Judy began.

"It could be anyone," said Swann. "The city's full of them. The only clue was a message scribbled in crayon on the front fender, 'Thanks for boxing me in.' "

12

Trailclearing

SUNDAY MORNING: sunny, mild, late September. I drove up the Henry Hudson Parkway, crossed the Hudson River on the top span of the George Washington Bridge, and trundled northward on the Palisades Parkway, which for much of its route parallels U.S. Highway 9w. I was not feeling too chipper. I had sat up late reading a book that Alec had thrust on me with grunts about its importance. It was called *Suburbia*, and it was by Robert C. Wood, political scientist at M.I.T., since made Under Secretary in the new Department of Urban Affairs. Alec said, "If you're going through Jersey, you ought to read this." And so I did, and found it illuminating; but at this moment its relevance was strictly that—having been engrossed in *Suburbia* until 3 A.M.—I didn't feel altogether in shape for the day's activity, which was a trailclearing expedition with members of the Atlantic Chapter of the Sierra Club. The Sierra Club announcement had said simply, "Trailclearing, Shunemunk Mountain, New York. Fine views, easy work. Bring lunch, water"; the announcement had also appointed a meeting place at the bus stop in Highland Mills, a small village on Route 32 just north of

Bear Mountain State Park. I got there at ten minutes past ten, and introduced myself to David Jung, the leader of the expedition, who in turn presented two other men and a girl who were already there.

"We're waiting for the ten-fifteen bus to come in from New York," Jung said. "Most of the hikes in the metropolitan region are announced in the travel section of the Sunday *Times*. We usually get a few people showing up."

While we waited, Jung, who was in his late twenties, moved some trailclearing equipment from the inside of his car to the trunk: long-handled shears, a folding bucksaw, and several grass whips. "Many people don't realize how wild it can be close to the city," he said. "In fact, as the metropolitan area expands, the wildness of the remaining wild parts seems to be increasing. Our club belongs to the New York–New Jersey Trail Conference which was set up to conserve wilderness areas and wildlife, to bring this sort of recreational activity to the public eye, and to build and maintain trails and shelters. In 1920, the conference helped lay out the Palisades Park trails and later on part of the Appalachian Trail. It now maintains nearly five hundred miles of trails in northern New Jersey and southeastern New York. Bear Mountain and Harriman State Parks have the largest concentration of trails to be found anywhere in the world so close to a big city."

Two young men got off the bus and joined us. Then in two cars we drove several miles up the road to the base of Shunemunk Mountain, a long, high shoulder that began steeply on the far side of some distant fields and woods. Jung said the mountain was 1624 feet high, and that we were 300 feet above sea level at this present spot; we would be climbing 1300 feet in the course of a mile. He distributed the trailclearing gear, together with some extra windbreakers and sweaters. The senior member of the party, Bob Eldridge, asked Jung if he had a snakebite kit, and Jung said he had, though he didn't think it was a good day for snakes; it wasn't hot enough, and it looked like rain. If, however, anyone encountered a rattler or a copperhead, the thing to do was stay at least five feet from it, more if you could. "If they're mean enough," said Jung affably, "they'll strike twice —once to get close to you and then a second time to get you. They don't see well, but they react to the heat of people."

We left the cars parked on a wide grass verge and turned in along a foottrack that crossed a field, past a sign that said: "WARNING. Hunting, Fishing, or Trespassing Forbidden. All persons hunting, fishing, or trespassing on these premises will be prosecuted according to law. Star Expansion Industries, Inc., Mountainville, N.Y." No one paid any attention to it.

The first part of the hike on the sloping ground up to the foot of the mountain was a little like the first day of a sea voyage: people got used to the novel conditions and talked about themselves. I found out from David Jung that he was a Californian by upbringing. He now lived in a garden apartment in Mamaroneck and worked as a financial analyst for I.B.M. at their Mohamsic laboratory on the Taconic Parkway; he was carrying a knapsack and wearing a New Mexico Indian serape-waistcoat, given him by his girl friend, Pam Farley.

Pam also lived and worked in the suburbs; she shared an apartment with two roommates in a Victorian house in White Plains and worked as a market research assistant for General Foods. She said that, if you were a single girl, finding accommodation in Westchester was even more difficult than finding it in the city. There seemed to be more and more jobs but nowhere to live. She had come from Buffalo, studied at Sarah Lawrence, and was wearing a sweater, blue jeans, and new hiking boots, a present from David Jung; instead of a knapsack she carried a B. Altman shopping bag.

We came into some woods and followed a path that led across the Erie Railroad tracks, running along the base of the mountain. Ahead of Pam Farley walked a tall contemporary of David Jung's, Bob Burtness, who had grown up with him in California. Burtness had trained as a pilot but suffered from air sickness, and so was now flying a desk at McGuire Air Force Base in southern New Jersey. He was wearing a white sweatshirt with the name of a Californian conservation group—San Gabriel Valley Council—printed on it, and on his head, briefly, appeared a red deerstalker hat with a "Vote for Goldwater" button pinned to it. Since he seemed a sensitive type, Burtness may have removed the hat and pin when he talked to Henry Bass and Roy Lisker, the two hikers who'd come up on the bus from New York City, and who gave the immediate impression of not being prepared to tolerate a vote for Goldwater just because Goldwater was a conservationist. Bass, with long, straight black hair, taught economics at Hunter College and looked rather fierce as he told me he was particularly interested in population densities —in why, for instance, 90 percent of the population of New York State chose to live in 1 percent of the available room. Lisker, a pale, bespectacled twenty-seven, said that he was a founder of the Free University of New York, whose courses cost three dollars apiece and were (he grinned) somewhat Marxist-oriented. He was going to work for a radical newspaper in the heavily Negro section of North Philadelphia. (When I later saw Lisker's name in print, it was in *The New York Times* several months after this, together with a photograph of himself and two others who had been arrested for burning their draft cards. I hope Lisker's social passions are not being wasted in jail. Judging from his performance that afternoon, he was happy to put them to good use in clearing trails.)

Beyond the railroad tracks we followed a gravel lane that became a gravel path, and this, getting steeper, turned into a rutted track with rough shards of stone sticking up in it. A stream carved down the hillside through a deep gully. We passed a shelter made—log cabin fashion—of old railroad ties, roofed over with tin. The chinks between the logs had been filled with pebbles and mud, which was a job recently done, Bob Eldridge said, since he hadn't noticed it when he'd been on the mountain two months before. Eldridge, in his late fifties, wore a floppy cotton hat, checked shirt, blue jeans, and high brown boots; around his collar was a lanyard fastened with a silver Indian brooch. He lived in Nutley, New Jersey, worked as a patent agent for the U.S. Rubber Company, and hiked not only with the Sierra Club but with many of the other twenty-three member clubs of the Trail Conference. (The names of some of these clubs and the years in which they were established are: College Alumni Hiking Club, 1922; Fresh Air Club, 1876; New York Ramblers 1923; Ramapo Ramblers, 1960; Suffern Historical Hikers, 1956; Torrey Botanical Club, 1867; Woodland Trail Walkers, 1937. Brooklyn and Flushing are strong centers of hiking enthusiasm.) At any rate, Eldridge not only hiked himself but sometimes brought along his wife and grandchildren. According to David Jung, he had "status" in the Sierra Club because he had led one of their summer camping trips. He led us up the first part of the Shunemunk Trail.

After the shelter the path began to get steep and the irregular rocks felt hard beneath the soles of my walking shoes. Far off one could hear guns, apparently firing on the West Point artillery range despite the Sabbath; they prompted Pam Farley to tell David Jung of Art Buchwald's suggestion for an easy way of demolishing the World's Fair, which was to give free admission to a couple of Viet Cong. The mountainside was forested with scrubby woods, and branches bent across the track above, while at ground level the shrubs and grass closed in on it. As he climbed, Henry Bass swung a grass whip to remove these intruders, and Pam and David pruned the shrubs and smaller branches with the shears. Roy Lisker, carrying the saw, had a chance to use it on a small tree whose roots had lost their hold on the stony hillside, so that the trunk had toppled across the path. This obstacle was too high to climb over and not high enough to duck under conveniently. Roy sawed it through in jig-time, and then, with a great deal of ill-coordinated exertion, the rest of us pushed the two halves over the edge of the trail into the gully. On the way again, Bob Eldridge pointed out various plants. "Try this," he said, handing me a small shred of dark green leaf. "Rub it between your finger tips and smell it. It's dittany. It makes a fine flavoring for spaghetti sauce." The dittany smelled sharp and sweet, something like sage or thyme. Eldridge also pointed out white golden rod, jack-in-the-pulpit, wild blueberries, and various kinds of fern. In fact, he was so intent on the plants that he missed a turning at a trail junction, and from the rear, David Jung called us back.

"The trail we're going up," he said, "is the Jessup Trail, which is marked with yellow blazes, or ought to be. This mark was obscured." He had a foot on a rock with a faded yellow splotch meant to mark the turn.

We now saw the reason for Pam's B. Altman shopping bag— it contained a quart of bright yellow paint and a two-inch nylon brush. From this point on the trail she painted or repainted yellow markings on rocks and trees. Here and there, in places where the trail went over long stretches of bare stone, causing us to make a wide sweep to find the continuation of the trail, we built small cairns of rock as bearing points, and Pam painted them with a stroke of yellow. Indeed, in the course of the afternoon she herself became a sort of traveling marker for the Jessup Trail, with her hands and her jeans liberally sprinkled yellow. "David said if we were doing the blazes on the Dark Hollow Trail it would be white paint," she said philosophically. "I like yellow better."

The Jessup Trail climbed the northeast flank of the mountain, through crags and gullies and over boulders, and then ran west-southwest along the straight top ridge of the mountain, sometimes through thick scrub, sometimes across rocky open spaces. We had two short rests to get our wind and wiggle our toes in our boots and shoes, but David Jung soon spurred us on. It was a sound hiking rule, he said, that short rests were valuable but long rests were tiring. The northeastern end of Shunemunk's ridge is double-crested, and when we reached the eastern crest we paused to admire the view. Eastward we could see the

Hudson highlands and the prominent bump of Storm King Mountain, whose top was just cleared by a layer of dark gray cloud. Rain seemed to be falling on Cornwall and on the Hudson, a little slice of which could be seen. Route 9w came over the back of Storm King's saddle, and some green golf-course-like fields of dairy farms were scattered among woods between our mountain and Cornwall. Eldridge said that on a clearer day than this you could see the Taconic range on the far side of the river.

We had lunch a mile and much machete-work further on— Barney and his sculptor friend would have been welcome additions to our force, I thought. We sat on the slope of the mountain top facing west, with rocks under us that were a purplish color, encrusted with a dry lichen that looked like gray-brown potato crisps. We ate our sandwiches and toasted the Sierra Club with a bottle of rosé that David Jung had brought along. Eldridge said that the Sierra Club was gaining quite a few more members who were attracted to it not only by its outdoor activities, but by the fight it was making to protect the California redwoods and the Grand Canyon. David Jung said that he thought more and more people were finding recreations like hiking or climbing necessary to enable them to put up with city life. Then for five minutes or so Bob Burtness talked about the fifty or sixty condors that were holding out in a small area of California. The condors live for fifty to seventy years and mate at thirteen. Burtness had brought a book about them in his knapsack, and this was passed around like the wine, so that we all had a chance to look at photographs of the giant birds soaring above the Sierras, and the photographs of the roads and houses that were driving them into a last retreat.

Earlier I had expressed an interest in the geology of Shunemunk, and David Jung, who seemed to be exceeding the normal benevolent duties of a hike leader, now dug around in his knapsack until he found the volume needed: the *New York Walk Book*, full of topographical information and pen sketches of mountains, first published in the 1920s and now in its third edition. The *Walk Book* located Shunemunk, not in reference to the village of Highland Mills, but to the Black Rock Forest in the northern highlands. Shunemunk was on the opposite side of the valley to the forest, and was geologically younger than the gneiss and granite highlands. It was composed, in fact, of sandstones, shales, and conglomerates of Devonian time, with Silurian strata at its base. Shunemunk was part of a long ridge of these strata which extended forty miles southwest into New Jersey, and which was formed of sediments deposited in a narrow sound of the ancient sea that once covered this area.

I learned something about the rock I was sitting on. "Conglomerate ledges are conspicuous on the long, level summit, with reddish purple matrix inclosing white quartz pebbles up to six inches in diameter—the remnants of erosion of streams from hills of the 'Old Land.'" But I'm afraid I skipped somewhat through the geology of the surrounding countryside, though intrigued by such terms as "Taconic Revolution," "Sedimentary Relations," "Ordovician formations," and "Lehigh and Hudson Railroad." The guide book related that the trail system on Shunemunk had been revised and simplified in 1947, when some trails—seldom used or hard to get at and maintain—had been abandoned to the encroachment of nature. These trails, the book went on, "undoubtedly will always appeal to those adventurous souls whose feeling for the wilderness will scarcely be dimmed by lack of blazed trails." The ridge of purple-gray hills I could see to the north were the Catskills—Slide, Cornell, Wittenberg, Plateau, Sugar Loaf, and Indian Head—while northwest were the Shawangunks.

Fed, rested, instructed, and inspired, we stretched, cleaned up the lunch site, and went back to the job. The encroachment of nature was going on on all sides. In some places we spent fifteen minutes clearing fifty yards of trail. Talking gave way to the steady sounds of shears and the grass whip. I took a turn at each of these devices, snipped at boughs, branches, and thick bushes, and felt that I was hitting back at woodland sprawl and in a sense clearing the grown-over fields of Wright Mills. Now and then someone would pause to straighten his back, and perhaps say something that carried to the rest of us, fragments like "Oak likes nothing better than to grow over a path," or "How does Chet Huntley pronounced Himalayas?," all of which hinted at unspoken conversations, trains of thought, running underground; we were too busy to talk. Meanwhile the rain had caught up with us. It came in short, light showers that weren't enough to get us wet. We concentrated on our task of gardening the mountain so that the trail would be open until the job was done again the following year. We went farther than we intended, beyond the junction of a trail, and Pam Farley's feet in her new boots got very sore.

The return trip was partly along the Jessup Trail and partly down the Dark Hollow Trail. It seemed rough and long. No one spoke; we kept our minds circling—like steadying gyro-scopes—around our weary legs and feet. Going down the steep hollow took more attention than climbing, for the rocks were big and round, and misplanting a foot could mean twisting an ankle. It was also hard to set a pace convenient for oneself; one felt irritated by the slower step of the man ahead or the stones kicked down by someone behind. When we finally reached the bottom and crossed the Erie Railroad tracks, descended through the woods and came out on a lane running through meadows for a mile back to where we'd left the cars, we felt as if we had truly been taxed and extended.

13

The Noble Stream

I WAS on the dock of the Tarrytown Boat Club at 10:30 the next morning in order to board Laurance Rockefeller's motor yacht *Dauntless*, which had just returned from taking her owner to work in New York City. (*Dauntless*, manned by a captain and a steward, makes the trip to a pier at 50th Street in forty-five minutes, roughly the same time as the New York Central commuter train; it is a trifle more private.) Already on board as I stepped over the rail were Conrad Wirth, former chief of the National Park Service and presently the executive director of the Hudson River Valley Commission; William Shore, information director of Regional Plan Association; and Carlisle Towery, an architect for the same group. The equinoctial rains had disappeared. Instead, out of a bright, clear sky, it was blowing about thirty mph from the northwest—what the Beaufort Scale, the mariner's measuring stick for such phenomena, calls Force 7, a moderate gale. "Sea heaps up; white foam from breaking waves begins to be blown in streaks." This was precisely the way the Hudson looked. A hundred yards offshore from the dilapidated Tarrytown waterfront a dredge was lying awash; it had come adrift and sunk during the night.

Cautiously, the *Dauntless* backed out of its dock and pivoted in the confined space between two piers. Then at quarter speed she plunged into the open river, bucking over the combers, sending perforated sheets of spray flying out on either side. The *Dauntless* is a sixty-five foot characterful combination of a spacious between-the-wars river launch and a seagoing World War II PT boat. I sat below with the other passengers in teak-paneled comfort and watched the grubby piers of Tarrytown fall astern; it was a view now seen through rainbows of spray. I wondered for a moment what the wind was doing to the trees and the trail on Shunemunk.

The Hudson is a basic factor of megalopolis. Without it there would be no city of New York, and New York is the great generating center of urban sprawl. And yet, cutting across the spreading northeast city at right angles, an organic (to use Mr. Mumford's word) rather than a mechanical factor, the river counteracts in many ways the basic megalopolitan premise—it postulates the possibility of a city that could be a region made up of urban and rural elements—a city that could be altogether more generous, more human, and more real. Captain Marryat wrote in 1837:

The Hudson is a noble stream, flowing rapidly through its bold and deep bed. Already it has many associations connected with it—a great many for the time which has elapsed since Hendrik Hudson first explored it. Where is the race of red men who hunted on its banks, or fished and paddled their canoes in its stream? They have disappeared from the earth, and scarcely a vestige remains of them except in history. No portion of this world was ever intended to remain for ages untenanted. Beasts of prey and noxious reptiles are permitted to exist in the wild and uninhabited regions until they are swept away by the broad stream of civilization which, as it pours along, drives them from hold to hold, until they finally disappear. So it is with the more savage nations; they are but tenants at will, and never were intended to remain longer than till the time when Civilization, with the Gospel, Arts, and Sciences in her train, should appear, and claim as her own that portion of the universe which they should occupy.

It was clear what portion that particular mid-nineteenth-century man thought they should occupy: it was the entirety. Marryat, contemporary of Malthus and a good sea writer, was too dense and too puffed up with his "civilization" to perceive that the broad stream of it, pouring along, was soon to put in peril the Hudson itself, or to see that he and his descendants were also tenants at will—not, like the savages at the mercy of a more powerful species, but at the mercy of our own preponderance, our scientific cunning, and our shortsightedness. So that what was in his day and for half a century thereafter a marvelous landscape, used and considered and enjoyed by men, tenanted by giant palacelike steamers, by fishermen, and by a fine school of native painters, became in the short course of things a river little used and less regarded, heavily polluted, and with its banks in many places inundated by industrial and domestic slums.

The giant Chevrolet plant at Tarrytown is one of the better examples of the industry that has settled next to the river, for power, cheap land, or convenience. The plant used to occupy the old site of the Walker Steamer Car Company, but soon spread, taking half of a park as a parking lot and sixteen acres of land beneath the river, which were reclaimed. It now employs fifty-four hundred men and has produced nearly seven million cars. In other places, such as Yonkers, Newburgh, and Poughkeepsie, oil storage tanks, run-down factories, and automobile junkyards compete for the shore, and oil and raw sewage stain the water—no fish will come to take bait in it. And everywhere roads and railroad tracks tend to inhibit access to the water; people are turned inland and away from it, as they are in most places in the city. Even the river front towns give the impression, with their closed-up stores and run-down industrial areas, that the oxygen-depleted river no longer breathes life into them. People shop in the big highway shopping centers. To a town like Cornwall, the promise of a new Consolidated Edison power plant on Storm King Mountain meant, in the first place, a guaranteed payment of much of the town's heavy tax load; and to Con Ed, Storm King was a convenient place to pump water up to a height from which, when needed, it could be released to generate cheap power. But for the Hudson itself, the Storm King power scheme was the final straw that got snatched away just before it broke the camel's back. Having been approved by the Federal Power Commission and Governor Nelson Rockefeller, it ran into the opposition of conservationists; instead of generating power it generated a whole series of movements to protect the river. To many people in public life, it seemed to be a classic case proving the point that when people are given a dramatic instance to show them how out of hand things have got, they will subdue their individual passions long enough to act for the common good.

In March 1965, Governor Rockefeller appointed Mr. Wirth as executive director of the Hudson River Valley Commission, "to formulate plans and recommendations for the protection, development and use of the varied resources of the Hudson River Valley." Nelson Rockefeller's brother, Laurance Rockefeller, the financier and conservationist, was named chairman. The New York State legislature passed a bill making the Hudson a Historic and Scenic Waterway, and appropriated $275,000 to finance Mr. Wirth's commission. Meanwhile, in the 1965 session of Congress, thirteen different bills were introduced, though not passed, aimed in various ways at preserving the Hudson. Ten separate federal agencies declared an interest in the river. Where before no one had seemed to give a damn for it, now there seemed to be a likelihood of a dispute between the federal, congressional, and state forces to see who could do the most.

As the *Dauntless* ran upstream under the lee of the western wooded shore, Mr. Wirth and Mr. Shore discussed the route of a new riverside highway that had been planned to run from Beacon to the Bronx. The Bronx-Tarrytown section had now been canceled, after protests that it would effectively seal off the riverbank forever; the Tarrytown-Beacon section was still subject at that time to variation, though the bulk of it had been fixed. Mr. Wirth and Mr. Shore stood beneath one of the cabin windows that gave them a view of that shore, and with a map spread before them they seemed a little like two feudal lords discussing their common problems. I had the impression that Mr. Shore, of Regional Plan—believing his problems were part of the whole kingdom's problems—was a little readier to accept the overlordship of the federal government, while Mr. Wirth had sworn fealty to the governor, in Albany. Both of them, however, were in agreement that highway departments at all levels of government were altogether too autonomous, and should be sat upon firmly. In places this new highway was going to run on reclaimed land alongside the river. At one spot a beach club was being forced to move, and in another it was going to run inland, through a residential area. The important thing was to make sure that it didn't do more damage than it was worth; that the Highway Department of New York State, in this instance, didn't "over-design" it by giving it more lanes and a capacity for higher speeds than was needed. "We have a real job," said Mr. Wirth, a bulky, bespectacled, genial man in his early sixties, "convincing the Highway Department that a road is more than a means of getting people from place to place." Mr. Shore, a shorter, wiry man of forty-odd years, said that he thought it crucial that, where the road ran along the river, there should be large hunks of filled land beyond the road by the water's edge, and many bridges and underpasses to enable people to cross the highway to new parks and beaches.

Opposite Ossining we passed the mothball fleet, long ranks of gray freighters, so many of them lying so still they appeared to have lost the nature of ships. No plumes of smoke rose from their funnels. The *Dauntless*'s captain said that now and then one of them would be taken away, hauled out, and cleaned and painted. This was the river's widest point—three and a half miles from shore to shore. It narrowed abruptly at Peekskill, and took a sharp bend into the highlands, and where Bear Mountain Bridge spanned the gorge we came out once more into the howling gale. The *Dauntless*'s captain decided to pass up the yacht's usual berth on the north side of the dock at Iona Island, where the Hudson River Valley Commission has its headquarters, and we came in snugly to leeward.

Iona's designation as an island could be challenged, since it is surrounded by water on three sides, and marsh and a causeway on the fourth. In the 1880s and 90s it was a popular summer resort, with a hotel, ferris wheel, and merry-go-round; the river steamers called frequently, and John L. Sullivan was a habitué. In 1899 the Navy bought the island for use as an ammunition depot, and in both world wars Iona supplied bombs, shells, torpedoes, and depth charges for use in the Atlantic. One hundred and forty-six brick and concrete arsenal buildings, the gloomy legacy of this period, will be pulled down now that New York State owns the island. Indeed, the Palisades Park Commission intends to turn it into a riverside playground once more, with such attractions as a marina, swimming pool (people who have swum in the river itself say the taste of the water stays in your mouth for days), archery range, restaurant, and a museum.

With the *Dauntless* safely moored, we had lunch in the yacht's saloon: steak, pommes frites, and asparagus. Then, Mr. Ben Thompson, who had been Mr. Wirth's second-in-command in the National Park Service and was now head of the planning staff at Iona, took us up to the commission headquarters, which was a late Victorian compromise between a Norman tower and a four-bedroom house. Inside, groups of young men and women were working on charts, maps, and overlays, and upstairs, in a room temporarily vacated by two women who were compiling a list of statistics, Mr. Wirth and Mr. Thompson used some of the charts and maps to demonstrate to us what they were doing. As they did so, I felt something of the excitement a planner must feel at marshaling great forces. It isn't at all the dry job I'd always imagined, for it involves a conscious shaping of the environment—a knowledge that human growth isn't just vegetative, or need not be.

The Hudson River Valley Commission had taken as its province the river and its watershed, and its first step had been to investigate the present uses of the land. Eight graduate students were sent out in two-man teams, made up of one landscape architecture student and one urban planning student, to look at the land and record their findings on maps. Meanwhile the headquarters staff sought out particular problem areas, zoning data, and plans already drawn up by federal or state agencies (they asked for the cooperation of the Department of Agriculture's Forest Service and Soil Erosion Service; the Army Corps of Engineers; the Department of the Interior's Bureau of Outdoor Recreation, Fish and Wildlife Service, and National Park Service; the Department of Health, Education and Welfare's Public Health Service; the Department of Commerce's Bureau of Public Roads; and the Housing and Home Finance Agency, which had a division for urban renewal). Most actual planning was presently happening at town or county level, and from these local planning boards a great deal of material had to be obtained—such things as master plans and urban renewal proposals. The data acquired from the more than two hundred planning agencies had then to be matched with the surveys of actual land use, and matched with each other for possible conflicts, for what might work out well for one town might have a detrimental effect on a town across the river.

The next stage was to attempt to project the future: the population pressure, in this case, of thirty million people by the end of the century in New York State, with much of the expansion taking place in the river valley, with a consequent need for land for houses, industry, transportation, agriculture, recreation, and the preservation of historic sites. The Arthur D. Little Company, an industrial research and consulting firm, headed by former General Gavin, situated near Boston's circumferential Route 128, and staffed by many ex-M.I.T. scholars, was looking into the prospects of industry. The TriState Transportation Commission (New York, New Jersey, and Connecticut) was already looking into that particular concern. The Fish and Wildlife Service had been asked to see what changes the Hudson's flora and fauna had undergone because of human presence and activity, and to find out what changes could be made to restore or maintain the natural life.

"Out of all this," said Mr. Wirth, patiently, "we hope to arrive at a plan—or maybe I should say a plan for a plan. We are concerned with the right ways for getting a plan across, of putting teeth into it. One idea we're considering is a sort of supreme court of planning, which would rule on differences between one locality and another, or one agency and another. And we're looking at tax situations, which is where a lot of the trouble comes. Every little town wants industry, to help finance its schools and services. And they all want to put their factories smack on the river bank."

Mr. Shore said, "An idea that might make sense is treating all industry in the Hudson Valley as if it were in one city, so you could tax it and collect all the money through a central authority, and hand back the revenue to the cities, towns, and villages on a per-school-child basis. In that way, there'd be less competition to acquire industry; certain areas could be specifically zoned for it; and you'd remove the danger of industrial blight spreading the whole length of the river."

"I think that's true," said Mr. Wirth. "Of course, it seems pretty radical to the people in each small town. But that's the biggest problem again—getting the plan across. I've been going round with some of my staff here talking to civic leaders, the League of Women Voters, and any group of concerned citizens who'll listen to me. Getting to the unconcerned citizen, I'm afraid, is another matter."

"We feel the urgency of this," Mr. Thompson said. "We realize that no one waits around for a plan. Things happen every day. The Central Hudson Gas and Electric Corporation was going to put power lines along the river at Newburgh. Well, we talked to them, and now they're going to wait for a while. But people are still getting born, taking jobs, and building new homes. Roads are being widened and extended all the time. There doesn't seem to be any way of getting all the highway builders to take a year's sabbatical in Miami Beach."

Mr. Towery asked, "How far back on either side of the river does your province extend?"

"About a mile," said Mr. Wirth.

"And what about New Jersey?"

"We don't intend to study the part of the river basin that's in New Jersey. We have suggested, however, that Governor Rockefeller write to Governor Hughes, so that he can appoint a representative who would keep informed of our activities."

We left Mr. Wirth, who said he would hitch a ride home with Mr. Thompson, at work on Iona. Their plan was due to be announced on the first of February 1966, and they were hearing time's winged chariot loud and clear. The plan, when unveiled, proposed a twelve member commission (nine members from New York State, three each from New Jersey and the federal government) that would persuade rather than command in an attempt to control development. However, proposals were made for a $100 million fund (half provided by the federal government) to acquire important land, and the commission requested power to review plans for major projects in the valley for a sixty-day period. The plan also suggested the creation of a statewide system of historic parks, the marking out of a network of roads to form a Hudson River Tourway, the cleaning up of billboards and junkyards in scenic places, the use of the underside of bridges to carry power lines across the river, and the development of trails and walkways near dense, urban areas —one example, forming a long, narrow, Bronx-Westchester park, was to use the old Croton aqueduct system as a thirty-two mile long, sixty-six feet wide grass-paved pedestrian highway; a great idea. Laurance Rockefeller, owner of the *Dauntless*, de-

clared the commission's opposition to the Storm King Mountain
power project, and brother Nelson chose the occasion to with-
draw his previous support for the Con Ed scheme. In numerous
places the commission hoped to acquire access rights through
riverfront property to let people get to and use the water and
the beaches.

Mr. Shore, Mr. Towery, and I went back aboard the *Dauntless,* running downstream with wind, wave, and current; it was
a more comfortable if less interesting ride. I thought the river
was a good symbol of the force planners had to master if they
could. It was life continuously flowing—life generating life. Because the Regional Plan Association had, since 1929, been attempting to educate the public in the need for, and methods of,
such mastery, I asked Mr. Shore if he thought the Hudson
River Valley Commission was on the right track.

"Well," he gave a diplomatic grin, "to start with, the commission exists, and bills like Congressman Ottinger's have been filed
in Congress, and that is evidence of concern. You can't work
without concern. But from our point of view they don't go far
enough. Regional Plan Association has an extensive background
in the success and failures of planning, and we know how hard
it is to get an idea across and make it stick. But we've boosted
such design concepts as Rockefeller Center and a new suburban
center for Nassau County, and I guess by now we know as
much as anyone about the effect of expressways and taxation—
anyway, all along we've insisted that planning take into account,
not just one factor, like scenic resources, but all the other factors, like jobs, housing, water, and transportation. Clearly it
doesn't do any good to freeze the Hudson into a scenic backdrop, when it can also serve as a site for new towns, and new
industry, and new recreation areas."

Although this was five months before the Hudson River Valley Commission released its plan, Mr. Shore seemed to have a
grasp of what they would propose, and I asked him how Regional Plan's proposals for the river might differ.

"I think I could say that our plan would be more definitive eventually, though it might seem to do less right away. Congressman Dow has filed a bill that matches most of our proposals. We believe that first of all a physical plan for the *entire* Hudson River Valley should be drafted, and it should be drafted by a professional, top-level planning staff, advised and directed by a planning commission. That commission should represent not only the federal, New York, and New Jersey governments, but the thirteen counties of both states lining the river, and all river municipalities. As the plan is being completed, the commission should work out what authority and funds will be needed to implement it."

"And the plan itself?"

"The plan would, in general, identify stretches where housing is appropriate, or parks; where farms should be maintained, or space for industry provided. It might press for the consolidation of freight piers and railyards along the lower Hudson—many are vacant now—and suggest new uses for the land. Those purposes should be coordinated with New York City and Jersey City. Parts of the river can possibly be ignored for the time being. In other places, as Mr. Thompson said, the developers are breathing down our necks. In some spots the plan might propose rerouting a railroad or changing the design of a road."

"You don't think the Hudson River Valley Commission goes far enough?"

"We think the whole river has to be planned at once. For one thing, people are alerted now. Moreover, the plan *has* to be comprehensive—there are heaps of small-scale plans already. New York State is planning, New York City is planning, the Iona group is planning, Westchester has a brilliant planner, and so does Dutchess County. Even Bergen County is rumored to have a master plan. The plan has to have great scope because it's stupid to plan beaches downriver if pollution continues upstream. There's no point in spending fortunes to renew a crummy waterfront while at the same time upriver a virgin stretch is being bulldozed. It is New York that suffers when

West New York tops the Palisades with apartment buildings. And while national parks are certainly a good thing upstream, as time goes on and it gets harder for a city dweller to get out of the city for a day of recreation, parks and boating facilities should be available on the Hudson actually in the city, and in Westchester and Bergen counties. In fact, among the important factors the planners should consider are the social problems of the central city. Furthermore, all levels of government should be represented on the commission because these days all levels are involved in any public program of this size. Such representation would ensure that two different points of view—that of the visitor and that of the resident—were always put forward."

I said that the big question seemed to be, how to achieve the plans' recommendations. (The Hudson River Valley Commission's plan fell into a thoughtful silence on this point, depending on a sixty-day review period. There was no sign of Mr. Wirth's supreme planning court.)

Mr. Shore said, "Right now every riverfront municipality has the power to control land use. All levels of government have parks along the shore. The federal government controls navigation, regulates electric power, and has the authority to allow land to be created by fill along the banks. The states control over-all real-estate tax policy, which influences the way municipalities zone land. Meanwhile everyone—landowners, businesses, government agencies, or counties—exploits and develops the land for his own purposes. What the plan does first is say what the Hudson would look like at its best, and how best it would serve most people. This is advice to the people and institutions whose decisions determine what actually happens. The second half of the plan should consider the leverage needed to get the decision makers to follow the first half.

"In some cases, all you have to do is show the government units or individuals that their own interest is aided by the plan—the tax-sharing idea, benefiting the towns and properly located industry, might be an example. Landowners' concern for their property rights and the public good might be balanced with purchases of development rights or scenic easements, by which the owner continues to own his land but agrees for a price to keep it the way it is. The plan would suggest where action should be taken at once, as in the cases of the World Trade Center and a new West Side Highway, neither of which should be built without relation to an over-all plan for the Hudson. The commission should stay in business after the plan is made, therefore, and encourage and put pressure on the many different agencies and levels of government which would have the job, maybe over a long period, of carrying it out."

Lifting over the short, steep combers, the *Dauntless* came down the wide Tappan Zee. Seen from the water, as an entire structure, the Tappan Zee Bridge is pathetic—it has four different rhythms; it sprawls, it builds up slowly from the western shore for a leap but when the leap finally comes, it is clumsy, and the landing is a painful belly-flopper.

"A cheap bridge," said Mr. Shore, whom I was beginning to regard as one of the unsung heroes of the urban catastrophe. He was, in any event, a man who propagated hope that the growing mess of the city could be organized, coordinated, and controled; who gave the impression that the urban future might just be bigger and better rather than bigger and worse. "They built it here because this was as close to New York City as they could get without being within the cosmos of the Port Authority. What a way to locate a bridge!"

The northwest wind helped us in toward the decrepit docks of Tarrytown, and the captain did a brilliant job of negotiating the *Dauntless* into her berth against one of the piers. Having bade good-bye to Mr. Shore and Mr. Towery, and having thanked the *Dauntless* crew, I drove a mile or so to a friend's house in North Tarrytown, which is a pleasantly old-fashioned suburb—or rather, a village that has become a suburb, with wide, tree-lined streets, and large, unobtrusive houses set back in slightly shabby gardens. My host taught science in a local high school, and a friend of his, an engineer in a space-age electronics company, was at dinner. We sat up late having one of those conversations that are common among undergraduates, complaining loudly about the world as it is. We discussed the theory of inertia and the theory of the magnet (which someone defined as the more you've got, the more you get). We discussed the lobbies for the automobile industry, the oil industry, the steel industry, and the cement industry. We discussed the lack of a lobby for R. & D. and the good life. Rather late, I dimly remember, someone said that there were only thirteen billion nerve cells in the human brain, and therefore there was a limit to the number of facts the brain could hold. And therefore, we were soon to reach the end of deductive reasoning. It was time we got back to first principles.

14

The Radburn Principle

IN THE morning I drove across the Hudson again and went down into New Jersey. The sun was out and the wind had gone. On the Jersey road map the city of Paterson is shown by a square patch of yellow, in the northeast corner of which appears the word Radburn. Paterson was founded in 1791 by Alexander Hamilton and other promoters of the Society for Useful Manufactures; its plans were worked over by Pierre L'Enfant after he was dismissed from the job of planning the capital city of Washington; and it became notable as the chief silk manufacturing town in the country and as the home town of the doctor and poet, William Carlos Williams. Radburn is less generally known, although it appears in the glossaries and indices of most modern works on architecture and town planning. Intended to be a new town, Radburn was founded in 1928 by Alexander Bing, a New York financier, and was planned by Lewis Mumford's friends, Clarence Stein and Henry Wright. In that year the George Washington Bridge had not yet been built. Radburn was as distinct from Paterson as both were from New York City. Now, of course, it takes some finding among the hundreds of suburban communities that have spread out over northern New Jersey, and I was glad, as I drove along Route 4 through Teaneck, Paramus, and Arcola, past shopping malls, subdivisions, and industrial parks, that I had been there a year before and knew my way. For out there, a person accustomed to either the dense city or a New England village may feel more than geographically disoriented; he begins to realize what it means to say that New York is the largest urban agglomeration in the world, with a population (at the last count in 1964) of 14,114,927, which is some 4 million more than Tokyo, the second largest: and that New York is "urbanizing" at the rate of 50,000 acres per year and absorbing 600,000 people yearly in this expanding perimeter. What it is like on the edge of the perimeter was illuminated in a *New York Times* story not long ago about the hitherto semirural village of New City, in Rockland County, New York. A resident of the place told the reporter, Paul Montgomery, "It's going. But you can't fight progress, can you? I believe that New City will be another Queens by the time I'm gone. These people want everything to stop just the way it is the moment they arrive, but then the next fellow comes, and the fellow after that. What you're getting is Queens."

It is difficult to be unemotional about suburban dispersal. Historians have fancied that they saw the first signs of the crumbling of the Roman Empire in the move of rich Romans out of their city to suburban villas, and Englishmen who appreciated the sharp contrast between grass and brick, between country and city, saw the industrial revolution as the creator of a monstrous London. It was, to William Cobbett, a "great wen," and to Smollet, "an overgrown monster; which, like a dropsical head, will in time leave the body and extremities without nourishment and support." In America, the cities overspilled their boundaries before the Civil War. According to Robert C. Wood, Brooklyn was New York's bedroom as early as 1845, and by the end of the century suburban communities were scattered along the spokes of iron rails radiating from the

center of the city. Lord Bryce pointed ouᵗ, in 1888, that rich
men were moving to the suburbs to escape city taxes. Writes
Mr. Wood, in *Suburbia:*

> The coming of the automobile intensified the migration, for now
> the open spaces between the spokes could be filled in. Henry Ford,
> stubbornly pushing the logic of production to its ultimate conclu-
> sions, offered the Model T as a car both cheap and reliable, and
> other manufacturers followed suit. . . . No longer dependent on
> streetcar or train, or at least having new access to them, families
> could settle where they chose. Given a breadwinner sufficiently
> healthy and complacent to endure the commuter schedule, access to
> work was assured. Highways began to ring the city and pierce it
> directly and buses and trackless trolleys went wherever the popula-
> tion grew. The metropolitan area was in being, and as land values
> soared within the city and along its farthest perimenter, the inter-
> mediate land filled up.

The Depression slowed this suburban growth, but it did not
stop it. Out of the New Deal emerged the Federal Housing
Administration to insure millions of mortgages, and after World
War II the Veterans Administration independently underwrote
millions more. By 1955 one out of four Americans was a sub-
urbanite; by now the figure must be nearly one in three, for
people were encouraged to become one, as Mr. Wood puts it, by

> the shortage of housing in large cities, aspirations for space and
> separate family accommodations and for home ownership, a drive
> for higher social status, the rising birth rate, the tradition of rest-
> lessness nourished and intensified by the Depression and the war
> prosperity, and the family ethic.
>
> But not the least of the forces at work was the persistent ideal:
> the image of small town life that every migrant held in his mind and
> that every real estate speculator raised as a conscious symbol. In
> some ways the ideal comprehended the forces which were at work:
> the desire for space, family life, and the homestead were part and
> parcel of the image itself. In other ways, the ideology determined
> the uses to which modern technology would be put. It diverted the
> urban population and their governments from efforts to rebuild
> their central cities on a substantial scale or to devise new residential
> accommodations there to house the growing number of children.
> Instead, it fostered investment in transportation facilities rather than
> urban renewal, in automobiles in place of more extensive develop-
> ment of urban land.

The suburbs that thus grew as an alternative to the central city were economically part of it but socially and politically independent. While, financially, they tended to grow at the expense of the central city, depriving it of taxes and income, they also soon found it fairly expensive to support their independent life—their own schools, fire engines, garbage collections, water supply, streets, lighting, and sewage. The fragmentation of political authority among so many communities—there are roughly fourteen hundred governments in the New York metropolitan area—might strike some as the chief contribution to urban chaos the suburban dispersal has made, although, as Mr. Wood stresses, it can also be seen as a decision to retain the most important elements of small town democracy, an expression of the desire to keep things small as all around they get bigger and bigger. And if the suburbs seems particularly vulnerable on aesthetic grounds, it is possible to make a defence on utilitarian grounds. Allan Temko writes, "The much disparaged 'split-levels' and 'ticky-tacky boxes' represent the most spacious and hygienic mass housing in history, filled with ingenious and indubitably useful appliances." Indeed, criticism of the suburb, and the particularly exaggerated form that has grown with the speed of crabgrass across northern New Jersey, could be dismissed as strictly from the ivory tower, if no practical alternative had ever been demonstrated, as it was demonstrated at Radburn.

Tuesday morning, and the main roads were crowded. However, Fair Lawn Avenue, which as a country road was marked on a map of George Washington's, had little traffic on it: delivery and service trucks, and a few women out shopping. In the gardens of some houses elderly women with neither children nor shopping to worry about were raking leaves. I drove through Fair Lawn, which gives the impression of being an area full of ranch houses set on quarter-acre lots rather than a town, and suddenly, in the middle of it all, I was once again in Radburn. At the junction of Fairlawn Avenue and Plaza Road, opposite an ordinary shopping center, was the Radburn Plaza, a red brick complex of shops and offices. And behind this, on both sides of the avenue, were two areas that, on close inspection, show evidence of being unlike the Fair Lawn housing that has since surrounded them. In each area was a park, which was rimmed by houses or garden apartment buildings. The architecture of the houses was not very original—the buildings were mock-Tudor and mock-Colonial—but for American middle-class houses they were rather close together; their gardens were at the front, rather than at the back; and it was at the back where the main door appeared to be, opening on a yard and driveway leading to a service road, itself a cul-de-sac, that opened at one end on a perimeter road. The houses all fronted on the park, and paths at some distance from the roads (or going beneath them in underpasses where the path and road converged) led to playing fields, swimming pools, tennis courts, and the school. At 8 A.M. and 3 P.M., these paths are crowded with children.

The idea of a garden city had been proposed by Ebenezer Howard in England at the turn of the century; at Welwyn and Letchworth garden cities were built, and the idea went on to affect the New Towns constructed to reduce the pressure on London, after the war. In America, Howard's idea was discussed and modified in conversations held at the Hudson Guild Farm, in Netcong, New Jersey, where in the 1920s such people as Mumford, Stein, Wright, and Catherine Bauer met on weekends to thresh out ways of improving the American city and countryside. To Howard's notions were added the facts of American life and some of its brighter architectural heritage—in particular the work of Frederick Olmstead and Calvert Vaux in Central Park, Manhattan, where a network of paths, sunken roads, bridges, underpasses, and green spaces neatly and safely separated pedestrian, equestrian, and vehicular traffic. Stein and Wright were also impressed by the superblocks the Dutch had had in Nieuw Amsterdam in 1660, with rows of houses surrounding a core of farms and gardens. They were fortunate to have a client in Alexander Bing, who was equally impressd and who saw things on what they considered to be a large enough scale.

In 1928 the borough of Fair Lawn, still mainly rural, had not adopted either an orthodox zoning law or a gridiron street plan. The site chosen for the new town was two square miles of gently undulating farmland, sixteen miles from Manhattan—a site large enough, the architects felt, for a town that would eventually contain twenty-five thousand people and would have its own schools, stores, and factories, served by the Erie Railroad. Stein had worked out that the park, around which the first houses began to go up, could be paid for by lower costs of the cul-de-sac streets and superblock pattern; in fact, the savings from street construction and shorter utility lines and pipes also covered the cost of grading and landscaping the play spaces and pedestrian paths. The houses themselves were not avant-garde, although they were turned back to front, facing the parks instead of the streets (which fitted between the green spaces like interlocked fingers), and—despite the fact that Paterson was losing its silk industry—they sold well. It was at this point, when Radburn's future seemed assured, that the stock market collapsed. The construction of Radburn slowed down, so that in 1933 only twelve houses were built; no industry came; and people who had so recently bought houses on mortgages held by Bing's corporation had to forfeit them to the corporation, which then found it hard to rent out these properties. With an expanding economy the scheme might well have succeeded, but with a shrinking one it failed. Land prices went down to 10 percent of what Bing had paid for them, and the corporation went bankrupt. Radburn was lucky to survive as a miniature island in the midst of Fair Lawn.

I parked by the Plaza building, and walked down one of the lanes, conscious, as Radburn makes one, that walking is an important thing. A place where one can walk to school, to buy a newspaper or a loaf of bread, to sit on an expanse of grass or (as in Stonington) a heap of rocks and watch the swell lift the seaweed in, is a place with a decided edge in regard to the amenities of life. The Scots transportation expert Colin Buchanan has written:

> The simple act of *walking* plays an indispensable part in the transport system of any town. There is nothing fanciful in this statement. Walking accounts for many medium-distance movements, the final distribution from bus stops and car parks, and a vast amount of casual coming and going. Nor is it to be discounted as a medium for the carriage of goods, as in individual shopping for example [or, in Manhattan, one might add, the conveyance of wholesale clothes in the crowded garment center]. It is therefore common sense that pedestrian movement should be enabled to take place in reasonable comfort and safety, and this can be said without appearing to be telling people what is good for their health. Walking is also an integral part of many other matters, such as looking in shop windows, admiring the scene, or talking to people. In all, it does not seem to be far from the truth that the freedom with which a person can walk about and look around is a very useful guide to the civilised quality of an urban area.

Although Radburn squeaked through as a suburban rather than as an urban area, the ability to walk along its pedestrian paths is one fact that gives it individuality. Nearly five thousand people live there, all but a hundred families in their own houses. Sixty percent commute to New York. Residents pay a Radburn Association assessment as well as a Fair Lawn borough tax; the assessment covers the cost of parks, paths, library, and recreational activities—all sorts of summer sports for children, two infant play areas with trained superintendents, and two swimming pools, which are reserved for adults at certain hours. Radburn also has a community church, bridge and bowling clubs, a weekly newspaper, and an amateur drama group, which has done such productions as *Guys and Dolls* and *Sunday in New York*. Radburn itself is a sort of club, and is prized as such. The houses maintain a high value, come on the market infrequently, and are then often exchanged—with cash adjustment—between older couples wanting smaller houses and younger families wanting bigger ones. The association has nine elected trustees, a full-time manager and recreation director, and a well-framed set of protective restrictions, which regulate finances and demand that a house owner get the permission of the trustees and his neighbors before changing the color of his house paint or building on a carport. Most problems are of a standard suburban order—someone has left his garbage cans out all week, or has a garden television set that is too loud.

In thirty-odd years the Stein-Wright ground plan has been well tested. In the ordinary gridiron layout, pedestrians risk twenty street crossings every mile, and children are everywhere exposed to the dangers of through streets. The two traffic deaths in Radburn have both been on the main roads that split the community (the footbridge across Fair Lawn Avenue which once linked the two sections of Radburn was removed by Fairlawn authorities, who declared it unsafe, and replaced it by crossing guards). In the cul-de-sacs and perimeter roads the only accident involved a child's broken arm. The one problem with them has been with snow removal, since a plough can't push the snow out through a dead end, but wide sewer gratings might be an answer. The lanes were of course designed for 1928 cars, and even my Jeep bulked large in them. Mr. Stein has said that if he were designing Radburn again he would make the lanes larger and also provide more paved areas where children could play ball—for at the moment, because balls bounce better there than on grass, they play in the lanes even though they are not supposed to. The fine Radburn parks occasionally attract youths from less favored suburbs, who use the novel space to drink beer and break lamps, but the pedestrian paths and underpasses seem to have no drawbacks at all.

Indeed, as one walks along them one is amazed that Radburn could have existed so long in America and not been widely imitated. Although the trees, parks, grass, paths, and houses have a pleasant air of age and use, they seem absolutely up-to-date. Most of the British New Towns have followed a similar plan of cul-de-sacs and pedestrian paths, and such older cities as Sheffield and Coventry have rebuilt blitzed sections on the same lines. Radburn has influenced the layout of new towns in Sweden, Canada, and Russia, but until recently its renown in this country has been confined to textbooks. In the last few years, however, some of its innovations have become a little less unknown. Planners talk of "cluster housing" and builders, rather warily, consider it as a practical alternative to quarter-acre, free-standing houses. In the past, most of them have naturally built what they have known they can sell, and they have been backed in this attitude by the Federal Housing Administration mortgage policy. It is only now, when people begin to feel that the land is running out, that the advantages (in terms of rural space together with urban proximity) of Radburn over Fair Lawn, and all the Fair Lawns that have spread out from American cities, are finally being seen. William James put it well: "Tight fit is what shapes things definitely; with a loose fit you get no results, and America is redolent of loose fits everywhere."

There was a previous time when space in America seemed tight, and that was when the settlers were sandwiched between the coast and the Indian-infested interior. Behind the close-at-hand frontier, the Dutch in Nieuw Amsterdam built their superblocks, and in Sudbury, Massachusetts, Peter Noyes and his colleagues founded a closely packed village among their common fields. It is perhaps significant that the origins of the nucleated village and the common field system have been found by medievalists to lie in the increase of population; the increase rendered inefficient the old layout of scattered dwellings and more split-up, more widely separated, and—with a division for every new heir—smaller parcels of field. "Eventually," writes the historian Joan Thirsk, "as fields multiplied whenever new land was taken into cultivation from the waste, and as the parcels of each cultivator became more and more scattered, regulations had to be introduced to ensure that all had access to their own land and to water, and that meadows and ploughland were protected from damage by stock. The community was drawn together by sheer necessity to cooperate in the control of farming practices. All the fields were brought together into two or three large units."

15

A Green Lung

WITH THE right mixture of luck and judgment I found the Garden State Parkway and headed south. According to the map I passed by East Paterson, Rochelle Park, Clifton, Passaic, Montclair, Nutley, Glen Ridge, Bloomfield, Orange, Maplewood, and Irvington, but I knew nothing of them save that, after Irvington, I had to bear right through Union on Route 82. Even so, a brief exposure to this part of the metropolis brings out the grumpiness in the most tolerant of travelers. It makes one wonder if the old, clear-cut distinction between man and the other animals was ever valid: are we in control of our own destiny; are we conscious; have we, unlike them, a soul? Do people—statistically better-off, more comfortable, more highly taxed and educated than any other people in history—truly imagine that this is a fitting landscape, a proper city? Sheer necessity has not yet drawn the hundreds of autonomous communities together to cooperate in the control of the apparatus of urban living. Yet there are signs of consciousness in New Jersey, and after taking a deep breath to ensure survival in the chemically stained air and wiping one's eyes quite frequently, one can see them. *The New York Times* reported from Trenton not long ago:

Governor Richard J. Hughes called on the people of New Jersey today to escape the shadows of New York City and Philadelphia, discover an identity amid megalopolis, and rise to a new, collective greatness befitting a rich, urban state. . . . "As I look out upon the face of New Jersey I see a people and a state destined to be great from the moment of its birth as a colony more than 300 years ago. But we have too long been hidden in the shadows of the great cities to the east and west, too long in their corridor without our own identity, too long rich in private wealth but poor in public service, too long afraid to come to grips with our own destiny."

If one believes that in an urban democracy politicians don't tend to move unless they're pretty sure the public will kick them in that direction, Governor Hughes's second inaugural speech was evidence of the dawn of a new era in Jersey. If, on the other hand, one believes that in the mass age a few statesmen are concerned with the major problems of the time while the spokesmen of the suburban communities, like ostriches, bury their heads in the sand, one will note, with a grin, that two months after this speech the New Jersey legislature turned down the bulk of the Governor's financial program that was designed to bring New Jersey into the twentieth century.

The fact that one doesn't necessarily need a master plan, one just needs to have the wit to kick and scream is pointed up by the case of the Great Swamp. Indeed, there is a fair reason to believe that a master plan might well have indicated, as a minor plan did, that this swamp was the most suitable place in the metropolitan area for a fourth jet airport. The Great Swamp case also proves, however, that when people care enough, at the right time, plans change.

Route 82 brought me to 24, which heads toward Morristown, and halfway there, in Chatham, I turned left on a country road, Fairmount Avenue, which I followed for six meandering miles, past new houses set well apart among the trees like those on the road in Sudbury which Al Noyes had been rebuilding. This brought me to the hamlet of Myersville—a gas station, firehouse, luncheonette, half a dozen houses, and the field office of the Great Swamp Wildlife Refuge. In the luncheonette I had a medium rare hamburger with ketchup and a slice of raw onion, and a cup of coffee, and then I went next door to the refuge office to keep an appointment with Dick Rigby, the refuge manager.

Rigby, however, wasn't there. The one man who was, introduced himself to me as another visitor, a land-acquisition agent from the Boston heaquarters of the Fish and Wildlife Service's northeast region. He called Rigby on the telephone, and relayed a message from Rigby to me that he'd be along in twenty minutes, just as soon as he'd finished putting in a window in an addition he was building on his house. In the meantime I was to sit down, put my feet up, and read a report he had left for me on top of his desk. There I found four machine-copied pages. The land-acquisition agent said he would leave me in charge—he had to go to negotiate for some land. About two-thirds of the swamp was now government owned, though it had all been privately owned once, and most of the titles on the remaining third were so obscure that the government was taking it by friendly condemnation, paying a fair, negotiated price for each tract.

I opened a venetian blind over the Model A copying machine that had rather foggily reproduced the report, put my feet up, as suggested, on Rigby's desk, and proceeded to put myself in the picture in regard to Great Swamp.

Great Swamp is located in Chatham, Harding and Passaic Townships, Morris County, in north central New Jersey. It lies 85 miles north of Brigantine N.W. Refuge, 110 miles northeast of Bombay Hook N.W. Refuge, and 190 miles southeast of Montezuma N.W. Refuge. [These facts, useful for migrating ducks, can perhaps be supplemented by the fact that Great Swamp is 30 miles southwest of midtown Manhattan.]

On March 23, 1965, the Migratory Bird Conservation Council authorized funds for the acquisition of waterfowl habitat in the Great Swamp. Added to the 2680 acres already donated to the Bureau [of Sport Fisheries and Wildlife—an offspring of the Fish and Wildlife Service, which in turn is a division of the Department of the Interior] by the North American Wildlife Foundation, this will provide for a National Wildlife Refuge of approximately 5900 acres. This refuge was formally dedicated on May 29, 1964.

Great Swamp is best described as a shallow bowl, 7 miles long and 3 miles wide. Surrounding hills rise 50 to 200 feet above the swamp bed. The refuge area is roughly divided into 3200 acres of shrub and timbered swamps, 700 acres of marsh, 1200 acres of upland timber, and 800 acres of farmland in various states of neglect. The greater part of the refuge including most of the existing marshland is located within the watershed of Great Brook and its tributaries, Primrose and Loantaka Brooks. The southeastern portion of the refuge, consisting primarily of shrub and timbered swamp, lies within the Black Brook watershed. These two watersheds supply approximately 50 percent of the Passaic River's flow at Millington Gap, N.J.

For anyone interested in geology, Rigby's report had the details—how, roughly forty thousand years ago, the Wisconsin Glacier rumbled south, collecting vast loads of sand, gravel, and boulders. Twenty-five thousand years ago it reached its furthest point of advance along a line through Morristown, Madison, and Chatham. As it then retreated it left long ridges of glacial till, one of which blocked the outlet of an ancient river basin near Short Hills. Behind this natural dam a lake formed as the glacier melted its way back north, and although it was eventually drained by an outlet at Little Falls Gap, which created the Passaic River, the vestiges of the lake remain in the shape of the Great Swamp.

In 1708, in one of those bargain deals conducted at the time, the Delaware Indians sold a thirty thousand-acre tract that included the swamp to some English settlers "for the consideration of . . . 30 pounds in cash, ten stran'd water blankets, 15 kettles, half a barrel of wine, one barrel of rum, two barrels of cider, four pistols and four cutlasses." During the Revolutionary War lumbering operations in the swamp supplied a nearby hub and felly factory, and brick, charcoal, and potash manufacturing went on in the vicinity. The logging of the uplands produced cleared farmland, while the draining of marshes allowed the growth of good crops of "foul meadow hay." In 1844, about half of the swamp was cleared and drained by ditches; a few old residents recall that in the early 1900s the marshes were still hayed and the uplands were still cleared; by the middle of this century, however, the uplands had largely reverted to woods, and the neglected ditches had allowed the old marsh and swamp to reappear.

Great schemes for Great Swamp have not been lacking in the recent past. The army engineers, who have a professional interest in dikes and dams, have drawn up plans (none so far approved) for flood control reservoirs in the area which would submerge large sections of the swamp under several feet of water. The W.P.A. worked on a drainage project in the 30s, constructing or improving ditches, and although no effect was felt in the western half, the drainage of the southeastern part was speeded up. Then in 1959 came the proposals for the greatest scheme of all, which would have drained the swamp altogether. This was the Port Authority's jetport plan, and it constituted—in the same way as Con Ed's Storm King Mountain scheme—the necessary threat. Local residents formed the cunningly named Jersey Jetsite Association, whose object was to keep the jetport out of this part of New Jersey altogether, and wide support suddenly materialized from local landowners for the North American Wildlife Foundation, which had been trying for some time to organize Great Swamp as a refuge.* From 6000 people, and 462 groups, the sum of $1.2 million was raised to purchase 2600 acres. The duck hunting public, through the

---

* A group that has for some years been working on the principle that landowners can be the major factor in conserving land, particularly in a period of uncontrolled metropolitan expansion, is the Open Space Action Committee. A private group, the Open Space Action Committee has embarked on field operations in the New York metropolitan area, working outward from the immediate urban fringe and, proceeding county by county, canvassing every owner of tracts of open space twenty acres and larger. O.S.A.C. attempts to find out what the owner's plans are for his land and points out to him his ability to hold onto it, preserving it himself or through his community. The committee has published its program in a book entitled *Stewardship,* which it has sent to some seven thousand five hundred landowners, and it presents as successful examples of land stewardship the covenant agreed upon by ten landholders along the Bantam River, in Connecticut, who agreed that in perpetuity their land for two hundred feet back from the river's edge should be kept free of buildings or billboards, forbidding the removal of soil, gravel, and trees.

purchase of annual $3.00 Federal duck licenses, provided another $2.8 million to pay for a further 3267 acres. The land-acquisition agents have been dealing with 101 private owners, whose properties ranged from 1½ to 282 acres; the average price paid was $857 per acre, less for marsh, more for prime farmland.

"It's going to be a couple of years before we've taken in all the land," said Dick Rigby, when he arrived. "But right now we've got enough work cut out cleaning up the land we've already got." Rigby was a tall man in his mid-thirties, with bushy eyebrows, a Jersey-southern accent, and apparently constant energy. He was born in Pittsburgh, grew up in New Jersey, and in recent months—having been brought up from the Laguna Duck Refuge in Texas to run Great Swamp—he had been commuting over from Eatontown, near Red Bank, on the north Jersey shore, where his father is in the real-estate business. "We've just moved into our house here," he said. "It's owned by the Bureau, and I have to make my own improvements, like filling in the garden, which was mostly old beer bottles. Doing things yourself is what our Bureau trains you for. We're the biggest bunch of scroungers ever seen, mainly because we're so low on the federal pole. We built Brigantine Refuge using old surplus army equipment. But I shouldn't exaggerate, because we have funds now, and we're letting contracts for dike building and the demolition of dud barns and shacks. In fact, I miss the old rough-and-ready days. I was trained to build dikes, and contracting it out not only means we're a little less in control of what gets done, it also means there's less fun in it."

I asked what the dikes were for.

"It's the drought, five years' worth. You know how it rained the other night—well, that didn't affect the swamp one bit. We'll take a walk in a while so you can see. In the spring it's wet, but summer dries it out. If we didn't make dikes to impound the water, the waterfowl wouldn't come."

"Any duck right now?"

"I haven't heard of any, though there may be a handful in the marsh—we don't own much of the marsh yet. But when we do, and when we can keep it wet, we'll be able to support about thirty-five hundred duck and eight thousand geese every year. Our biologists say that right now Great Swamp accounts for eighty-five thousand waterfowl days—a waterfowl day being one bird using the swamp for one day. Fifty-one percent of the use is in the fall when they are going down the Atlantic Flyway, thirty percent in the spring, eighteen percent in the summer, and one percent in the winter. By then all the transients —the black duck, wood duck, pintail, widgeons, teal, mallard, and geese—have gone south. The count, by the way, is fairly accurate. In the old days in our Bureau they used to call the coot the refuge manager's duck. The coot isn't really a waterfowl, though it hangs around with ducks. In those days a manager was paid in proportion to the number of ducks on his station. You can see how the coot got its nickname."

Rigby suggested that we take a drive around the swamp. As we climbed into his car he told me something of the history of refuges, which hadn't really been needed until the turn of the century. Until then waterfowl had fared well in America, being widely distributed and shot primarily for home consumption. But the introduction of automatic shotguns and modern, more effective ammunition, together with continuous, year-round shooting and more hunting for the market instead of the domestic stove, began to cause alarm. In 1903, President Theodore Roosevelt established the first wildlife refuge in Florida to protect brown pelicans, whose plumage was then fashionable for women's hats. Other refuges were also set up by executive order, and, in 1916, Canada and the United States signed a treaty to protect migratory birds. Congress caught a touch of the fever in 1924, appropriating one and a half million dollars for waterfowl habitat lands along the upper Mississippi. Drought in the thirties, war in the forties, and government subsidized agricultural drainage programs in the prairie states in the fifties all caused depredations. By 1965, however, nearly three hundred refuges had been created with a total of 28,500,000 acres, which is an area not much smaller than Pennsylvania. Two hundred and twenty refuges are managed primarily for waterfowl, and on fifty-eight of them hunting is allowed in certain sections, at certain seasons.

We drove past the luncheonette and turned into the swamp on Long Hill Road. At first there were open fields with small farm buildings, then shrubs began to close in, and finally, thick trees. On a fifteen mile circuit we sometimes followed the periphery of the swamp and sometimes cut through it. Rigby pointed out places where the Bureau was acquiring land, where old buildings were about to be bulldozed, and where other buildings were to be improved for use as houses for the refuge staff, offices, or storage. Some owners would be allowed to remain in their houses during their own lifetimes, particularly if it was a hardship for them to move; but one man had just built a brand-new red brick house, and the bureau hadn't yet decided whether to buy him out or let him stay. "That guy irritates me," said Rigby. "He knew what the plans were, but he went on building anyway." Rigby was also anxious about six hundred acres of private wildlife preserve, whose owner didn't want to merge with Great Swamp, but some of whose land might be flooded by the Great Swamp water-impoundment schemes. He also showed me places he was proud of, where his clean-up crews had dragged away old cars and scrap heaps; where there stood a group of four hundred year old oaks; where there were wide fields of the lushest, greenest grass; and where, in presently unkempt meadows, he was going to plant millet for duck and winter wheat for geese. "That big field is going to be a real sight with a thousand Canada geese feeding on it," he said, with the pride of a proprietor.

The surrounding roads seemed to be in very good shape for such a sparsely populated area, and Rigby said that he thought they might have been improved for the possible jetport. "You know, that was a real battle. The first word about the Port

Authority plans leaked out in 1959. Someone said too much over a martini. The late Mr. Hartley Dodge, president of Remington Arms, heard about it, and he put up some $300,000 to buy marsh property. At first he was going to give it to the Morris County Park Commission, but he didn't think they'd have the power to withstand the Port Authority. So he approached the government through the North American Wildlife Foundation, which donated the Dodge land to our bureau. We had looked at this swamp in 1937, but we were a cowboy outfit then, and we couldn't afford it. Apart from Mr. Dodge, the other leader of the opposition was Mrs. Helen Fenske. She's forty-two, attractive, and a real, articulate, fighting politician. Also, she's smarter than I am. She went round giving talks to the local garden clubs and political groups. Then she lined up the right men, with the power and the money, who didn't want the jetport, and she organized the Great Swamp Committee, which collected some nine hundred thousand dollars. With this backing, and the approval of Governor Hughes, we took our case to the Migratory Bird Council. The council gave us the power to buy more than three thousand additional acres with the $2.8 million of duck stamp money. And that for the moment knocked the Port Authority flat."

Rigby parked the car in a small graveled clearing to one side of the road, with its borders delineated by neat creosoted posts. We got out. The sun was warm on the gravel, and in the treetops the wind soughed. Birds hopped around the edge of the clearing, or bounced from bush to post to tree to fern. Somewhere in the gravel a grasshopper was piping. We followed a little path that went through a meadow into the trees, and Rigby, walking ahead, said, "Around here the response to the refuge has been pretty good, especially in Harding Township, which is where most of the land lies. Harding has a lot of big estates, whose owners don't want to see a deluge of new housing. There have been a few grumbles that we're removing taxable property from the list, but we're giving the local authorities a share of some of the fees we get, for instance for the gas pipeline that passes through the swamp. And three-quarters of one percent of the $2.8 million purchase price will be paid every year to Morris County in lieu of taxes."

We came to a place where the path became an oak plank walk. The ground on either side looked damp and boggy, despite the drought. Rigby said that two thousand acres on this side of the swamp would remain inviolate as a natural area, and would be open only to serious students, such as the scientists who were already investigating the mosquitoes in relation to encephalitis, of which there were quite frequent outbreaks in Camden but few here. They wondered if air pollution did anything to trigger it. Rigby walked across a small wooden bridge that spanned a brook, and pointed out some bird boxes that had been built in the trees to encourage the nesting of wood ducks. He said black bear and red fox still lived in the swamp. The swamp was particularly interesting to botanists because it formed a meeting ground of northern and southern species of plants (rather like the waters off Cape Hatteras, where northern and southern fish meet). "There's a young beech starting up," Rigby said, bending a sapling. "We have one at the other end of the swamp that is sixteen feet in circumference. These depressions you see on the ground between the trees are either glacial pockets or else places where the loggers burned up all the scrap after they'd lumbered the area, and the fire burned down into the peat. Over there, just look the way I'm looking, see the deer, a yearling, she's staring right at us. Her tail isn't even flicking. I guess she's hypnotized by the sound of our voices."

The young doe stood scarcely twenty feet away; she was dapple brown, the color of the trees, leaves, and ground, with the sunlight sifted on them. Only her brown eyes gleaming brought her apart from the woods. She was standing so still that I turned my head to see what spell Rigby was casting on her, but of course my movement broke the frail hold we had on her. She whipped around and with a graceful flick of her heels bounded away.

"That was a treat," said Rigby, and I agreed with him.

The trail was a circular one that brought us back to the graveled parking lot. When we got there, Rigby said that there was another place in the swamp that he would like me to see. It was only in the construction stage as yet, but it perhaps gave a hint of what he hoped to do in Great Swamp. "The way I see it," he said, as we got into the car, "we have a chance of a million people a year coming through here. Within a fifty mile radius of this spot there are twenty million people, and more every minute. Twenty years from now the fence around Great Swamp will be the backyard fence of houses, all the way round. So what we save now is all we're going to save, and this place can have real influence. I want it to be the conservation center for the region. I want it to represent segments of other refuges, so that it demonstrates what we do in the way of water management, waterfowl production, and farming for feed. This place is important for producing ducks, but we can get more ducks out of other places. Its greater value can be in teaching people how to look after the earth. Man is the only animal that can control its environment for good or ill—but we haven't woken up to the responsibility yet."

Rigby pulled up in front of a new wooden gate that barred the entrance to a field. After he had got out, opened the gate, driven through, shut the gate, and had climbed in again to drive over the field in the direction of a copse, a quarter of a mile away, he said, "Did you notice that gate? Dandy piece of work. The man who built it can't read or write. He used to be a treeman, but a tree fell and broke his back, and now he's all wired-up. In the mornings he's slow, but you can't keep up with him in the afternoons. I wish he was still with me. He's gone to work for a gas station."

I asked Rigby why *he* was working in this particular job.

"My father is always asking the same thing. He wants me to go in the real-estate business with him and make some money. I don't know—I guess I'm in love with this. I used to be a pretty quiet fellow, but look at me now—I shout and roar until I get things done. I get told off every now and then for being so impatient with bureaucratic procedures, but the way I see it, it's the determination at my level, getting eyeball to eyeball with them, as Dean Rusk says, that produces results both up and down."

Having left the car, we walked past an immobile bulldozer to a little ridge; from the wide-spaced sprouts of new grass in the ridge, I gathered that it was recently man-made. Beyond was a serpentine-shaped depression, partly filled with water, that wound through other banks and ridges, with trees overhanging the far end.

"I'm controlling the environment here," Rigby said with a grin, "but I could do with some natural help in the form of rain. In fact, that thunderstorm the other night dumped a little water in the pond. You should have seen this place last year. There were seven buildings back where we parked the car—one of those backwoods farms, with chicken coops, an old cow barn, and pig pens—the trashiest place. We burned some of it and backfilled the rest. This area here was all silted-in marsh, and we used a dragline to dig out the channel, and the bulldozer to build up the ridges. There will be a series of interconnected impoundments. By next spring we should have plantings coming up—the millet in the big field will bring in the waterfowl."

I congratulated Rigby on his skill as a landscape architect.

"Well, this isn't just me," he said. "John Gottschalk, who was head of the northeast region and is now our boss in Washington, had this idea for a wildlife observation blind. A local garden club in Somerset Hills submitted the scheme in the annual National Garden Clubs competition for the Founders Award of three thousand dollars—and they won. That money is paying for much of this. There will be a lookout post on the ridge, camouflaged with earth and shrubbery, making it a good place to stand and see what goes on in a swamp. The Summit Nature Club has been putting up bird nesting boxes, like those we saw on the circular trail. All sorts of people have pitched in to help. Secretary Udall said that this project was the best demonstration of government and public cooperation he'd seen. One other thing we're going to build, probably in one of the houses we take over, is an information center, because as I said before, this place has got to teach. I had a visitor last week—a man who was writing a textbook for third-graders on conservation. I showed him round, and told him where to go to get some other material he wanted. That visit thrilled me—I think it was a good sign—because the care of the earth should be the primary thing taught in schools. Anyway, it seems to me that if we can get this across to the next generation, we may be all right."

The New York–New Jersey conglomeration doesn't yet have its circumferential road. Small sections of one, however, have been started, and the rest is on the books and—in the form of a dotted red line—on the road maps. I followed on more or less parallel roads part of the route this future U.S. 287 will take, through Basking Ridge, Bernardsville, and Pluckemin. The present highways are generally two-lane affairs, like the roughly surfaced country roads of New England, although here they seem to carry three times the amount of traffic. There was congestion in the late afternoon on Route 206, running south past Raritan to Princeton, where the open fields around the prosperous town were beginning to blossom with a permanent-looking harvest of modern factories and offices, similar to those that ring Boston on Route 128. Among those here were R.C.A. and McGraw-Hill, with space, a strategic position in the Corridor, and a nice proximity to the brains of a distinguished university. In Princeton itself I stopped for a cup of coffee in a superior sort of coffee shop. I sat contemplating a newspaper report that—unlike M.I.T.—Princeton's Department of Civic Engineering believed that 400 mph travel between Boston and Washington by 1980 was strictly science fiction. Princeton engineers thought the best way to improve transportation between those cities was by modernizing the existing railroads to allow trains to do 150 mph and carry people for low fares. (A few months later the Department of Commerce let contracts to several companies to work on the speed aspect of such a proposal, though no mention was made of lower fares.)

After Princeton I turned east through Hightstown and Freehold and headed for the shore, taking a jog north for a few miles on Route 79 in Freehold, and then east again on 520 toward Rumson, my destination. I passed through Holmdel, which was a small crossroads hamlet set amid farms, but which was also close to the Bell Telephone research laboratories, and hence was sprouting round its edges Colonial Splits and Ponderosa Ranches, advertised by prominent signs saying "Models Open." In the Holmdel gas station, where I refilled the thirsty Jeep (eighteen m.p.g), I remarked on the fertile farmland. The proprietor said, "Yeah, but it won't be for long. New homes going up every day."

I asked where all the people were coming from.

"Out from the city. They're coming out like flies."

Someone else who thought flies and people had a lot in common.

Toward Rumson the farms are horse farms, surrounded by well-kept white fences, the sort of gentlemen's estates that are also to be found in Westchester around Bedford Village and in Nassau County near Westbury and Oyster Bay. But when I turned the radio on, hoping to find a local station, I got the sound of the big city—the roar of a helicopter engine, and over it, the hoarse voice of the airborne announcer, peering down in the urban twilight and conveying the urgent news of the hour: traffic was backed up for two miles on the Bruckner Expressway. . . .There was a two-car collision on the West Side Drive at 42nd Street. . . . Things were beginning to free up on the F.D.R. Drive, while on the Cross-Bronx Parkway one lane was stalled, and a tow truck was on its way to a car that had broken down. I remembered what Rigby had said. If we can get to the next generation, we may be all right.

16

The Seashore

THE PATTERN on this as on the other shores of the northeast has been of small ports and fishing villages becoming coastal resorts which in turn become all-season towns. Here, as on Cape Cod (and on inland lakes), summer houses are converted into year-around residences, and new summer houses go up on hitherto deserted cliffs and dunes. I spent the night with Bill and Jane Robinson, who live in Rumson on the bank of the Shrewsbury River. Their house, formerly a summer cottage, faces the town of Sea Bright, which sits across the river on the thin strip of barrier beach running five miles north to Sandy Hook. The Robinsons have insulated the house, installed central heating, built a wing with a living room that looks onto the river, and have brought up three children in it; but they have never quite managed to waterproof it against the floods that periodically devastate this part of the Jersey shore. The Robinsons, however, are better prepared than most people for storm tides, for they are all accomplished boatmen—indeed, their garden is full of small boats of one sort or another, and when the water level rises above the front step they hoist the motor out of the furnace, switch off the electricity, and take to their boats. Bill commutes to Manhattan every day (car to Red Bank, train to Penn Station) to edit a yachting magazine. In fact, one summer he actually commuted by water, on an experimental hydrofoil from Atlantic Highlands, but the service was rendered uncertain by fog and the dangerous driftwood in New York harbor, and it didn't pay its backers enough to keep it going.

Perhaps because of the sea air, I decided to let the day take its own direction. I got up late. Bill had gone off to Manhattan and Jane to the local high school where she teaches. I had been given the run of the kitchen, and so I made myself some eggs and toast and warmed up the coffee, and then sat in the living room looking out on the river, on the end of a little grassy island where until the previous year a hermit had lived, and on the Sea Bright waterfront where a few fishing boats were tied up. Sea Bright was once known the length of the Atlantic coast for its fine skiffs, which were sea boats with exemplary performance in surf as they were launched from or landed on a beach. One eighteen-foot Sea Bright skiff, built there by William Seaman, was rowed across the Atlantic by two young Norwegian-born clammers in 1896. Samuelson and Harbo rowed the *Fox* from the Battery to Le Havre in fifty-five days, and won a $10,000 prize put up by the *Police Gazette*. In the 1880s and 90s, a journalist named Gustav Kobbé wrote some marvelous pieces about the Jersey shore, and in one of them, in *Harper's Weekly*, he described the activities of the fishermen of Sea Bright. From June to November five or six hundred men and some three hundred boats fished for blue fish, using long lines and pieces of menhaden for bait; after November some of them fished for cod. A good day's catch of blues amounted to five hundred pounds, and was cleaned on the way to shore, packed in ice, and shipped by steamer to the Fulton Street market in New York. Kobbé wrote:

About four o'clock one of the boats came in, and I stood on the beach to watch it. Sail was taken in just before the rollers were

reached, and the two men took to the oars. The landing in the surf
is the most dangerous part of the proceeding, and a steady head is
needed. The men in the boat waited for a momentary cessation in
the great rollers that tumbled in. This period of comparative calm is
called a "slatch" by the fishermen. As the boat lay to, with her head
to the wind, a mighty wave would seem to rise up from beside her,
and the boat was lost entirely to view. A moment later she rode over
the top of a great billow, and then went down, down, down, until
hidden again. For ten minutes she lay there, rising and falling, until
suddenly the men bent to their oars, and the boat shot ahead a little
distance, and then stopped, while a roller passed under and broke
on the sand. Then ahead she went for a few yards, stopping again;
after a minute a sudden calm seemed to come, while the men pulled
hard. A small roller came up close upon them, and waiting until the
curl of the wave passed, the boat went swiftly in on top. This
performance was repeated several times; and finally a greater wave
began rolling in, and lifted the boat up to the shore, when the men
jumped out into the shallow foam and pulled the boat high and
dry—just in time, too, for the slatch had passed.

According to the local historian, George Moss, Jr., the fishing
skiffs, reduced to a handful, were last launched in the surf in
1949. In 1964, only three boats worked out of Sea Bright, and
they were power boats that moored in the river opposite Bill's
house; to reach the old fishing grounds they had to make the
long run up around the Hook and back down along the ocean
beach.

After my leisurely breakfast I drove over to Sea Bright by the
bridge across the Shrewsbury, and parked on the main street,
Ocean Avenue, off which there are small alleys with close-
packed houses. On the beach side stand the bathhouses and old
fishing shacks, and several big shingled hotels and beach clubs. It
is a town built of wood on sand, and it gives the impression that
a good fire would sweep it all away. Indeed, when I passed
through Sea Bright three years before, a large fire had gutted one
of the two adjacent grocery stores. Now, on this later morning,
I went into Gardella's Market, and I overheard a conversation
between two women shoppers about the two fire alarms that
had sounded the night before; apparently part of the tennis club
had burned down. Gardella's had given shelter to its burned-out

competitor during the rebuilding, but it was now once more on its own—a very high-class purveyor of wines, spirits, meats, vegetables, and groceries. I bought some materials for a picnic lunch—fresh Italian bread, Bel Paese cheese, cherry tomatoes, a few slices of Genoa salami, and a small bottle of white, dry Orvieto. I asked about the tennis club fire, and the man behind the counter, a tall, urban-looking fellow, said, "I wasn't there, but I bet there was a good crowd. Fires are a social occasion here. Some of the houses on the side streets are only eighteen inches apart, and they're built of the remnants of tarred lobster pots. When the "A" whistle blows in Sea Bright you can pretty well take a census of the whole community. Most fires are good ones. We have a saying that the fire department has never lost a foundation."

My informant introduced himself as John Gardella, a member of the third generation of the Gardella family to run the store. He wasn't very happy about some of the social change he saw roundabout. "Over in Rumson a new street opens up every week," he said, "and here in Sea Bright the old places are coming down. The next to go is Peninsula House, the big, old, brown shingled hotel on the beach, with the gray shutters and white trim. One of those nine-story apartment jobs is booked for the site—a condominium. It's the same all down the shore— apartments, apartments, apartments. Our sewage plant can't handle the load, and I don't think the beach clubs will last much longer. The property they're on is getting too valuable, for one thing, and it's impossible to get to them in mid-summer, when the crowds are here—it can take you two and half hours to drive a mile. People in Rumson used to drive over here just to fill up with gas, but they don't in summer anymore. The woman who runs the garage opposite says the traffic has killed her business. I know people in Rumson who leave town in June and don't come back till September, though once this was the swishest place on the shore. Some of the people who shopped in here had fifteen servants. Now the big estates are being broken up—first the main house gets sold off cheaply to a big family, then the grounds are split up into lots. I live in the gate house of one of the old mansions."

I said it sounded as if he missed the good old days.

"Well, they *were* the good old days around here," Mr. Gardella said. "Of course, we've had our bad moments too—that fire next door, and the storm of 1953, when the water in here came up within three inches of the drawer in the cash register. Any time there's a real threat of a storm, everyone in Sea Bright clears out to Rumson. Anyway, I shouldn't complain. We have the last of the carriage trade, and at this time of year, as you can see, there's no rush. I can stand here and chat to some of the old people who are sure the town hasn't been right since the railroad tracks were taken out. The trains used to come right down the other side of Ocean Avenue. You got a ferry from New York to the terminus of the line, which was first on Sandy Hook and later at Atlantic Highlands. The ferry boats sometimes carried half a million people a summer between the city and the railroad—it was the Long Branch and Sea Shore Railroad, and a very friendly outfit too, at least for its regular patrons. The conductors always stopped the train right in front of the store to let my grandfather out. Then there was a Mr. Galif, a munitions magnate, who didn't want to have to go eight blocks too far and so built himself a private station. Now we've got the commuter bus service—an hour and ten minutes to the Port Authority—but it isn't the same."

Taking my provisions and a corkscrew which Mr. Gardella had thoughtfully provided for the wine, I made a U-turn on Ocean Avenue and drove north up the beach road to Sandy Hook. I paid the fifty cents admission to the State Park gateman and left the Jeep in a visitor's parking lot halfway up the Hook. For its last mile or so the Hook is off-bounds to civilians, for although its position commanding the ship channels into New York harbor is no longer of great strategic value, the site of the military post has proved useful for a Nike missile base.

I climbed over the dunes to the beach, which was demarcated by a row of huge granite boulders. Their crevices were jammed with chunks of driftwood, beams, fenders, piles, and planks. The wind blew offshore, and I sat on a rock with my back to it, and the sun on one side of my face. Loose white clouds were rushing toward Coney Island; on the right horizon were the highrise brick apartment towers of Sheepshead Bay; and, panning left a little, one could see the distant white peaks of Manhattan, curiously in focus, like the Rockies seen from the Nebraska prairie. The sea horizon itself seemed high, perhaps because the land was flat and low, and the cloud shadows rushed across the dark green water, flecked with white caps, toward the freighters that hovered off the Scotland lightship, waiting for pilots or tides or an empty berth at a pier. The freighters bobbed like models in a toy seascape. More convincingly real were the big jets that came coasting down the Hook, one behind the other, a few minutes apart. With their swept-back wings and tails, black exhaust streaming from their engines, and their noses gently depressed, they varied only in the manner in which they deliberately slowed down, some swinging inland a little and then out, and some banking out to sea and then in again before making the wide, counterclockwise turn that brought them down with head to wind into Kennedy Airport.

Sitting in this place, I ate my lunch and drank some wine and felt thoroughly fortunate. A few fishermen stood at intervals along the beach, casting into the surf that just then was breaking with remarkable softness on the shore. That early megalopolitan man, Walt Whitman, came here on one occasion in the 1880s and put it with his usual *brio:* "The attractions, fascinations there are in sea and shore! How one dwells on their simplicity, even vacuity! What is it in us, arous'd by those indirections and directions? That spread of waves and gray-white beach, salt, monotonous, senseless—such an entire absence of art, books, talk, elegance—so indescribably comforting, even this winter day—grim, yet so delicate-looking, so spiritual—striking emotional, impalpable depths, subtler than all the poems, paintings, music, I have ever read, seen, heard. (Yet let me be fair, perhaps it is because I have read those poems and heard that music.)" The thump of the waves on a beach, as Matthew Arnold also noted at Dover, puts one in mind of eternity; if one feels sad, it is because one feels transient.

Sandy Hook has had a human history, however short, befitting its position as a prominent landmark and seamark. The local Indians prized its wild harvest of beach plums. Because of the shoals that stretch to Coney Island across the lower bay, any explorer making for New York Harbor (as it now is) had to pass in the narrow channel close to the Hook, and some, like Hudson in the *Half Moon*, got driven onto it; in Hudson's case, he got off unscathed. After some twenty thousand pounds worth of shipwrecks in the first months of 1761, New York merchants promoted a lighthouse, which is still there, the oldest operating marine beacon in North America. Several military actions took place on the Hook during the Revolutionary War, and in later years it was deemed a suitably isolated spot for the testing of rockets, boilers, and other explosive articles. In the days of sail, when small cargo schooners carried most of the trade up and down the Atlantic coast, this was like a major interchange of a turnpike, and despite the lighthouse and a fog bell there were dozens of shipwrecks on the Hook. Now, with efficient depth sounders, vessels generally manage to avoid the land but in the confined channel sometimes do a less efficient job of avoiding one another.

In the afternoon I drove south. In some places the road along the ocean front was the main road, and in other places it was simply a bumpy concrete drive in front of the summer houses. The bigger houses were already shut for the winter, and large signs warned out-of-season vandals to keep off. Autumn was indicated by the empty garbage cans being blown over by the gusty wind. Deal and Asbury Park, however, gave the impres-

sion that they still had some of the affluence that had originally
built their mansions—Deal allegedly being the place where a
hooch pipeline coming in from just outside the three-mile limit
had its terminus during Prohibition. The greatest wealth on the
shore was concentrated between lower Long Branch and Loch
Arbour, where one Protestant parish, St. James, on Ocean Avenue, claimed pewholders with an aggregate wealth of $120,000,-
000. Much of this money went into the houses built between
1890 and 1910, such as the one-hundred-room palace of Solomon
Guggenheim and James A. Hearn's million-dollar-scaled-up re-
production of Shakespeare's homestead in Stratford on Avon.
Along here, as elsewhere, people moved to a place because it
seemed scenic and then proceeded to complain when they
found that the scenery smelled. "As late as 1928," writes John
T. Cunningham, "a court action to halt fishing failed, despite
fervent protestations to the court that noisy commercial fishermen got up too early and that their fish smelled."

There is perhaps more than ever a quick-buck, shiny-
Cadillac flavor to the Jersey shore. Big billboards advertise new
colonies of waterfront houses all the way from Belmar to
Barnegat and from Manahawkin to Cape May. The realtors and
the Chambers of Commerce are fighting a neck and neck battle
with the conservationists and the forces of nature, which now
and then—as in 1889 and 1962—give the dunes and marshes a
thorough scouring. The storm of March 5–8, 1962, lashed the
Atlantic Coast from Georgia to Long Island, but was particularly severe in New Jersey, where it wrecked 2400 houses and
partially damaged 8300, inflicting some $80 million worth of
damage. Ian McHarg, a landscape architect I met in Philadelphia, had made a study of this storm; he has written:

Almost all the damage was caused by ignorance of natural process
and the resultant destruction of the natural defenses against flood.
The theory of dune formation is well understood, as is stabilization
by vegetation. In the Netherlands the value of dunes and their
stabilizing grasses, and the important role of ground water, is
known and valued—not, however, in New Jersey. Although beaches

are tolerant of human use, dunes are not. The development of the Jersey Shore has included breaching of dunes for home building, beach access, etc. In many cases no constraints have been placed on use of dunes, so vegetation has died and the dunes have become unstable. No effective restraints were made to control withdrawal of ground water—vegetation growth was therefore inhibited. Considerable areas have been waterproofed by buildings, roads and parking areas, which have diminished recharge of the aquifers. The consequences of all this are inevitable. With its natural defenses destroyed, the shore is vulnerable in great storms and is extensively damaged.

I had a piece of cake and a cup of coffee in a restaurant on the municipal dock at Barnegat, a scrappy, sandy place in the marshes at the edge of the bay. One elderly couple was standing side by side with fishing rods propped up over the edge of the dock. In the empty restaurant the lady proprietor apologized for having run out of homemade apple pie; the cake was store bought. She also seemed to apologize for the vacancy of the place, for she said it was a little livelier in the early mornings around five thirty, when the crabbers went out in their garveys from the local creeks, and later at eleven thirty, when they got back to the dock for a late breakfast.

The late afternoon sun had gone in behind high gray clouds as I turned inland toward Philadelphia. My route took me across the least inhabited part of New Jersey, forty miles without a single town or village directly on the way. Here and there a few shanty houses had been built, and abandoned. From the highway, which ran straight as a Roman road, other roads occasionally ran off at right angles. They were dirt-surfaced, and may have been intended as little more than firelanes through the scrub.

This extensive region, the Pinelands or Pine Barrens, forms roughly a quarter of the state and is very much unspoiled. Before piecemeal development begins, it would seem to be important that a good plan for the area be made. A group of planning consultants in West Trenton, Herbert Smith Associates, believe that the Pinelands would make a first-rate spot for the new international jet airport the New York conglomeration presently needs. The ground is fairly high, with a good weather record and not much fog. Present highways would enable more people to reach such a location in less time than it would take them to reach Kennedy. Philadelphia is twenty minutes away, and New York City fifty minutes, and the Smith outfit feels that with this airport as the chief airport of entry for the eastern seaboard, Kennedy could become domestic, Newark would not need to be expanded, and La Guardia could be abandoned altogether. (The Port of New York Authority might, of course, have somewhat different feelings.) In conjunction with the airport, a new city could be built, though the problems presented by the environment would have to be carefully considered.

Ian McHarg, who has also considered them, writes of the Pine Barrens that they are "a unique ecological community. Most important is the fact that they are dependent on fire. They will burn, sometimes with minor annual fires, often at longer intervals with more ferocious fires. This hazard to settlement is at least as great as hurricane danger on the dunes. The principal plants are pines, oaks, and sweet gums. The forest is more open than the beech-oak-hickory forest. It overlays sands and gravels with abundant ground water, upon thin acid soils. There is little topographic variation." Settlement in the region would be facilitated by the abundant water, obstructed by the problems of waste removal, and limited by fire hazard and the instability of the environment if vegetation were removed and the sandy soils were exposed.

One other authority on the Pinelands is Gustav Kobbé, who wrote about them in a small, privately published guidebook to New Jersey he brought out in the 1890s.

The Pines are the wildest section of the state. Except for the settlements along the railroad, the forest is broken only by a few lonely roads—almost abandoned old-time stage routes and lumber tracks; by narrow, swift, resinous-colored streams flowing silently through the colonnades of pines . . . or by deserted, decaying shanties, grouped around the ruins of the forges which this region harbored in the days long since passed, when the manufacture of iron from bog ore was one of the most important industries in the country. . . .

In those days, in the 1830s and 40s, many taverns were scattered among the pines; where there was a forge there was also a still. The taverns were called jug-taverns because their entire stock consisted of a jug of applejack. In summer, according to Kobbé, the natives gave huckleberry parties, and in winter oyster parties, at which they danced to a fiddler playing "Hi, Betty Martin," and "The Straight Four." Then as now schools were few and far between. One teacher made a thirty-mile circuit every day while his wife, at home, mowed their meadow and built a chimney on their pine-log house. In the neighborhood of the furnaces, the charcoal burners worked, and the mid-nine-teenth-century traveler coming through the pines at night would often be presented with the weird effect of the flaring and smoking charcoal pits, whose guardians lay in small lean-to sheds with the side toward the fires open for warmth.

17

The Possible City

A TRAVELER can come charging toward a city, hit it at the wrong angle, and bounce off. My feeling about Venice will always remain inextricably related to the fact that for the two days I was there it rained solidly and my one pair of good shoes collapsed from so much walking on pavements as wet as the canals. It is also possible to arrive in a city in such a way that an initial shove sends one from one encounter to the next, like the steel ball in a pinball machine, causing bells to ring and lights to flash, which is more or less what happened to me in Philadelphia.

Where the Pinelands end in good agricultural soil, there are a few farms which almost immediately turn into developments. The developments become Camden. Expressways and bridges lead one over the Delaware River and over the docks and downtown Philadelphia into the last rush-hour traffic, and my first impression was that this—the fourth largest city in the country —was like the other northeastern seaboard cities, swamped by the forces of megalopolis, of which the most visible at that moment were too many people trying to get home at the same hour in an inefficient form of transportation; most of the cars had just one person in them. And when I arrived at the solid, stone house of my friend, Jack Justice, on Midvale Avenue, a pleasant, tree-shaded street, he immediately recommended that we move some bicycles and the lawn mower so there was room to park the Jeep alongside his car in the garage. He said that occasionally a gang would make a raid in the neighborhood and loot any cars left out on the streets. Not often, mind you, but now and then.

I have known Jack since college, when we shared such experiences as a 1931 A.J.S. fabric-body saloon with no syncromesh, and a hitchhike ride to Paris with a drunken Dieppe fisherman who, as we sped down a slippery Route Nationale in the pouring rain, kept turning to me in the back seat to explain a joke, taking both hands off the wheel for the necessary gestures. Jack was now a partner in the eminent Philadelphia law firm of Drinker, Drexel, Biddle, and Reath, was active in the Reform Democratic movement, and was a member of a nonparty activist group called the Philadelphia Committee on City Policy, which met once a month to discuss city problems and ways of solving them. At dinner he proceeded to fill in the background for me. "Just before the war," he said, "a group of young lawyers including a man named Walter Phillips formed the Committee of City Policy, which had experts come to address it on city finance, planning, etc. The Committee lobbied, became politically active, badgered the big corporations, and generally screamed and yelled until the city reorganized the Philadelphia Planning Commission and made it effective. So there were several vehicles for action when, in the late forties, people here got the feeling that the city was almost uninhabitable; things had got so bad that something had to be done. In 1947, the City Planning Commission assisted by the City Policy Committee and friends like the architect Oscar Stonorov put on the Better Philadelphia Exhibition, which included a scale model with working parts of the central city, as it might be improved. This exhibition drew nearly four hundred thousand people to see it in a downtown department store, and it aroused businessmen to form the Great Philadelphia movement, which has furnished the indispensable backing for all the changes that have since been made. The fact that much of the renewal here was private rather than municipal not only made it work but contributed to the general excitement. There was real action here in the fifties. Joe Clark came in as the Reform Democrat mayor. The Pennsylvania Railroad decided to tear down the elevated tracks to the Broad Street station—these tracks had cut the city in half. And there were suddenly lots of new, professional people in pivotal jobs, like Ed Bacon, director of the Planning Commission, who did such things as going around to the public schools getting the children to make models and drawings of what they wanted their neighborhoods to look like. There were problems with bosses and political machines, but in Philadelphia there have always been ways to get round them. Moreover, the unofficial establishment here is more important than the official one; it makes things move; it has great economic power. Another thing, City Hall is in the center of the city here, where it can be reached—it isn't downtown the way it is in New York. And maybe Philadelphia is also fortunate in still being a manageable size, with a tradition of public spirit and enlightened self-interest. The result, in any event, was that we were off and running before any other city."

In the morning Jack and I walked two blocks down Midvale Avenue to a small station, and there, after a congenial five-minute wait in the open air, we boarded a self-propelled electric train made up of four stainless steel cars. The train was just crowded enough to make one realize its popularity, without making it uncomfortable. Jack and I stood for the ten-minute ride to the center of the city, the last few minutes of which were below ground, and he told me that like Boston, Providence, and San Francisco, Philadelphia was in the process of setting up a Regional Transit Authority to run and coordinate the commuter and city transportation systems. Our ride ended at the Penn Center station, and we came up some stairs into a sunken courtyard paved with cobblestones, on which the sun beamed down through elegant iron railings that rimmed the sidewalk above. If one has to arrive at one's downtown job by an underground route—and the tendency in cities all over the world is to build subways if they haven't got them already— then this is the kind of hatchway to the upper world one wants, rather than the mean burrows of the New York system. (It might be worth noting that when the New York Subway system opened, on October 27, 1904, *The New York Times* reported that the first man to give up his seat to a woman was a gentleman from Philadelphia, Mr. F. B. Shipley. Said the *Times*, "He was on the official train and the lady was good looking, but he said that made no difference—in Philadelphia everyone was polite.") Stone stairs out of the courtyard brought us up into Penn Center.

Philadelphia was designed by its founder, William Penn, in the late seventeenth century in a gridiron covering the narrowest point between the Schuylkill and Delaware rivers, and the influence of the great man kept his master plan intact until the Revolution. Anthony Trollope, passing through on his way from Boston to Washington in 1862, wrote, "I do not like the right-angled building of these towns, nor do I like the sound of Twentieth and Thirtieth Street, but I must acknowledge that the arrangement in Philadelphia has its convenience." Having, in the course of the next ninety years, got clogged, choked, and altogether run-down, the "arrangement" is now in process of being made not only convenient but attractive under a plan that has a good chance of being well-implemented by 1976, the two hundreth anniversary of the Declaration of Independence; in which case Philadelphia will be as up-to-date as the M.I.T. High-Speed Ground Transport System.

Urban renewal is a term loaded with the dullness and desperation of bureaucracy, but what is happening in Philadelphia is urban renewal by definition only. In fact it is the re-creation of a city center and the master work of Edmund Bacon, director of the city Planning Commission, who has been contemplating the possibilities of Philadelphia since he was an architectural student at Cornell in the 1930s. For Penn's gridiron, thirteen blocks wide by twenty-four blocks long, Bacon has devised a linear spine. The center section of this spine—Penn Center—is for the most part already built adjacent to the Victorian, French-Baroque City Hall (a building of fine scale and great character). Penn Center is a complex of banks, hotels, shops, restaurants, offices, underground concourses, sunken gardens, transit services, and pedestrian malls. The courtyard into which we came from the Penn Center station is part of it. The complex cost roughly $125 million, which whether compared to the cost of an Agena rocket or a pound of sirloin seems an astonishingly small price to pay for such a magnetic, indeed such a *central* section of a city. Beyond the city hall, toward the Delaware, the spine will continue as far as Independence Mall in the form of Market East—a seven block "megastructure" of shops, parking garages, offices, and hotels, connected by plazas, walkways, and glass-enclosed arcades—a sort of giant stranded ocean liner designed to separate pedestrian and vehicular traffic as people shop or stroll or go about their business in a downtown city that is, perhaps for the first time since its founding, both safe and exciting. William Penn's gridiron will also be spanned by a pedestrian way, running parallel to the Penn Center–Market East spine; for this purpose Chestnut Street will be reserved for trees, walkers, and an electric trolley system. Although a great deal of this construction and conversion will take place in the next ten years, already it has encouraged development elsewhere in the gridiron core of some four hundred million dollars' worth of new office buildings, apartment buildings, peripheral parking garages, plazas, schools, and private house rehabilitation. The effect is revolutionary, perhaps because many of the ideas themselves are from the well-founded past: arcades, malls, traffic separation, and the notion that private interest is best served by a profound concern with the common good.

Jack had suggested some people who might furnish an indica- tion of how and why this renaissance had come about, and I called first at the office of one of them, Drayton Bryant, a handsome gray-haired man of fifty, who certainly fits the Renaissance prescription for *L'huomo universale*, being by pro- fession an economist, planner, and housing consultant, and by avocation a farmer, writer, linguist, philosopher, agitator, and whirlwind talker. Bryant sat behind a table covered with maps and books and began speaking in short, energetic bursts. "Jack probably told you how things got started here—the exhibition —the bankers took an interest—good government is the feeblest of appeals. As Lincoln Steffens said, 'making money is better.' And then the major property holders felt action had to be taken because the city was so congested, so grim. Philadelphia had the awareness of all this before other cities—and that's why I'm here—and yet we're not keeping up with it, the train is rushing down the tracks and our urban thinking is going alongside at walking speed."

Mr. Bryant threw his hands up and took a breath. "Most Americans grew up in small towns, and they still think they live in them—all those suburbs. In fact, two-thirds of the country now lives in urban areas, and the number is increasing; we're on the way to several giant Los Angeles trailer-camp type of cities, which as far as I can see are not only ghastly places to live but a pretty fast way to a breakdown of the democratic process. We have to believe in our power to control our own environment, and to do that we will have to take big steps. Julius Caesar said 'There are to be no chariots out after midnight.' The Bulgarians have said that their capital city, Sofia, can grow only so much, and other new building has to go to satellite cities. But satellite cities or new towns, which are once again being mentioned here, have to be properly mixed—unlike Reston, the much talked-about new town near Washington, which looks to me just like Beverly Hills set in Virginia. Our society is already getting excessively specialized and segmented, with the bottom economic group particularly cut off by the problems of race and automation. For a society, this is like the hardening of the connecting membranes between various organs that comes with human old age. We have too many lobbies, related to short-term selfish interests—concrete lobbies, highways, big universities, and southern congressmen. What we call planning is just a means of escaping from the past half-century; we have as yet no comprehensive urban policy, and this endless conurbation we seem to be building will be a disaster."

I remarked that, considering this gloomy prognosis, Mr. Bryant looked cheerful. He said, "Well, I know that things can be done when a problem is recognized by people. I'm president of the Education Television Council here. It took us a long fight, but finally we got Channel 12 for it, and a million-dollar-a-year budget. Now we can reach six million people. And all that started with half a dozen of us talking one night in Jim Klein's apartment."

In the course of a day, Mr. Bryant is preoccupied not only by educational TV, but by the several Philadelphia community councils of which he is an officer; by the Philadelphia Committee of Higher Education, to which he is an aide; by the Council for International Visitors, of which he is a board member; and by Oak Lane Park, Inc., of which he is, again, president. Oak Lane Park was to be a cooperative apartment house, designed by Oscar Stonorov and Frank Haws, with 272 apartments, no corridors, two elevators serving each apartment, community music rooms, arts and crafts rooms, a theater, a coffee shop, and a medical service room. The building expresses a number of Mr. Bryant's ideas about community, which he feels most modern "housing" does little to engender. He also makes a living as a planner, advising towns on such problems as the aged and traffic—in two recent cases he managed to convince one town to incorporate

old people in various buildings in the center of the city, rather
than in an out-of-the-way project, and he persuaded another to
see that its traffic engineers' plans to speed up traffic by a few
miles per hour would tend to destroy residential and commercial values and push the town faster toward bankruptcy. He
reads Russian architectural and engineering textbooks, corre-
sponds with scholars in twenty countries, and addresses meetings of planners, groups of industrialists, and anyone who will
listen. "It's a job," he said to me, "making everyone realize that
a city shouldn't just be an accumulation of all sorts of unplanned results. It should be a corporation, expressing the
mutual creativeness of people."

Some of Mr. Bryant's creativeness was going at that moment
into a bootstrap operation called Queen Village, in a decayed
neighborhood a few blocks south of Center City; he had a meeting to attend there, and suggested I come. We drove in his big,
dark blue station wagon, having collected it from a nearby parking garage, for he needed the car afterward to drive to a conference in Atlantic City. Halted at traffic lights or in jams, Mr.
Bryant was silent; when the traffic moved again he spoke of
Philadelphia, which he said despite its great progress still shared
most of the problems endemic to the late twentieth-century
American city. About one hundred and fifty thousand people
had left it in the last five years. There were one hundred thousand unemployed. The educational system was in bad shape, and
in higher education public facilities were so poor that the Federal Space Agency, which required bright young employees, had
never put Philadelphia on its list for consideration as a site. Con-
currently, there were racial segregation, poverty, and slums, of
which north central Philadelphia (where Roy Lisker had intended to work) was one of the worst in the nation. Housing
projects succeeded only when they had people of great will and
imagination leading them, and in Queen Village (which was an
upgrading sort of name that they had given the old neighborhood after Queen Christina of Sweden, for Swedes of her time

first settled the area), he and his associates were avoiding new housing projects altogether. Instead, they were trying to encourage the community to help itself, with the support of a corporation that was buying dilapidated old properties, fixing them up, and then selling them to people who would in one way or another help the neighborhood, perhaps just by their presence. People who were thinking of moving out of the neighborhood were being exhorted to stay, helped to purchase better houses, or improve their own.

The state of the half square mile that was bounded by Sixth Street, Bainbridge Street, Delaware Avenue, and Federal Street was quickly apparent. Most of the houses that formed the neighborhood were narrow, two-story brick buildings with dormers poking up through their tarpaper roofs. The solid rows of houses were broken here and there where a building had been demolished, or had fallen in, and a few stood with empty windows or an unhinged door. The cars lining the curbs were beat-up Fords and shiny five-year-old Buicks, barely preserved by their owners' pride or indignation from the fate made manifest by others—squatting on the road with their wheels gone, and their doors and seats and headlights missing. For a residential area at this time of day a lot of people were about, which meant unemployment. In some places alleys led back to courtyards, where the squalor was Dickensian, almost too exaggerated to be real. Garbage cans overflowed, perhaps from the plentiful packaging that accompanies cheap food. Windows were cracked and the brick was unpainted; the houses gave the impression of rotting, and the people who sat about on stoops and crates looked as if they were rotting too. Mr. Bryant pointed out a new public housing project, of gray concrete, and he indicated the place where the proposed Delaware Expressway was apparently going to come blasting over the neighborhood at the height of the famous spire of Gloria Dei church, cutting off access to the river, and requiring the demolition of houses and the relocation of their occupants—Mr. Bryant and his friends were still fighting it. Some houses were in reasonable shape, and spotted here and there like banners were buildings that the Queen Village Corporation was fixing up. We passed one, on Fitzwater Street—an eighteenth-century brick house, with a basement, three rooms on the first floor, a small yard, three rooms and bathroom on the second floor, and a third floor studio or extra bedroom. It had fine, old wide-board floors, but new plumbing, new electric heating, and a sliding glass door giving access between the kitchen and the yard. It had just been sold to a young engineer for $10,750. "We had a real struggle to get a mortgage for him," said Mr. Bryant. "The banks are a real inertia force in rehabilitation—they're scared to death of a tricky neighborhood like this. But after a battle we got the financing, and the F.H.A. has now agreed to insure our mortgages. The area is lower class and lower middle class, two-thirds white and one-third Negro, and some people move every two months while their neighbors may have lived in the same house for forty years. If we can keep the place sound, we'll keep it stable."

Having passed a piano factory, a professional music school, and five of the six churches—Lutheran, Catholic, Baptist, and Jewish—that had sponsored Queen Village, we arrived, rather late, at the real-estate office of Louis Plumer and Son. This was a ground-floor, shop-front establishment, whose windows also advertised insurance and check cashing facilities. The Plumers had been in business in the neighborhood for forty years, owned a good deal of local property, were active members of the neighborhood synagogue, and felt, Mr. Bryant said, every incentive to improve the area. We were let through a locked gate in a cashiers' counter, and entered a back room into which light filtered through a dusty, barred window, disclosing some chairs, an old dark wooden desk, a big black safe, half a dozen religious and professional framed diplomas, and three men—Mr. Plumer, his son (both small, round), and Mr. Meyer Madway, with a moustache, the manager of Queen Village, Inc.

The meeting was to consider putting on the market the second rehabilitated house. Mr. Bryant did little talking, but seemed to draw forth questions and answers from the others: that the advertisement should state that the price was $10,700; $400 downpayment, $73 a month on a thirty-year mortgage. Would it be a good idea to say how much less per month if the downpayment were larger? What about the necessary phrase "qualified buyer," which meant someone whose credit was good? What about a letter to the city relocation agency, telling them the house was available? What hours should the house be open for inspection on the following weekend, and should coffee and doughnuts be served? Had invitations been sent out to the neighbors, churches, and old so-and-so, who was still trying to sell them some of his dilapidated properties at an inflated figure? (The old houses had to be bought at a realistic price, around $200, in order that they could be properly fixed up and sold at an attractive price—certainly less than $11,000 seemed reasonable, even with the difficulties of the area thrown in.) Having sorted out the advertisement, the meeting discussed some other Queen Village problems, such as a row of falling-down houses that the city had just certified as historic buildings, thus putting on the pressure to have them speedily restored. Mr. Plumer, Jr., had got wind of a developer who was scenting out the neighborhood for a site on which to build small town houses for rent, and who was maybe considering an abandoned school nearby, or a certain parking lot. Mr. Bryant thought Queen Village should consider purchasing both those properties, building houses, and *selling* them, which would be better; he would look into it, if they wanted him to. They did. Mr. Plumer, Sr., said, "Drayton, you'll be glad to hear we got that service station and garage behind the new house to clear away all those old wrecked autos."

A young planner who worked in Bryant's office was buying a piano, secondhand, from the factory and warehouse we had seen, and Bryant had said he would inspect it for him. As we walked down the street toward the place it occured to me that I had just been present at one of those collaborations between the forces of business and of the imagination that—perhaps on a larger scale—had done so much for the renewal of central Philadelphia. For this the scale was right, the effect considerable. In the warehouse a workman directed us to a back section where several dozen pianos of various shapes, sizes, and condition were stored. Mr. Bryant examined the tags and finally found the one he had been asked to see. It was a shiny black upright by Bailey and Company, Brooklyn. He struck a few notes and said, "The keys are a bit light, but the tone is fine." Then for a few minutes he played Brahms.

I caught a bus along Walnut Street (which is still an ordinary traffic artery, one way westbound), and on the other side of the Schuylkill River got off by the stadium of the University of Pennsylvania, and walked for a few blocks to the landscape architecture department, with whose chairman, Ian McHarg, I was going to have lunch. "He's coming right now," said the girl in McHarg's office, and when I looked around it was to see the double doors of the adjoining lecture room swing open, with two students holding them. There was a huge burst of applause, and McHarg strode out, six foot two inches, Battle of Britain fighter pilot's moustache, clad in the loudest possible brown and white checked tweed suit, saying to me and the secretary, in an authentic Caledonian growl, "Ay, I was in top form this morning!"

When the Scots leave Scotland it is often to become engineers on ships (as on so many Conradian freighters) or gardeners (I think of McAllister, Lord Emsworth's head gardener at Blandings Castle). McHarg, who came as a graduate student to Harvard in the late forties, is now—apart from his University of Pennsylvania professorship—a partner in the firm of Wallace-McHarg, landscape architects. Wallace-McHarg is involved in making a comprehensive landscape plan for the National Capitol

Planning Commission, in Washington, and (in conjunction with Whittlesey and Conklin, architects) a similar study of lower Manhattan for the New York City Planning Commission. Moreover, in top form McHarg is one of the most articulate spokesmen for what he calls ecological determinism—the view that nature provides the best guide and form for a city. We had lunch at the faculty club. The food was terrible but there was only one brief moment I considered it, and that was when Mc-Harg's sonorous Scots voice halted for a moment as he sketched a series of contours on the back of a table mat, and I found myself looking at the cold and greasy turkey casserole, with a piece of soggy Wonderbread at its base, which I was—per-adventure—eating.

McHarg had been describing the modern metropolis, which now covered thousands of square miles, sterilizing and water-proofing the land. The animals had vanished, and so had in-digenous plants. Rivers were foul, the atmosphere was polluted, and a million acres of land were annually transformed from farming to hot dog stands, gas stations, ranch houses, billboards, car cemeteries, and the like; slums were accruing faster than the new buildings that were meant to replace them. "Epidemiolo-gists speak of urban epidemics," he said. "Heart and arterial disease, cancer, neuroses, and psychoses. We record stress from sensory overload and negative hallucinations responding to urban anarchy. When you consider that New York may grow by fifteen hundred square miles of low-grade urban tissue—Mumford's phrase—in the next twenty years, you may then recall Loren Eiseley's image of our cities as gray, black, and brown blemishes on the green earth. These blemishes have dynamic tentacles extending from them. They may be evidence of a planetary disease—man."

McHarg is by no means a follower of what he calls "the historic Western anthropocentric-anthropomorphic tradition" which relegates nature to a position as backdrop for man, the ruler of the cosmos. He cites instead Duns Scotus, Francis of

Assisi, Goethe, Thoreau, and the nineteenth- and twentieth-century naturalists and scientists who insisted that nature demands deference and reverence, and that whenever man interferes with or alters nature he does so in a way that recognizes his interdependence with it—the way in the past thousand years the Japanese have enriched their land while farming it intensely, the way the Dutch have "created" Holland, or the way the English, in the seventeenth and eighteenth centuries, transformed their denuded medieval landscape into a rich and genial countryside that is still apparent despite the later Industrial Revolution and a century of urban sprawl. McHarg said, "If you want a closer example, take the Amish, Mennonite, and Pennsylvania Dutch farmers. But then farmers generally understand these things—they know where their food comes from. They know a crop is directly related to the organic materials, fertilizer, water, and sunlight that go into the soil. They know from experience they have to separate septic tanks and wells, and they recognize what happens with erosion, runoff, flood, drought, differences of altitude and orientation—which way a field faces and slopes. A farmer will give over the high ground and steep slopes to forest, as a source of timber or game and an element in controlling erosion and providing water. He uses meadows on the gentler slopes for orchards or pasture, and in the rich valley bottom puts his intensely cultivated fields. He allows woods to shelter his farm buildings, which he has built well above the flood plain."

For McHarg, the rules of the farm are not only practical but produce beauty, and the city requires similar rules. "If you take water as the most important factor—the most specific determinant of a large number of physical processes—you can isolate certain natural areas, each of which has a function, such as the surface water in rivers and lakes, the surface water in marshes, the flood plain, agricultural land, steep slopes and forests, and so forth. If some of these areas in a city—river, marsh, flood plain, and steep slopes—were protected and remained natural, the city would have a planned watershed and would at the same time be immensely improved. It would benefit from flood control and a good water supply. For instance, Philadelphia, with a twenty-two-mile-long waterfront on the Delaware, all in flood plain, and requiring at the most eight miles of it for port and industry, would most benefit—not from costly levees and dams—but from a protected, natural waterfront park.

"Then, apart from its usefulness, such areas are what determine the humanity of a city. One reason people flee to the suburbs is for a more natural environment. It's a self-defeating move, but it shows the value people set on nature, on space, on gardens. In a city, nature has to have the correct, expansive dimensions in order to perpetuate itself, but what a worth it has then! It induces tranquillity, introspection, an openness to order and purpose, and a sense of the place of values in a world heavy with fact. You can respond to it as you can to works of art, and yet nature is, or could be, abundant, and art is rare."

McHarg stopped a passing waitress and ordered coffee. "I go on like this so passionately because it seems vital that we have these terribly simple rules. Most of our present trouble is of our own making. Seventy percent of the municipal money in Philadelphia is spent on highways and streets. If you want to control floods and air pollution, you have to make sure you don't fill in marshes. You have to leave uplands forested. You have to build in the right place. And maybe the word is getting around. David Wallace and I seem to be getting consulted, anyway. There are our two jobs for Washington and lower Manhattan, and we've recently completed a plan for Green Spring and Worthington Valleys, near Baltimore—some lovely countryside that was suddenly made vulnerable to suburbanizing pressure by the opening of an expressway. Our plan requires the landowners to join in a syndicate with the developers, conceding their ownership of the land in return for stock, so that—instead of piecemeal building—the development of the valleys can proceed on planned lines, following our design, which is based on the natural form of the valleys and preserves large areas of them. So far we haven't been able to form the syndicate, but we're lucky that most of the people who live there are sensible enough and rich enough that they don't want to sell their land for a quick profit. Here at the university we've just finished a big research project, supported by Pennsylvania, New Jersey, and the Urban Renewal Agency, to establish criteria for the selection of metropolitan open space in the Philadelphia region, criteria that we've discerned by examining the major physical and biological processes of the region, like water supply. It's time this was done. For in the last hundred years the city has been a great success at providing jobs and social services, but as a physical environment it has been more and more of a failure. We're beginning the absolutely vital counterattack. It's simply that if we don't find a place for nature in the city, we'll soon find that nature no longer has a place for man."

Running late, I took a cab back across the Schuylkill and into Center City in order to meet Walter Phillips, one of the original bright sparks of the Committee for City Policy, a Reform candidate for mayor, holder of various municipal offices, and most recently the director of a project to explore the possibilities of regional city government. Drayton Bryant had said that one of the most urgent metropolitan problems was the lack of political apparatus to run efficiently the spreading city. Philadelphia, like New York, is becoming a region, and by 1975 will have 750,000 more people than it had in 1960, 170,000 new houses and apartments, 140 square miles of land made into suburbs, 460,000 more cars on the road, and 3 million more road and rail trips every day. Immensely greater quantities of water will be consumed, and more air will be breathed, while if the present trends continue the inner city will be inhabited largely by the poor—and particularly the Negro poor—and the middle-class people who work in the city will live in—and pay their taxes to—a suburban community, putting an increased tax burden on those who remain in the city and are least equipped to cope with it. Political scientists have been frustrated by the problems of adapting state and local governments to the requirements of such giant metropolitan areas, especially where the areas cross state lines, as in Philadelphia's case. Finding a new organizational structure is less hard for the experts than suggesting means of effecting a changeover to it, for as the city gets larger, the smaller units of government seem to harden and strengthen in reaction.

Walter Phillips is something of an expert's expert in this field, a new type of professional—half politician, half political scientist. From 1959 to 1964, he ran a regional city project called Penjerdel, which covered an eleven-county region in Pennsylvania, New Jersey, and Delaware on both sides of the river between the cities of Wilmington and Trenton, and included the usual confusion of counties, towns, townships, boroughs, school districts, and autonomous authorities looking after fires, health, and sanitation. Penjerdel was basically a research project that hoped to provide information about regional problems to those who wanted it, and it was financed by the Ford Foundation with matching local funds. It ceased to operate when the local funds ceased to come in.

"The local authorities apparently felt that Penjerdel wasn't giving them a program or recommendations for action that would help solve their immediate problems," said Phillips, who was a tall, Roman-faced man of forty-six. "And in that—in the fact that they want a program—lies hope. But in any event we got a few things started in those five years. We dug out a number of people with a natural flair for civic leadership. We held conferences and published reports on such regional topics as open space, transportation, and air pollution. We acted as a clearing house for federal and state aid programs, and we helped coordinate them. Maybe the best thing we achieved was the Regional Conference of Elected Officials, in which we brought together the people who run the four hundred and thirty-seven little governments in the region. We established a constituency, in which people began to realize the region's unity and inter-dependence."

"But they still wanted their independence."

"Yes. It's the same with the suburban communities around New York or Boston—they all imagine they're bastions of small town democracy. They haven't yet faced up to the fact that most of the important municipal functions in the region are now regional in scope, and need an interstate regional organization empowered to perform them. We're still stuck with the frontiers that history and geography have dumped on us. The Penn-Jersey Transportation Committee has recently been turned into the Delaware Valley Regional Planning Commission by the Pennsylvania General Assembly, but New Jersey hasn't passed any similar legislation, and Delaware wasn't even a member of the original committee. Trenton, Camden, Philadelphia, and Wilmington are all competing as ports, instead of working out what each can best do for shipping and industry."

I asked at what point he threw in the sponge.

Mr. Phillips shook his head and grinned. "Hope isn't lost," he said. "The key is water."

I said that Ian McHarg also considered water to be what he called a specific determinant in working out the rules for a city.

"I know, and the fact that he is working from the ecological aspect and I am working from a political one is encouraging. What gives me hope in particular is something I helped create— the Delaware River Basin Compact. For thirty-five years there were disputes about the uses of the Delaware water, and of course without the Delaware there would be no life in this region. New York City, New York State, New Jersey, Philadelphia, Pennsylvania, Baltimore, and Delaware were all involved because of their need for the river water, and they were all unhappy. There were unsatisfactory agreements about how it should be shared. Needs and supply fluctuated. In August 1955, there was a great flood. Then there was the long drought.

All of this helped create the right climate for the compact, which included the federal government, and which set up a commission with over-riding powers in regard to water development. Now, no other public or private authority can take any action materially affecting the region's water resources without prior approval from the commission. The commission can also take positive action, initiating various projects of its own. This was the first occasion in United States history that four states granted such extensive powers to an agency operating in all of them, able to act by majority vote anywhere in the basin, and with the federal government as a party to the compact."

Mr. Phillips looked for a moment around his office, as if for a book. "I'll try and find a pamphlet I wrote on this," he said. "But anyway, you see that it makes a good precedent for a regional government. It demonstrates the process that can produce similar results. We had the helpful circumstances of the flood and the drought, and the change of administration in Washington brought top-level attention to the matter. But there were three pre-eminent factors in the process—first was the formation of a six-man committee made up of people directly appointed by the mayors and governors—the appointed men had high authority, great curiosity, and none of the usual governmental timidity of men with jobs to hold and pensions to get. They also had an adequate budget and staff to probe, deliberate, and negotiate. The second factor was the interest and support of the business leaders—something we had learned here in getting through the plan for central Philadelphia. In the region, many of the big industrial users of water were happy to continue with things as they were, partly because there was no strict pollution control. The fact, however, that the governors' and mayors' advisory committee already existed, the prospect of a government study supported by the Ford Foundation, and the ardent leadership of one farsighted investment banker whom they respected—all these things made them sit up and think. They began to see the over-all picture of the water problem, and when they saw that, they saw the need for change. In fact, they contributed money for a public information program to spread the word. This program was our third factor. We sponsored meetings, lectures, films, radio and television programs, and publications. We created such an atmosphere of concern about water that the legislators of all four states together with the congressmen and senators became aware of it all, were friendly to the proposed compact, and at the appropriate time supported it."

The following morning I spent an hour or so walking round the city. I began in Fairmount Park, the three thousand acres of green space which nineteenth-century beneficence gave Philadelphia, and for a while I wandered along the banks of the Schuylkill, which weaves through the park, the home water of such magnificent oarsmen as Jack Kelly. Two single sculls were out practicing, the oars wafting the boats forward in a fast, easy rhythm, marked by a thin wake and two lines of rippling circles where the tips of the oars came out. The Museum of Art stands at the south end of the park, and from it Benjamin Franklin Parkway cuts like a Parisian boulevard diagonally across the gridiron core to City Hall. William Penn wanted Philadelphia to be a "greene countrie towne," which it isn't any longer, if it ever was, but it has apart from Fairmount four greenish squares at each corner of the central grid—Rittenhouse, Washington, Franklin and—with a traffic rotary inside it, causing it to change its name—Logan Circle. Walking past Logan Circle, I appreciated the way the architect, Oscar Stonorov, had matched its circular shape with an adjacent cylindrical apartment tower. I headed toward the Delaware and saw the skid row section where the Benjamin Franklin Bridge (which I had driven across on the way in) debouches its traffic; then I took a quick look at the mall that runs down to Independence Hall (the mall out of scale, too expansive, making the Hall seem smaller than it is) before I walked on to glance at some town houses designed by

I. M. Pei, in the rehabilitated zone of Society Hill. Society hadn't, as yet, moved back in; only six of the twenty $35,000 houses had been sold, but since Alcoa was the sponsor, and had already had the wit to pick such a site and architect, they presumably weren't in the rush a speculative building firm might have been in. I decided that something of Penn's intention had stuck in Philadelphia—the quality of being a town, rather than a vast city. It remained comprehensible, a place in which a provincial person like myself could easily decide it would be possible to live.

Jack Justice had suggested the night before that some of the steam had run out of the Philadelphia movement; too much emphasis had perhaps been placed on strictly physical renewal, and not enough on the quality of life engendered by the city. Talent was lacking in teachers and social workers. There weren't enough people like Drayton Bryant. Furthermore, the political reform movement had lost its impetus (the present mayor, Mr. Tate, was considered a run-of-the-mill ward politician) and the young radical Democrats, with whom Jack lumped himself, were trying to find new ways to achieve their ends, such as backing Republicans whenever that traditionally more conservative party came up with a dynamic candidate. There was, however, one person whose steam had never run out, who had been and who remained a prime source of inspiration for the movement, who in a not necessarily very logical way managed to convey what it took to change the life of a city from bad to good: the ideas, the passion, the hope, and the charm. That person was the architect Oscar Stonorov, designer of the Logan Tower and Drayton Bryant's Oak Lane apartments. Jack had arranged that the three of us have lunch together at the Racquet Club.

Buckminster Fuller's demand of the modern architect that he be an all-around man, "a manager, a planner, an administrator, a scientist, and an artist," who sees the problems of human environment in comprehensive terms and not simply in terms of highways, or slums, or open space, is well met by Stonorov, who also happens to have the qualification I was finding almost common on this trip—that of being a farmer. On this day he was wearing a medium gray double-breasted suit, a cream-colored linen shirt, and a dark blue silk tie, a small, dapper figure who seemed as if he would have been more at home if one had heard, from the side rooms off the ornate club lobby, the rattle of a roulette wheel rather than the rustle of morning papers turned by portly Philadelphian community pillars. His English was of a cosmopolitan European variety, not always syntactical, but almost always thought-provoking, and he indicated at once that, despite these man-of-the-world manifestations, he was first and foremost a Philadelphian.

"We have a saying here," he said, drawing a meandering line down the back of the menu that had been handed to him by a plump waitress, "that the oceanfront from Maine to Virginia is owned by Philadelphians—so we are charter members of megalopolis. This megalopolis, however, is a subject full of great paradoxes. I believe London and New York have more in common than New York and Philadelphia"—he made two stabs at the line, denoting these two latter cities—"for the people who live in New York and London have more in kin while in Philadelphia, we have more in common with Boston—the same feeling for living, our suburbs a little more connected to us. Of course, we are also both, in a sense, satellites of New York, looking for an identity of our own. New York cannot be planned. The tempo is too fast, it is too exciting, it is the one city in the world that is not being cocacolonized. And yet it puts all the rest of us in danger unless we assert our own identities, and to assert them we have first to find them. To me New York is the night club, the cultural center, and the telephone exchange of the new world city; it is necessary that Philadelphia and Boston be two of the universities. It is also necessary for us here in Philadelphia to have a definite connection with this other megalopolis, this ring of cities that is forming around

the world—New York–London–Paris–Milan–Moscow–Bombay–
Tokyo–Los Angeles–Chicago–New York. In ten years it will be
easier and faster to get between any of these places in the two
thousand mile per hour plane than it will be to get from Boston
to Washington. This plane is the herald of world culture, and it
is essential that Philadelphia have a pipeline to it.

"Two factors therefore: the World Trade Center and the
new jet airport. I am most anxious about this huge World Trade
Center that the Port Authority and David Rockefeller intend to
build in downtown Manhattan. I think, if it is built, it will be
the number one address—every important firm in the world
will want space in it. If it is successful it will reduce demand and
therefore rents for midtown New York office space from eight
dollars to four dollars per square foot, and that will make our
Philadelphia office space—which is presently doing nicely at a
competitive five dollars a foot—seem exorbitant. Then, the jetport, which the New York area needs. On some days, Kennedy
has an average lag in landing time of forty minutes, and by one
of those curves they use to show population figures increasing,
that will be a lag of ten hours in ten years time. So the best spot
for the airport is in the Pinelands, and that would be very good
for Philadelphia; that would be our connection. But David
Rockefeller says the Pinelands are too far away from the World
Trade Center. Do you see how these things connect, and how
they can affect the fate of cities? But don't misunderstand me. I
believe in world trade. It is the only way to world peace—there
is no communism or capitalism in world trade."

Mr. Stonorov took several quick gulps of vichyssoise to catch
up with us, and I said that I had been reminded of the early
competition between the cities of the eastern seaboard, when
Philadelphia, Baltimore, Washington, and New York had all
fought for the trans-Appalachian trade by building separate
routes into the interior. Baltimore and Philadelphia had chosen
roads, and Washington and New York plumped for canals, and
it was New York's Hudson-Erie route that eventually won,

opening up the West, bringing back cheap wheat, and incidentally contributing to the depopulation of New England and the hegemony of New York City. It seemed to me that since the interstate highways and railroads in the Northeast Corridor were similarly big factors in the growth of a sprawling city, surely one way to control it was by controlling communication and transportation.

"Agreed," said Mr. Stonorov, who had finished his soup, and added several more lines, rings, and obscure sets of figures to the back of the menu. "This megalopolis is a problem, on a larger scale, like the Tennessee Valley before Roosevelt got the T.V.A. set up. We need a five-city compact to work out what each of us can best do and how we are going to help each other best be ourselves. And this authority, set up by the compact, would also have the same object that T.V.A. had, which was to prevent the erosion of the land. At the moment, as you have seen, it is mostly still *laissez faire*. My neighbor can sell his fifteen acres for fifty houses, and that is it, megalopolis, the city out of hand. All the land enclosed by our cities should be under the final control of the inhabitants, the community, and not just the individual. Not so long ago Justice Bell, sitting in the Pennsylvania Supreme Court, declared that the compulsory fifty-foot set-back of office buildings was confiscation, contrary to the American way of life."

"That's what we're up against," said Jack.

"We are, and we are fighting," said Mr. Stonorov. "There are two further approaches to this megalopolis monster. One is quality. The twentieth century has done very little one can call quality—it has been building a great number of slums, in projects or subdivisions. Now look instead at the stuffy capitalistic Victorians. Nothing we have done in Philadelphia yet matches what they did in Fairmount Park—the Art Museum, the Franklin Parkway, destroying in the process a hundred blocks of slums—a great endeavor. I think if we aimed higher, at great things, whatever else we did would be finer too—we would get more done, we would make city life more fit for human beings. For that would be another purpose of the anti-megalopolis authority—to prevent not only the erosion of the land but the erosion of the urban human being. How many poisoned, wasted lives are there in the black centers of our cities, in grim places like north Philadelphia? Humanity is a matter of being in touch with life, with living things—and that is something we have lost and should regain. I would say that of the quarter of a million school children in Philadelphia, two hundred and forty thousand have never touched a cow. They've never seen a pig. On my farm, the pheasants are everywhere; somehow we have to get them into the essence of our cities. Without grass and animals, there will be no life other than what you can get out of cans in a supermarket."

Jack said, over the coffee, "Oscar, you had two approaches. One was quality, which led us to your pheasants. What was the other?"

Mr. Stanorov smiled, perhaps detecting the suggestion that he hadn't been hewing to a resolutely direct argument. "My second approach is also Victorian—it is money. I think the most vital revolution in this country in the past few years has been the realization by bankers of the technology of money. It isn't the simple thing it used to be of just paying a man for a day's hire. Walter Reuther convinced General Motors it was in its own interest to let a worker retire three years early on a hundred dollars a week. We are finally seeing the importance of rent subsidies. Can you therefore imagine what we could do if the government shifted twenty billion a year from defense to peace? If most cities were given half a billion a year with which to solve their problems, they wouldn't know how to spend it.

"What I am thinking of is the year 1976—the two hundredth anniversary of the Declaration of Independence here in Philadelphia. This would be a different kind of world's fair. It would show the force that is possible for doing things on a world scale in the city of that declaration, the city of Penn and Franklin, and the city with a stain like that in north Philadelphia. By 1976, we could create in that grim section an environment which is not a hand-me-down but which would be, as Fairmount was for the Victorians, a demonstration of what our society promises. We now have missiles going up two hundred and fifty miles. From there on you can become an angel. What we can do in space we can do on earth. It is all possible."

18

Brand-new Columbia

IN 1796–97, a gentleman called Francis Baily, who was later president of the Royal Astronomical Society, visited the United States and wrote a journal entitled "A Tour in the Unsettled Parts of North America." One of the unsettled parts he toured was the stretch from Philadelphia to Baltimore, which he traversed by stagecoach at a fare of six dollars—more expensive than the rail fare today. At one point his coach became mired in a bog so that the passengers had to abandon it until the next morning. The road between the two cities had the reputation of being one of the worst on the eastern coast, apparently because both Baltimore and Philadelphia were more concerned with their rival routes into the interior.

Today there is still an element of the uncoordinated about the trip. To get from Philadelphia, in Pennsylvania, to Baltimore, in Maryland, I also drove through New Jersey and Delaware. This was said to be the swiftest route. I first headed back across the Delaware River on the Walt Whitman Bridge and once in Jersey turned southwest, parallel with the river, on Interstate Route 295. This, however, proved to be incomplete, and for ten miles or so I was forced to take a heavily trafficked two-lane concrete strip known as Route 130. Big trucks were bombing along in both directions, tailgating slower cars, swaying as they went out to overtake or cut back in, and displacing such quantities of air that even the steady Jeep rocked as they roared past. I kept an anxious eye on the vibrating hood lest one of these blasts shake it loose and fling it up across my vision.

I crossed the river again on the high, narrow span of the Delaware Memorial Bridge, where the weight of traffic was being recognized by a matching span in the process of construction nearby. The bridge arcs several hundred feet above the water, and on a clear day one should be able to see Philadelphia thirty miles away. But Wilmington, Delaware, the Du Pont town, and Chester, Pennsylvania, lay between. The air was grey with smog from refineries and chemical plants, and it was a relief to come down to ground level and join Route 95 that runs to Baltimore, across the skinny neck of the so-called Delmar peninsula and southwest along Chesapeake Bay. Delmar sounds like a beauty treatment, which the area doesn't at all need. Although the highway generally runs out of sight of the bay, it crosses at a lofty height a superb stretch of the Susquehanna, and most of the way the countryside is equally splendid, with great rolling green meadows and solid dark clumps of veteran trees. Unfortunately the landscape did little to alter my mood, which had been established by Route 130, and which might have made good material for those San Francisco specialists who have been investigating highway tensions. Various rattles and bangs came from different parts of the Jeep. They may have been caused by uneven tire pressure, or by some reaction between the length of the vehicle and the uneven road surface, but there were moments when I was almost certain that a tire was getting flat, that the kingpins were on the point of wearing through, or that the remnant of the red-hot tailpipe was beating its way into the gas tank.

I meant to stay on the fringe of Baltimore, and to that end

took the beltway round to Towson, not far from which I had an appointment with the builders of a new city on the following morning. In Towson, however, I had the unsatisfactory experience of being told there was no room in the motel; it was full because of a horse show just up the road. Having got oneself into the right state of mind to stay in a place one has never seen before, it is unsettling to be told one can't stay there anyway. (I suppose I should have been grateful that horse shows can coexist with beltways and suburban sprawl.) I drove on into downtown Baltimore, and was later glad, for it was an instructive drive. From the circular beltway, my route was a radius of the circle, and as I headed for the center I realized what a definite target pattern the American city had assumed—the outer circle white, the middle circle black, the inner circle more or less white again. In this case the middle band of black—at any rate in the segment of it I passed through—was not in bad repair; it was formed of similar streets of two-story, red-brick row houses, with scrubbed white stoops and flat roofs. But the central white in Baltimore's case was even more of a bombsite than Providence, Worcester, or New Haven. Several tall modern edifices were rising out of the vacant lots and junkyards, and past a Mies van der Röhe office block and a new, modern "legitimate" theater, cars jounced over the pot-holed one-way streets, while the pedestrians scurried from side to side. Outside the Lord Baltimore Hotel, where I found accommodation, I was accosted by an elegant, moustached Negro of my own age, wearing a black suit, white shirt, and black bow tie, who caught my attention with a forthright look as he thrust forward a tin can marked "Independent Pentecostal Church." He may have said, "Do you mind helping us?" or something of the sort, but I had put a quarter in the can before I was aware of any spoken question. The situation was the question, and—despite the doubt I had as to whether I was contributing to a religious charity or a private cause—the coin was my abashed, immediate answer.

Charles Dickens remarked of a hotel in which he stayed in

Hartford that it was very conducive to early rising. The air conditioner in Room 820 at the Lord Baltimore was conducive to the insomniacal speculation that American civilization was all right as long as it worked. Very little air flowed through the machine, and what came out was not cool. Although the machine's dark brown simulated walnut sheen and bulky curves seemed to date it to an era coeval with the Chrysler Airflow or the first Blue Ribbon voyage of the *Berengaria,* the problem did not seem to be entirely the air conditioner's fault. As I saw when, on the second try, I managed to raise the Venetian blind, the chief culprit was the floor plan of the hotel. The window of Room 820 was at the foot of a U-shaped well let into the building. Although it afforded the dim light of day to my room, the well also placed my window a few feet from the window of another room on the side of the U. The air conditioner of this window approached mine at right-angles, so that, nearly touching, the two machines were fighting for the same slim quantity of air, and were at the same time gulping each other's exhausts. I found that if I turned off my machine and opened the window I got the foul air directly from its colleague. If I closed the window and continued to run the machine I got the exhaust indirectly. So I turned off the machine, spent an hour in the bath, and turned in, trusting that the air already in the room would hold out till morning.

From the center of Baltimore to the center of Washington is thirty-six miles. From the edge of one metropolitan area to the other, measured from the circumference of each city's beltway, the distance is twenty miles. From the border of the latest Washington subdivisions to the farthest extension of Baltimore's roadside sprawl is less than ten. The gap is closing fast. One reason it is doing so is that Washington is the fastest growing metropolitan area in the country, expected to increase its population from a present two and a half million to nearly four million in 1980. Baltimore, no laggard, ranks ninth in the national rate of city growth. Between these two expanding cities lies Howard County, Maryland. In the last decade Howard County has doubled its population, and indeed in 1962, when it contained forty-four thousand people, many of whom had come to it seeking the countryside, the majority elected an administration of county commissioners on a platform of no new development for the county. (As that man in New City, New York, said, "Those who come want to keep it the way it was when they got here.") This desire, of course, scarcely reckons with the human demand for space and the quick profit to be got out of selling it. Nor did it reckon with a Baltimore mortgage banker named James Rouse.

In Rouse's ambition come together such elements I have already touched on as new towns, the Connecticut General Company, Mumford's organicism, McHarg's ecological determinism, and a rational transportation system. Rouse intends to build with the financial backing of Connecticut General a new city of 110,000 people in which every possible aspect has been considered in the light of numerous disciplines to make a coherent dwelling place, a good and civilizing community.

A project of this size has in other countries been government sponsored, and in this country never previously attempted at all. Most of the other "new towns" being built here and there across America are fancy suburban subdivisions, for the shadow of Alexander Bing's failure remains long, frightening investors, and most builders are naturally conservative, building what they know they can sell to people seeking space outside the city. But the space shrinks, and the city spreads. James Rouse decided to find some truly open space, and rather than extend an old city build a new one. A site was found in Howard County, and after—rather rapidly—considering such local names as Poverty Discover'd and The Mistake, he decided the name of a crossroads hamlet would best fit the bill. It was called Columbia.

Rouse, at fifty-three, is a bespectacled, professorial-looking man, who made a great deal of money out of lending cash and advice to builders, and who finally took some of his own advice and built his own shopping centers. He currently owns eight of them, with an over-all occupancy rate of 98 percent. He is also an elder in the Baltimore Brown Memorial Presbyterian Church (which he has advised on setting up suburban branches, where much of its congregation has gone to live) and a counterpart in Baltimore center-city redevelopment to those Philadelphia businessmen who supported Edmund Bacon's plans. From Baltimore his influence has spread to Washington, where he helped push the notable Southwest Renewal Project and worked on Presidential housing committees and neighborhood improvement organizations. All of this worthy activity brought him in touch with up-to-date thinking about cities and city life, and his well-rounded knowledge has been demonstrated in lectures to specialists at Harvard and members of the Chicago Chamber of Commerce.

To Rouse, a believer in good works and the possibility of the good life, the most pressing concern is where and how the seventy million people who are going to be added to the population of the United States in the next fourteen years are going to live. He doesn't see much general hope for the great environment such architects as Stonorov demand—the sprawl will continue. The reason, he believes, is that not only the nation is unprepared for the problem but so are most urban planners and designers, who concentrate on everything but the crucial factor, which is people. Rouse claims that the true and proper end of planning is to develop people's concern for one another. This somewhat religious conviction is backed by the idea that the broadest range of friendships and relationships occurs in a small town; that there is a greater sense of responsibility for one's neighbor and a greater sense of support; that out of this comes a strong sense of self-reliance, and a closer relationship with nature and with the process of life. Rouse thinks that most serious social problems stem from the fact that the city is out of scale, dwarfing or deracinating its inhabitants. He said in a speech at Berkeley, "Our talented designers need to be hauled away from their myopic view of buildings as man-made works of art, and lifted up to the bigger view of communities as gardens in which we are growing people and a civilization."

Rouse was drawn to the notion of building a complete city in which to play out his theories, spurred on by the experience he now felt unsatisfactory of financing and building various urban components that had been "splattered over the countryside in unrelated bits and pieces." Having set up for the purpose a company (Community Research and Development Incorporated, whose "R. & D." space-age label indicated some of the skills Rouse felt should be called on), the next hurdle was considerable. In the 1960s there is no easy equivalent to walking out into the woods and swapping some beads, hatchets, and firewater to a group of Indians for their land. Three hundred years after the settlement of Sudbury, the agents of C.R.D. had to roam the entire eastern seaboard looking for an appropriate site for a new city. Proceeding from the necessity of such urban elements as a hospital, college, museum, and shopping core, with a hundred thousand people to support them, the C.R.D. scouts went searching for at least twelve thousand acres. They finally settled on Howard County—the land was there in farms, with development only just beginning. The county was in the direct crossfire of Washington and Baltimore, as one can see, driving down one of the built-up roads and looking at the newspaper boxes—Baltimore *Sun*, Washington *Star*, Baltimore *Sun*, Washington *Post*. . . . For that matter, it was inevitable that Howard County be developed one way or another.

The next step was getting the money. No bank would lend the amount of funds needed to acquire and hold this kind of land. The biggest source of lending capital is the life insurance companies, but they have traditionally been hesitant to invest in land development until the project is well advanced. Consequently, among the smaller firms that are willing to help at the critical financing stage, gamblers' rates prevail. Here, however, after he had acquired as a beginning, in 1962, one thousand Howard County acres, Rouse gained an ally in Frazar Wilde, of Connecticut General, which agreed to advance $24 million to buy the land. No repayment was called for until the actual building began. Indeed, to the insurance company, land between Baltimore and Washington seemed a safe investment. Although he made no guarantees, Rouse thought he could acquire another twelve thousand acres over the following three years at fifteen hundred dollars an acre. In fact, in nine months, C.R.D. managed to gather in 15,200 acres at an average cost of $1485 per acre.

In those hectic months C.R.D. worked through various front organizations and dummy buyers, using real-estate firms and lawyers to acquire various parcels of land. They worked fast because they didn't want one land sale to cause the sudden escalation in the price of the piece of property next door. Many buyers didn't know who was paying them. There were clandestine meetings, cash payments, and drugstore tipoffs. It didn't take long for word to get round the county that a lot of land was changing hands along Route 29, one of the two main roads between Baltimore and Washington. One rumor said that British or Russian money was behind the land grab. Someone claimed it was going to be for an African diplomatic colony. Someone else said it was intended for a U.N. cemetery. On October 31, 1963, Rouse appeared before the county commissioners in the county courthouse to explain that he was the head of the firm that now owned one-twelfth of the county—an area the size of Manhattan; assuring them of his honorable intentions, he said he would be back in a year to let them know what C.R.D. was going to do with it.

Columbia was set out a year later in a newspaper size pamphlet delivered to all Howard County taxpayers and, more fully, in a handsome spiral-bound book for the county commissioners and officials. These presentations contained the gist of the planning ideas and decisions that had been made since the land purchase, and which C.R.D. has continued to work over in its offices at Cross Keys, a Rouse housing development cogently situated near the point where the Jones Falls Expressway running north from Baltimore meets the beltway, running around the city (this was the expressway that had made the Green Springs and Worthington Valley vulnerable to suburban development, thus interesting McHarg in protecting them). At Cross Keys, I met W. Scott Ditch, a tall ex-Marine major who is Rouse's intelligence officer. With the aid of maps, slides, models, a tour of the office, and a trip out to the site itself, Mr. Ditch showed me what C.R.D. intended to make of Columbia and how they had arrived at it.

The first step was to act on Rouse's opinion that there was no dialogue going on between urban planners, who study cities, and the teachers, sociologists, and ministers, who study people who live in them. A work group was set up to carry on just this sort of conversation for four days and two nights every month for five months. The group included architects, planners, and fifteen experts in such fields as public administration, community structure, family life, recreation, local government, transportation, psychology, economics, education, and health. The group as a whole consulted with authorities on churches, libraries, rivers, flora and fauna, roads, light and power, sewers, and golf course design. What came out of these discussions was perhaps not revolutionary, but simply the discovery, or rediscovery, of sensible principles for a city. For just as Stein and Wright at Radburn had found that a plan of cul-de-sacs, parks, and paths was more economical than the orthodox pattern of streets and lots, so here, seeking a community that would at the same time best serve its inhabitants and not bankrupt the individual developer, the work group decided strongly in favor of *shared* facilities—junior and senior high schools placed where they could use the same, better auditorium, library, and gym than either would have had alone; and also placed in the centers of residential areas where the school facilities would be useful for adult education. In the same way, office buildings and shopping centers, which in most suburbs are on their own, would here share a common parking lot, thereby creating a nucleus that with restaurants and cafés would be an attractive, urbane central area. Village centers of this kind would put people within walking distance of stores, offices, schools, and park. Although some residents were expected to commute in and out, the goal aimed at was self-sufficiency, with a home in Columbia for anyone who worked there, whether company director or school janitor.

The plan for Columbia was under the direction of William Finley and Morton Hoppenfeld, who had served on the Washington National Capital Planning Commission, and it was influenced by the work-group discussions (one member reported that the academic consultants were the conservatives, while Rouse himself made most of the radical suggestions) and by such vital factors as the nature of the site and the necessity to make a profit. Rouse said, "The profit purpose was alive and creative throughout the planning. It was casting the votes for what people want and care about enough to pay for. It was continually moderating the temptation towards sentimentality and sophistication. It hauled dreams into focus with reality, and produced bone and muscle solutions." As for the land, the fifteen thousand acres contained fields, woods, and streams, of which a careful study was made to record landmarks, features, and views, while foresters, surveyors, and wildlife experts each studied their own concerns. Since development had already begun in the county, C.R.D.'s property looked like a piece of Swiss cheese, and the different shapes and conditions of the "holes" had to be taken into account. Some were subdivisions; some were unpurchasable farms and woods. In any event, all the irregularities, natural or man-made, precluded for Hoppenfeld "any geometric or homogeneous solution." Columbia—which the chief planner calls "the next America"—would be broken up into various neighborhoods clustered around a village core. There would be ten such villages, each with roughly twelve thousand people, with many of the neighborhood houses on cul-de-sacs of the Radburn pattern. The villages would be separated by streams, valleys, woods, lakes, and parks totaling thirty-two thousand acres of "open space," while they would be connected by roads, bridle paths, and a minibus service running on its own right-of-way to provide frequent (one bus every five minutes) and cheap (ten cents' fare for adults) transportation, the aim being to make unnecessary a second car. This bus service would connect the villages to the city core, downtown, with its stores, hospital, offices, library, and a sort of Tivoli amusement park that is Hoppenfeld's pet project. There would also of course be a shopping center, which Rouse would continue to own, having sold off parcels of land to other builders who would build under C.R.D. supervision. The city core was expected to have a genuine downtown bustle.

I went with Scott Ditch on a tour of C.R.D.'s one-story Polynesian offices at Cross Keys, which were also bustling. Some seventy people were sketching, typing, making models, lettering signs, studying maps, working out engineering calculations, having conferences with utility specialists, or talking to Mr. Rouse's secretary on the off-chance that he might have a moment to see them between his call to Frazar Wilde of Connecticut General and the next call to David Rockefeller of the Chase Manhattan Bank. (At this point, so many of the haphazard elements of my trip were dovetailing that I wouldn't have been surprised to learn that M.I.T. or Mrs. Griswold had a hand in Columbia—Fantus, in fact, had.) The offices were brightly planned, with open ceilings planked with West Coast woods and colorful partitions, while the atmosphere was cheerfully tense, as at a race course before the big event.

Following Mr. Ditch's car—by which he would return to Cross Keys—I drove out around the beltway and then south-

southwest along Route 29 toward Washington. What had been a gray day was now a wet one. The windshield wiper in front of me was not only out of phase with its colleague but was working erratically, staggering part of the way up its arc and then, collecting its energies at the zenith, rushing downward. Concentrating on the road and on Mr. Ditch's car, I didn't have much opportunity to survey Howard County, but what I did see, beyond the initial roadside ribbon development, looked as if it matched its description as rolling and green. We came eventually to an isolated roadside ranch house that C.R.D. had taken over and converted into an information center—all the better to let the people of Howard County know who had gobbled them up, and why. The ranch house sat on a knoll overlooking Route 29 (which is here a rather grubby two-lane road, though soon to be widened to four), with a fine view of the woods and fields and valley beyond, which will be a lake and the city center of Columbia. Within the house was a convincing display of the advantages Columbia presented to oppose the usual form of piecemeal development. The house also had the advantage of being close to an absolutely first-rate country inn; and to that hostelry, having seen the exhibits and models, Mr. Ditch and I repaired for lunch.

Part of our conversation there concerned what happened in November 1964, when Rouse released the C.R.D. plan for Columbia. At that point Howard County gave no hint of budging from its backwoods reputation; it had given more of its votes in the previous election to Governor Wallace of Alabama than it had to its own Senator Brewster. It had gone on record as not wanting any industrial development. Its influential County Citizens Association was vehemently opposed to either quarter-acre zoning or multiple-dwelling units. Columbia with its suggestions of *plan, industry, town houses, and apartments* brought out in the county a lot of over-my-dead-body spirit. The county commissioners' legal counsel termed "illegal" C.R.D.'s first move to obtain the new zoning laws needed for Columbia to begin.

A second move was made six months later, in May 1965, and by then a sense of what Rouse and company were trying to do had begun to seep in. The C.R.D. brochures and propaganda made much of the fact that a rise in Howard County population was inevitable. In 1965, it was 48,000—Columbia would raise it to 158,000 by 1980, and state planners had already predicted a rise without Columbia to such a total in the 1980s. Columbia, said C.R.D., would organize the growth and make it possible to increase services without raising taxes, which were at that time rapidly going up in adjacent "suburbanizing" counties. Columbia residents would pay for their own amenities. C.R.D. men also canvassed the county, addressing informal and formal meetings, at which hot discussions took place. Columbia is intended to be racially "open," but integration may be hard to achieve without one village becoming black and the other villages white. The frequent question was framed by one man: "What are you going to do about the coloreds?"

Ditch replied, "Do you know of an American city of 110,000 that has no Negroes?"

"No," said the man, "but here's a good chance to make one."

Despite qualms on this and other scores, the education process worked; the hearing of May 1965 approved Columbia. Every county organization turned up at this event, including the Farm Board, the League of Women Voters, and the various village improvement societies. The only man at the hearing who spoke against Columbia said that he did so as an individual, but he thought that the commissioners should be for it.

Zoning changes were the next hurdle. The Citizens Association feared that other developers less conscientious than Rouse might take advantage of the changes made for the benefit of Columbia. There was also a certain amount of thinking to the effect that C.R.D. should build a bit of Columbia so that Howard County citizens could see if they liked it. "This," one local lady editor said, "is like asking a gal to get a little bit pregnant." The zone changes, however, took place in August 1965, and the first ground was broken in the spring of 1966.

C.R.D.'s plans for the first village began to go into effect, with support from Frazar Wilde, David Rockefeller, and William Greenough of the Teachers' Insurance and Annuity Association, whose companies had joined to provide fifty million dollars in long-term mortgage bonds. Together with the village, construction has started on part of downtown—an office building and shopping mall—and the minibus route that links town and village. Already several engineering and research firms have located there, and C.R.D. is after more, with high hopes of getting them. Fantus declares that Columbia rates high in twenty-eight out of the forty-five most important criteria in industrial location, and apparently in a few years' time it will be tops in forty-one of these profitable ingredients.

One thing Columbia will lack from an ideal point of view is a surrounding greenbelt to separate it from the enclosing sprawl of the two neighboring large cities. There will be, however, plenty of green throughout the new city, whether in ten-acre private estates, along the roads and trails, or in golf courses, parks, and gardens. Altogether there will be five lakes, and, as in Radburn, the residents will be members of an association that will assess them for the added recreational and communal amenities. Rouse expects the total of this charge and the county tax to remain less than the taxes paid in the surrounding counties, whose development has not been so well planned. One of the first of such benefits to arrive, apart from natural ones, is the Washington National Symphony Orchestra, which plays its first summer season in Columbia in 1967. The auditorium is a large tent made of three-quarters of an acre of canvas, designed by the San Francisco architect James Leefe, to seat three thousand people with room for three thousand more partly outside, under the sloping canvas arches. In the meantime, the space and amenities already present on the site are not being wasted—indeed, following Rouse's insistence that Columbia be a money-making propositon, seven thousand acres of the C.R.D. land were leased to local farmers; four thousand acres were devoted to a selective timber improvement program; and two thousand acres were used for company farms, nurseries, and pasture land. Some two hundred and fifty thousand trees are being planted every year and will be transplanted to various locations throughout the city as they are needed. Sod has been sold to the Maryland and Virginia state highway departments, and a game preserve began its second season in 1965 stocked with 2750 pheasants, 1000 quail, and 1300 duck, and with hunting facilities for a dozen hunters using four separate areas of roughly a hundred acres each. Several field trials for horses and dogs have been held there. Over the whole Columbia area a long-range study is being conducted by the Bureau of Sport Fisheries and Wildlife, Rigby's parent outfit, in order to compare bird population trends in Columbia with that of the rest of the state. The bureau thinks this is a good chance to investigate the effects on birds of a sudden shift from a rural to an urban environment.

The effect on people will also be of interest, though perhaps harder to chart. Columbia is meant to be a city where individuals feel that participating in community affairs is a "good thing," without feeling any sense of summer camp regimentation. Scott Ditch told me that people in Howard County were already using planners' jargon, and the county library has installed a shelf for books on urban studies. In Hoppenfeld's plan for the city center there is a Columbia library, surrounded by various shops, facing a small informal park that sits above the lakefront among the cafes, Tivoli gardens, and concert hall. Some architects have complained that something of the essential city will be missing without tall buildings, but they may merely be rationalizing their resentment against an endeavor in which for the first time in this country the design of single, brilliant structures has been subordinated to the design of a work that may well be a complete, new, and better city.

19

Conversations and Speeches

IT WAS raining hard as I drove into Washington, and the windshield wiper in front of me finally expired—it twitched and thereafter refused to move. I stopped at a garage on Route 29 where the mechanic said from underneath the dashboard, "Yeah, it's the transmission cable. You have to order it from Toledo. Take at least a week." I drove on. The pelting rain hit the windshield and ran off in all directions, so that the world I saw through straining eyes was gray and unfocused: blurred cars, the line of the curb, dim traffic lights, and—as I got into the city—dark people, children pouring out of school and across the streets, their elders shopping, strolling, or simply standing on the sidewalks. That everyone was Negro was a surprise. I had been driving south for two weeks, and I was now there. I was also lost, for the system of a gridiron overlaid with diagonals, and streets named with the same numbers and letters in each quarter of the city, had me completely foxed. *"L'Enfant terrible,"* I muttered, as I pulled into a corner gas station to ask my way to Georgetown, (where most of the city's white 37 percent live), and to Thomas Jefferson Street, which was my immediate destination there. Five Negro men hovered under the gas pump canopy, and they came to the car window, looked at my map, showed me where I was, and how to get where I was going. What struck me then was the complete lack of tension, overtone, even of difference, in this encounter, unless it was the quite normal difference between a stranger and residents; it was their city.

Eventually I reached Thomas Jefferson Street. It was a small side street, off M (N.W.), Georgetown's main street. It ran downhill with a bump of a bridge over the Chesapeake and Ohio Canal and with small, brick houses, one of which had been the third President's, on either side. The effect of the street was intimate and fine. Thomas Jefferson produced the program for the architectural competition for the White House and the Capitol, and in an anti-industrial revolution mood once wrote, "The mobs of great cities add just so much to the support of pure government, as sores do to the strength of the human body. It is the manners and spirit of a people which preserve a republic in vigour."

Just beyond the bridge were the offices of Chloethiel Wood-ward Smith, who is married to Bromley Smith, executive secretary of the National Security Council; she was formerly married to the son of the Radburn-designer Henry Wright, and is currently the most notable "lady architect" in the country—a compliment which some of her admirers believe obscures the fact that she is, quite simply, one of the best architects, planners, and thinkers about cities now working. Mrs. Smith's colleagues call her Chloethiel, as they call Mies van der Röhe, Mies, or Corbusier, Corbu; she is a handsome, well-groomed, rather maternal woman in her early fifties, and although I was by now more than late for the appointment I had arranged with her, she received me with great courtesy in her light, sloping-ceilinged office overlooking the canal. The pale fronds of a willow brushed against the window. Mrs. Smith asked a secretary to bring two cups of coffee and told me to sit down and put my feet up. She said, "I don't think there's any substitute for living in the center of cities like Washington or New York. I love cities, and I love this one particularly, although it has its problems, which in some cases are all its own, and in others are the problems of other northeastern cities intensified. For one thing, eighty-seven percent of the school children in Washington are Negro. A large percentage of the adult Negro population is ill-educated, ill-equipped, and either unemployed or underemployed. This puts a huge burden on the city. It gives the white middle class a reason for thinking they should move out, and in some ways you can't blame them, because they want a good education for their children, and Washington public schools are just too crowded, too harassed, too full of the backward and unprivileged to provide that. There is also the problem of being the capital. From the very beginning, the city has been a sort of poor relation of the federal government, which gives the city money to get dolled-up whenever it strikes Congress that its own dignity will otherwise be impaired. The city is run by the oddest collection of committees, councils, and volunteer societies—there's no mayor or city council you can elect or throw out if they're no damn good—and the devil in the picture is the House District Committee, which is run by a bunch of elderly southern congressmen who like keeping the local liquor prices low and seem to feel that the city's racial imbalance is just what it deserves. In many ways we're like a small town with winter people and summer people, and a lot of transient visitors who don't feel they have a stake here—Congress being the summer people, up on the Hill, which in L'Enfant's time was called Jenkins Hill—he thought it would make a good spot for the Capitol.

"Then we have a planning commission, which exists in a sort of political void; it has no power. Nat Owings of Skidmore, Owings has, however, a temporary commission that's got up a great plan for the Mall and Pennsylvania Avenue, which has at last been declared a historic site. We've got a code so that new

246 / THROUGH THE GREAT CITY

buildings will be set back fifty feet. It's amazing how many small things are needed to make a dent on the situation. The Kennedys got it moving—they gave the city square shoulders for the first time. But I often wonder what L'Enfant would do if faced with the problem of the northeast coast—we need something that cuts right to the core of the problem, something big—how we need R. & D. money for environment, as well as for defense and space. Space right here! The defense of individuality! Instead we're ruled by committees, and we nickel-and-dime everything."

Mrs. Smith gave her coffee cup an exasperated glance. She said, "Here, have another cup while I read you something." She passed me the coffee jug and began to look through a desk drawer. "Every now and then I go away and make a speech. Last year I went down to Miami and talked to the Institute of Traffic Engineers. I tried to get across to them how they had changed the land with all that asphalt and concrete before we knew how we wanted it changed. We've let the endless city happen because we didn't know what kind of city we wanted. Even good architects have this sense that they are adrift, and they don't know if they are designing what's really needed. But I cling to the hope that this mass extended ugliness of the democratic city will finally be fought when people realize that it is destroying the independence and individuality they make so much of. Here, I've found what I was looking for. It's a little pamphlet by August Heckscher—a speech he made in Geneva. Listen to this:

" 'The result of technological forces—combined with increased numbers of people, increased weath, increased mobility and increased leisure—is to threaten the existence of every place which is separate and distinct, every integrity which gives to the individual the possibility of standing apart and meeting the world on his own terms. The man who can withstand the mass is a man who has his own place. He may not be isolated; he need not be a hermit. But he must have a sense that he is surrounded by space to move in, time to think in—an environment which is congenial and in some sense an enlargement of his own being. If this space is eaten away, he is himself diminished. If it disappears into a homogeneous and unindividualized nothingness, then the individual has in effect become part of the mass.' "

Mrs. Smith put down the pamphlet; she looked melancholy. "In the past," she said, "everything took time. A place was a matter of slow accretion, an accumulation of what all sorts of people did and said over the years. Now, in order to oppose the fast accretion that's happening all up and down the coast, we're going to have to build whole cities from scratch. Like Brasilia, or Columbia and, in a way, Reston. It frightens me. It's like screwing in a whole set of new light bulbs at once—they're all liable to go out at once too. We have to try to find a way, in fighting this massive explosion, to create something like this canal, these houses around it, the bridge, the tree, this view from the window—all the pieces had a purpose, and the collection of them is mainly good luck and now seems marvelous. We have to *plan* this sort of thing. That's where it gets tricky."

Mrs. Smith's architectural firm is involved in numerous projects across the country, although in Washington her name is particularly associated with the Southwest Urban Renewal Area, for which she was master planner as well as one of the architects, and with Reston, the nearby Virginia new town, for which she has designed "town houses." Elsewhere she is doing office buildings, shopping centers, and parking garages, and is trying hard to get someone to commission her to work on a bridge covered with shops and buildings, like the Ponte Vecchio or old London Bridge, which would span the Washington Channel from Southwest Renewal Area to East Potomac Park. Her parking garage in Brookline, Massachusetts, is ninety feet below grade and has a built-in waterfall. Because apartment houses are generally rather dull looking by day, and yet interesting at night when apartment lights go on in a random pattern, she has designed an apartment house where the windows are of

different shapes and sizes, scattered all over the façade. The
effect may strike the observer as a trifle wayward, but Mrs.
Smith feels it is justified—that only human, sometimes haphazard architecture will keep people in a city.

"One thing the planning statistics never take into account,"
she said, "is that there are some people who don't want to live in
split-levels, surrounded by half-acre plots of grass to mow, or
even in Colonial houses in the middle of open country. There
are urban people who want to live in the centers of cities if you
make it reasonably possible. What we tried to do in Southwest
was make a place for this sort of person, who will put up with
racial problems and school problems as long as what they have is
first-rate and open to life. You should go down and see it. It has
mistakes, but it has human corners—it isn't like those huge
lonely projects in New York. There are 1740 families living
there so far, about 15 percent of them Negro. We have floating
lights in one of the pools, which drift around in the wind. The
Harbor Square section is going to have the world's largest willow tree. But you know when I tried to get a reflecting pool for
Capitol Park, the first section to open in 1957, *they* wouldn't
give me a permit. They said the rats would come and drink in it.
They said people would fall in. I went through weeks of bureaucratic hopscotch pestering officials and researching regulations. It was no, no, no. Well, I finally found an ordinance
permitting fountains, and so I put a fountain in the middle of
my hundred foot pool. That fixed them. You can't believe what
it was like getting a sort of café-bar in the corner of an apartment block I've just done in St. Louis. You'd have thought I was
asking the federal government to go into the white slave trade.
Oh, I got it. We have to fight city hall. It's worth the struggle."

I asked Mrs. Smith if she didn't have a streak of country-
liking.

"I do. We have an old house, sixty-five miles from here, that
looks down the Gettysburg Gap. I get there at midnight on
Saturday some weekends. I find it hard to get away from here.

Now and then at night leaving here I go over to Southwest at dusk when the lights go on, and I learn things by watching people. Who knows, they might just get used to all that air, space, and the best views in town—it might start a trend! One night there I was stopped by an elderly, military sort of gentleman. He said, 'I guess you're new here, the way you're looking around.' I had a moment in which to make a decision—should I say I'm the architect, and then face the stuff you have to face when you're the author of something? Instead I said, 'Yes, I'm new.' And he replied, 'Oh, you're going to like it. Especially when the azaleas are out and the fountains are on. You'll like it.' It was the nicest thing that's ever happened to me."

After leaving Mrs. Smith's I walked for a while along the Chesapeake and Ohio Canal. The rain had stopped, and the sun shone in a hazy, humid sky. Eastward from the bridge the canal went downhill at the rate of one lock per block. The ground was wet and the towpath muddy, overhung with old mill buildings and willow trees, although in places it broadened out in green lawns or was paved with cobblestones. In one lock the *Canal Clipper*, a narrow barge restored by the parks department, was moored. In the pool at the foot of the lowest lock gates a tree had fallen, and muddy water brimmed over the thick, brown creosoted timbers of the gates and splashed among the branches with the force of several fountains.

The canal is perhaps more valuable now than it ever was as a commercial venture. During construction it gobbled up money, and even when it was finally completed as far as Cumberland, Maryland, from which point it was hoped to connect it to the headwaters of the Ohio, the lower channel of the river in Georgetown began to silt up. What happened was a demonstration of ecological ignorance. As the upper valley of the Potomac was cleared of trees for settlement, the spring rains washed down the denuded hillsides, and the soil came down to fill up the once-navigable Georgetown channel. For that matter, although the canal continued to operate until 1923, it ran into the fierce competition of the Baltimore and Ohio Railroad, which headed west on more or less the same route from Baltimore. Nowadays it is much used as a park, along which Washingtonians hike and cycle, or on which they canoe and take summer barge trips.

Of course, a city in which it is pleasant to live is more than just houses, security, a job, transport, or recreation; it is also good society. In this respect, Henry James thought the American city went drastically downhill after the Civil War—New York, in particular, fell in his opinion. He came to prefer the "less bristling" Philadelphia, or Washington, with its slower and more interesting conversation. I had an opportunity that evening to sample Washington's conversation at this later date, for having left the Jeep and my belongings at the house in Arlington (a suburb beyond the Potomac) of my friend Frank Getlein, a writer for the Washington *Star*, we headed back to the city for a social round. The first stop was in Georgetown at the eighteenth-century town house of an English newspaper correspondent. Figures of the great mingled with those of the humble, and conversation seemed to be flowing as freely as the liquor in the generous hands of the butler. Our host, a dapper, middle-aged man, darted about the narrow room that ran from back to front of the house, moving and introducing guests like a novelist trying to get all his characters to say something. I was introduced to a pretty girl with an Iowa-or-thereabouts accent who turned out to be a secretary in some obscure government department, and the date of the tall dark C.I.A. agent who was chatting with the British ambassador. The ambassador was wearing what appeared to be his "demob" suit, the gray flannel non-mod civilian garments handed out to soldiers leaving the army at the end of World War II. He had shaggy red hair and wore bright red wool socks. Then I was introduced in turn to an elderly woman, the mother of the secretary, and an Englishman who talked about the past cricket season; he, it seemed, was the guest of honor, a leading economist. Next I talked to a woman editor who said she hoped I was going to Reston, and went on to tell me what grim things Congress had done the previous summer to the administration's "new towns" proposal —which would have provided federal loans and grants to state and local governments, and loan insurance to private developers, to make it easier for them to assemble land, plan comprehensive towns, and create good public facilities in them. Under opposing pressure from the mayors of several big cities (who didn't want any more competition for industry and citizens), from southern congressmen, (who thought the whole scheme would encourage "race mixing"), and from the developers of orthodox suburban subdivisions, the plan failed. I was interested in hearing more of this, but my informant was dragged away to be introduced to a small mysterious figure who was identified for me as Robert McNamara's right-hand man.

Frank and I stopped in at several other functions that night, but the party that made the greatest impression on me was at the Corcoran Art Gallery, a splendid specimen of the Beaux Arts style, with heaps of marble, high halls, and sweeping staircases. Having failed in the dry goods business, Mr. William Corcoran founded a fortune by negotiating government loans for the Mexican War in 1846, and he expanded his fortune in the buying and selling of western lands—all of which enabled him to spend the Civil War in comfort in Paris, buying pictures. The exhibition opening that night at the Corcoran was of the work of a New York artist, Romare Bearden. The crowd, mostly in black tie, was nicely unsegregated, which may have been partly due to the Washington population bias and partly because Bearden himself is Negro. It was the first opening of the Washington art season. There was white wine in the hallways and whisky, in a further room, for art critics. As usual at such affairs the art itself wasn't getting too much attention, although after a preliminary drink I noticed that people who, chatting competitively about their summers in Ischia or Northeast Harbor, entered the two rooms where Bearden's pictures were

hung, came out five or ten minutes later looking rather har-
rowed. And when I left the crowd and plunged in myself, I
saw why.

Bearden called his works "projections." They were the end
result of a process that started with snippets of various photographs, made into collages, and then photographed again and
enlarged to make a black and white "projection" some two feet
by three feet in size. The chopped-up elements within them
were of Negro faces, scattered playing cards, broken windows,
city streets, bottles, southern field cabins, a guitar, a cow, a
cigarette, all masterfully organized to frame a world more real
and poignant than any simple photograph could show. It was a
world of poverty and lost intentions. The pictures were so moving that one was tempted to say, "This isn't art, it's propaganda," though one then wondered if this seemed the case
because it was a long time since one had been moved by contemporary art at all. It seemed, at any rate, an art that caught and
held some crucial aspects of the spreading city.

Frank said, "When I was in Italy during the war there was
this general who thought it would be nice to doll up the officers'
club with a little art. He requisitioned a local man, Sergeant Bill
Mauldin, to come down from the front and paint some murals.
Mauldin did. On either side of the bar he drew a porthole, and
inside these he drew portraits of his two tough rifleman characters, Willie and Joe, staring in at the carousing. They looked
absolutely beat up and resigned to death. This strikes me as the
same kind of confrontation."

Next morning I drove out to Reston. It was a bright, breezy
day, the Fairfax County fields blue-green, the trees dark green,
shaking in the wind. It was autumnal, full of change, and a good
day for looking at Reston's then half-finished first village. Black
cat's-paws chased across the waters of man-made Lake Anne,
which is named after the wife of R. E. Simon, a former president of New York's Carnegie Hall and the developer of Reston.
Horses trotted along the perimeter roads to trails in nearby

woods, and in the small gardens of several already occupied town houses by the lake people mowed their lawns and pruned their roses. I went round with a small group of prospective house buyers. I chatted with a public relations man. I spent ten minutes with a couple who had moved in earlier that summer after their retirement from the foreign service. And after a visit to the golf course and a sandwich in the clubhouse, I decided that if this was, as Mr. Bryant had said, like Beverly Hills, then I had been wrong in my assumption that Beverly Hills was a frightful place.

There is no doubt that Reston, in many ways a smaller version of what Columbia will be, has at the moment an upper-income air that Columbia supposedly will eschew. (Reston has gone through some of the same financing and zoning troubles as Columbia, and shares its Radburn influence and the same golf-course designer, Edmund Ault.) But if the lower and lower-middle classes aren't much in evidence in the as yet thinly settled new town, neither is any pandering to orthodox suburban taste. Indeed, everything I saw at Reston had been designed with style and intelligence, which may perhaps be as limiting a factor as high cost in the creation of a community. That aside, Reston is situated where William Finley's Washington Plan for the Year 2000 calls for a satellite town, and such is the need for new housing in the vicinity it can probably be filled with people who work in Washington, have good jobs, and make money. A private developer like Simon is clearly pressed to seat the well-paying customers first, and then try to find room for some of the workers who would not only be needed there but would remove the atmosphere of the place being a high-class dormitory. Some of the government subsidies laid out in the presently stalled New Towns program would make possible the building of lower-income homes at the start. Certainly Reston has generated interest among all sorts of people. After the grave of the late President Kennedy, it attracts more visitors than any other place in Virginia, running well ahead of Williamsburg, which of course is not free. Roughly three thousand people turn up on Sunday afternoons, few of them to buy houses but simply to wander around and gaze at the wonders Mr. Simon and his architects, with the help of the Gulf Oil Corporation, have wrought.

Gulf was to Simon what Connecticut General is to Rouse—an angel, enabling land to be bought and development on a large enough scale to begin. The land at Reston did not need to be assembled. It came in a ten-square-mile chunk that had been held by one family since the eighteenth century, its trees used for barrel staves and its lush fields for grain to make Virginia Gentleman bourbon. (The distillery remains, a steady influence on Reston's seven other burgeoning industries.) The Gulf money also enabled outlays to be made for such amenities as the lake, at one end of which is a small rectangular harbor that gives its own shape to a line of houses, shops, cafés, and stores running around it, with a dent made by a small circular plaza. At one side of the harbor entrance, like a pharos, rises a fifteen story office and apartment building. It can be seen from a distance over the Fairfax County woods, and with a crane on its summit while it was being built it helped broadcast the news over the countryside that here a new town was being built, which it might be worthwhile going out of one's way to see.

The plan for Reston and the design of stores, houses, and apartments round the harbor were made by the New York firm of Whittlesey and Conklin, who are associated with Wallace-McHarg in the landscape study of lower Manhattan and have worked, in upper Manhattan, on a project similar to Drayton Bryant's Queen Village, where they have attempted to produce a proper mixture of new building, rehabilitation, and slum clearance in a beat-up section of East Harlem. "Mixture" is a term that also fits Reston. Even with piles of bricks and a stray cement mixer sitting at the harbor edge, and a few workmen or tourists wandering through, the unfinished village center had a delightful quality that was partly a result of various buildings that would have different functions, and also a result of different materials—brick, wood, concrete, tile, and steel—used in many visible and tangible ways. A sculptor called Gonzalo Fonseca had built three play sculptures for children to climb on, which were nicely assembled heaps of the materials used in the nearby stores. William Conklin has expressed an interest in finding out what effect this "mix" of uses in a small area will have on people. "Just think what might happen to investors if they saw mothers pushing baby carriages down Wall Street every day. Business might become less abstract, investments more involved in human issues. And who knows what else?"

The people in Reston do not include any stockbrokers with offices there, as yet, though they probably include a fair number of investors. Some 50 percent of the new owners work for the government. A Negro air force colonel has bought a lot on which he is going to build a $50,000 house, and a psychiatrist has taken an apartment high in the fifteen-story apartment tower. Town houses sometimes have a disagreeable connotation to people brought up in or near the long, monotonous row houses of Baltimore and Philadelphia, which are now generally homes of the poor, but here in Reston, Mrs. Smith's town houses by the lake were selling well at prices from $23,000 to $44,000. The effect sought and successfully achieved was somewhat Provençal: varying roof heights, different pastel colors, small balconies, wooden decks, oriel windows, and skylights. Inside, the houses had fireplaces, circular stairs, and a standard of house carpentry that—judging by some of the poorly mitred molding and mantlepieces I saw—didn't seem to be up to the standard of design. This problem didn't seem to have arisen where it might have done more readily, in the construction of the Whittlesey and Conklin, and the Goodman houses, which used a great deal of concrete. The Goodman houses looked resolutely modern and rather small. But grouped around a central common, and with a common parking garage underneath, these houses surprised the members of a house-hunting party I encountered in one of them with their interior space and sensible layout. A three-level house had a kitchen, large living-dining room, and utility room on the ground floor; three bedrooms and bath on the second floor; and a bedroom, bath, and wide roof-terrace on the third. All the houses in the first village could be connected to a master air-conditioning plant, which would help make endurable the muggy Virginia summer. Outside the villages, on the residential roads, the architect-planner's control extended to the lots sold to private builders in that the house location was specified on each lot, so that the house best fits its own ground, and the surrounding houses.

In their Chloethiel Smith town house by the lake, former Consul General and Mrs. Grady gave me some of their feelings about living in Reston. They had run into a few problems, but they didn't feel these were more than any customer got with a brand-new product, hot off the assembly line. Mr. Grady, who now runs a management training business, was annoyed by the light outside the front door for which—four months after they had moved in—the electrician had still not installed a switch by which they could turn it on. The house hadn't been ready on the promised date, and there had been some minor service problems. Starting a new town involved trash collections, plumbing adjustments, police and fire protection. All in all, however, the Gradys were very happy with their home. Mrs. Grady had managed to make most of their bulky antiques fit in, and having acquired a passion for gardening while Mr. Grady had served in England, they were pleased with the results of their work on the front garden. They didn't mind Reston's laws forbidding one to cut down a tree more than four inches in diameter without permission, and with a deck overhanging the lake they thought it very sensible that outboard motors should be banned. (Electric motors, sails, paddles, and oars are all allowed.) Mr. Grady said, "These laws, as I see it, make us free. It's the kind of planning that liberates us from the really strict conformity of the average American suburb. We're sold on it. I go to work a few miles from here, but it seems to me that this place will be ideal for people who work in the new research plants and offices that are coming in. Imagine the joys of not having to commute. It should be enough to make every young man study electronics."

A party of prospective buyers came trooping down the hill, and one bent to sniff the Gradys' roses. They then walked toward the lake, staring through the windows at the furniture and crossing what—in most small towns—would have been marked as the Gradys' back lawn. I asked the Gradys if they minded these intrusions. "Well," said Mrs. Grady, "it's a weekend and that's the worst time. It's generally pretty quiet. Even so, you know I rather enjoy it. We're demonstrating that this is a good place and a good way to live. We're the pioneers."

Frank and I had a late lunch at an Italian restaurant near the Washington vegetable market. Then, full of antipasto and pasta, we took a walk through the Southwest Urban Renewal Area—a clumsy, irritating title for so interesting a section. Renewal, of course, was going on; blocks of apartments stood raw and unfinished; there were piles of construction material, as there were at Reston, though here the roads were not new—they were old, patched, and bumpy, and the grass verges were in need of care. Mrs. Smith, however, had in no way oversold her product. Southwest was indeed a place. One felt it in the very act of walking, which was pleasant there. It was possible to fling out one's arms, to stand and stare at things or people, to admire the views, or to breathe the air that was being blown in fresh gusts from the river. The scale of Washington was well preserved in the wide spaces between the low but solid buildings, and in some ways I thought Mrs. Smith's genius as a master planner was shown in a brighter light than her talent as an architect, at least as demonstrated in the black and silver façade treatment of one set of apartment buildings, which gave the thirtyish impression of being an architectural good-bye to Berlin. Even so, these buildings were more successful than an unrelievedly plain I. M. Pei apartment structure, whose expanse of glass windows at that afternoon hour was totally backed by an expanse of fawn curtains, all closed, and all the same color and tone as the masonry. Here the uniform reaction of the tenants to too much light produced a uniformly drab quality about the building, and made an effective demonstration of the point that what suits office buildings north of the fortieth parallel does not necessarily suit buildings south of it. The high standard of the conjunction and arrangement of the Southwest buildings was better matched by Mrs. Smith as architect in a series of town houses and a great set of brown-red apartments called Harbor Square. These did a finer job of being influenced by the work of the Chicago master Louis Sullivan than some buildings do of being original. Frank and I sat for a while by the edge of a pool and fountain in a spacious courtyard of Tiber Island, another apartment group, and watched a young girl sketching. It was a sight one would see in Paris or Rome and think nothing of; but here, amid these new elements of a city, it was a surprise and a tribute.

Dickens called Washington the city of magnificent intentions, with "broad avenues that begin in nothing and lead nowhere." The intentions are finally being fulfilled, and there are ends and beginnings. There also remain things that would undoubtedly make Major L'Enfant unhappy, such as the temporary World War II buildings on the south side of The Mall, but Washington is a city whose brilliant plan alleviates individual horrors, whether on that scale or the larger one of the House of Representatives' Rayburn office building, the apotheosis of waste and tastelessness. The Mall, having served time as cattle enclosures and vegetable allotments, is the center of that plan, and it has been fully reinstated as the "publick walk" L'Enfant intended this once low-lying land along Tiber Creek to be. It is a fine, wide space channeled between public buildings on either side and blocked dramatically by the scarp rising up to the Capitol, over which the planner of the city wanted to redirect the Tyber waters in a hundred-foot-wide cascade. The grass expanse enables one to walk with a spring. Cars passing along the roads seem small, and the public buildings that delimit the space take on an appropriately symbolic quality—Justice, the National Gallery of Art, Health, the Smithsonian (haven of curiosity and philanthropy); so many monuments to remind one of mortality. Beyond the Capitol on the way to the station are such institutionalized forces of human nature as the Teamsters headquarters and the Standard Oil of New Jersey building. The plan seems to have collected them, and regulated them, and it appears to be not only fine in itself like all great works of art but a diagram of a plan for a greater and farther-reaching city.

Where L'Enfant wanted the cascade to be, I found, instead, General Grant. It was no disappointment. On a raised marble terrace this memorial to the Civil War hero is in larger-than-life-sized parts. On one side a cavalry troop charging; on the other an artillery battery, slogging through hell; and in the center, flanked by four lions, the General on his horse. The sculptor's name is chiseled in the base—Henry Mervin Shrady, 1906. That was the year cubism was born, and although—for that year—Mr. Shrady's art may seem archaic, the result is magnificent. As I climbed up to it, a small Negro boy was spinning round the central base, alternately standing and crouching on a skateboard, whose wheels clattered on the marble paving. Above him the horse rose high, its feet firmly planted, its head cocked to one side. The General, riding it, wore a large field hat whose brim was bent downward on all sides, so that even on this clear October day one felt the incessant rain beating down. Grant himself stared at the ground a dozen yards away. He had the abstracted gaze of someone taking a few seconds out from a long and difficult task to think of anything else—a meal, a drink, a warm bed. Yet there was something in the way he sat that let one know that, although his attention had momentarily wandered, his resolution had not.

20

Last Frontier

THE QUESTION that remains: Do "people" know what is happening; do they care; can they do anything about it?

One day in early December I boarded the Jeep again and made a rapid excursion to Flemington, the chief town of Hunterdon County, in northwest New Jersey, somewhat away from the central megalopolitan stream. I reached Flemington at six at night, and even though it had been dark for some time I knew from the lack of lights along the road that I had been traveling for the last three-quarters of an hour in relatively open country. Indeed, Flemington's main street, dressed overall with Christmas decorations, still had a country flavor that was emphasized by the houses interspersed among the shops, and the barrels and baskets hanging on the porch of the hardware store. I bought that day's Hunterdon County *Democrat* and asked the newspaper store proprietor, a woman, what was a good place to have dinner. She said, "Well, if the Courtesy House is closing, you'll have to eat at the hotel." The Courtesy House, a luncheonette, was closing, sparing me a choice, and so I climbed the wooden steps of the Union Hotel, a long three-story white clapboard structure, with a wooden porch that looked as if it needed a few rocking chairs, and a men's bar handily adjacent to the front desk, so that the same man could tend both. Behind the desk he read his copy of the *Democrat*. Behind the bar he pulled fifteen-cent beers for the regulars, adjusted the tuning of the television set which was showing a Japanese movie about pterodactyls taking over the earth, and mixed me a rum and tonic in an orange juice glass with one lump of ice in it—the price, forty-five cents. I had a feeling the city hadn't got here yet.

This feeling, however, was countered by the scene in the tin-ceilinged dining room, with hand-painted murals of the last Mohicans, where elderly waitresses were running around as they hadn't run since the entire New York press corps was down in Flemington in 1935 for the trial of Hauptmann, convicted kidnapper of the Lindbergh child. At two or three long tables were seated groups of men who looked a shade more prosperous than newspaper reporters. They were, in fact, members of a younger profession; they were planners, and some of their shoptalk and gossip wafted over to me on the breeze stirred-up by the scurrying waitresses: ". . . three thousand acres down Princeton way . . . landowners like a little activity . . . phasing-in new regulations . . ." I thought of something Mrs. Smith had said—"City planning has a sanctimonious air, and it's small wonder that men seek the familiar chaos and reject the unfamiliar, sterile order." Then I considered the statement made by Mr. Heckscher in another part of that pamphlet Mrs. Smith had read to me. "What is the planner? He is, essentially, the man who disciplines the engineers and subjects their power to humane and rational ends. . . . To give full weight to the insights of the planners, that is the first step—and a very important one—in reaffirming the place of individuality in our society. . . . It means not only tempering the arrogance of the engineers. It means also, very often, limiting the profits of the speculator. It means putting long-range values above the enticements of immediate gain. . . . The planners may in the end do more for us than the psychiatrists."

The planners were in Flemington, as I was, to attend a meeting that night at the County Agricultural Building, and they were welcomed in an editorial in the paper I read while I had dinner. I read the *Democrat* rather the way I'd read the New-town *Bee*, and the quick impression of the area I got from it (which was bolstered by the reason for the meeting itself) was of farming country feeling the first threat of the out-reaching city. There was a lot of farming news in the paper, and an agricultural machinery firm was having a sale of Ford tractors, advertising the fact in the sort of display ad that in most towns in the Northeast would be used for family cars. The local farmers' cooperative was offering "best prices" for local wheat and corn. The average price of farmland in New Jersey is the highest in the country ($640 per acre), which is a direct result of the pressure of urbanization, and it was the sort of price beginning to govern in Flemington, where real-estate activity also figured highly in the news. Acreage was in demand by several developers for housing sites. A group of residents of Raritan township, not far from Flemington, were seeking support for an ordinance establishing a minimum lot size of 150 front feet by 200 feet in depth. Although they were written up in a news story, the group had also taken an ad to say, "We are afraid that with sewers there will come smaller lots, mass developments, lower well tables, increased school costs, and an undesirable change in the character of our community." The jetport—by now an old friend—was apparently also breathing down the neck of Hunterdon County, for despite a promise from Governor Hughes to shoo it away, the *Democrat* seemed to think that the collision between the two airliners in the holding pattern over Danbury would renew the menace. The editorial welcoming the planning and zoning experts to the meeting declared that, although Hunterdon had so far been far enough away from the big city to avoid most of its bad effects, the crush was coming, and the paper trusted that when it came, the county would be ready for it with a complete set of planning and zoning laws.

The County Agricultural Building on Route 69, just outside the town, was a large, solidly built modern building, and by 8 P.M. nearly a hundred people had collected in the basement auditorium. In one corner stood a Christmas tree with colored lights. There was something of the atmosphere of the town meetings we have in Stonington, though a good deal less dramatic and emotional. Mr. Wiles, of the Hunterdon County Planning Board, opened the proceedings by saying that they were all there to learn something, thanks to the New Jersey Federation of Planning Officials, which for the past twenty-seven years had been attempting to give local planners and zoners the benefit of its collective experience. Mr. Haas, of Flemington, outlined the situation of Hunterdon as a rural area that had the chance, and he thought the willingness, to learn how to cope with the onslaught before it arrived. The basic problem of planning was that God had stopped making land some time ago, but was still making people.

A speech from Mrs. Griswold might have heightened the atmosphere, but there seemed to be a quiet sense of urgency at the seminars that took place in each corner of the auditorium, where a quartet of experts talked and answered questions about subdivisions, zoning problems, open space, and the functions of planning boards. People with a particular concern found the appropriate group, while others moved from group to group. Afterward, a summary of each group's proceedings was delivered to the whole audience. I moved around for a while, and found that some problems—such as septic tanks—were being mentioned in several seminars at once; subdivision committees of town planning and zoning boards were being advised to go out and actually walk the land on which a decision had to be made, rather than just studying the contours on a map; zoning adjustment board members were learning about such technicalities as setting time limits on variances and how to handle "hardships," especially when they came in the common form of "I gotta sell my lot, I need the money"; and such factors in the control of change were discussed as taxation, health laws (enforcing sewers and treatment plants), and the purchase of land by the county for use as future parks—something that Bergen County had had the foresight to do in 1946. A solid core of interest was displayed at the seminar discussing open space, for clearly what preoccupied most of the ordinary citizens who had turned up at the meeting was how to keep Hunterdon County green. The expert running this seminar was named Alvin Gershen. He had been a house builder before he became a housing consultant, and he did a fine job of drawing forth the people who didn't know quite what density they wanted, though they wanted space, and the directions in how to acquire that space and make it truly useful. Without appearing to be promoting them, Mr. Gershen told of ways counties could buy private golf courses, which were being gobbled up all over Jersey, and of the economic advantages for a builder in cluster housing, which left more open space for everyone. He noted the trend toward campuses that the whole town could use around elementary schools, and he spent some time on the details of flood-plain zoning, which helped preserve marshes, water meadows, and river valleys. He said that he was shy of using the term "master plan," which made some people think of the Russians, but it was important that they know that a community had to have a master plan committed to paper before it could receive federal grants for open space, or indeed any such aid. He reminded them, as Ian McHarg had earlier reminded me, that successful farmers had been master planning for a hundred years.

Afterward, I heard a lawyer who had led the seminar on zoning problems say that, ten years before, he had nearly been run out of town when he came to the Flemington Grange to attempt to talk local officials into planning and zoning. Hunterdon County now had planning and zoning, and the number of citizens at the meeting seemed to indicate that the county intended to learn how to make its regulations work. Planners have a saying, "People don't mind doing the planning, they just don't want to be planned for," and I detected in the modest applause that closed the meeting a note of unsanctimonious concern that the people there didn't want to seem to be planning for the people who were not. As far as I was concerned, however, they were showing that they recognized that, under the increasing impact of the city, things were getting unhealthy, and therefore they were taking the county's medicine for it. I felt that their applause was not only for the experts but for themselves. It was deserved.

Bibliography

SUMNER CHILTON POWELL. *Puritan Village*. New York: Anchor, 1965
M.I.T. STUDENT PROJECT. *The Glideway System*. 1965
THOMAS JEFFERSON. *Notes on Virginia*. New York: Harper, 1964
JEAN GOTTMANN, *Megalopolis*. New York: Twentieth Century Fund, 1961
H. G. WELLS. *Anticipations*. London, 1902
A. A. ARCHAMBAULT. *Mill Village*. Boston: Humphries, 1943
JOHN COOLIDGE. *Mill and Mansion*. New York: Columbia, 1942
H-R HITCHCOCK. *Rhode Island Architecture*. Providence, 1939
CHRISTOPHER TUNNARD. *The City of Man*, New York, 1953
WILLIAM CHUTE (ed). *The American Scene* (including *Madam Knight's Diary*). New York: Bantam, 1964
COLIN BUCHANAN. *Traffic in Towns*. London: Penguin, 1963
CAPTAIN MARRYAT. *Diary in America*. London: Longmans, 1839
ROGER TORY PETERSON. *A Field Guide to the Birds: Eastern Land and Water Birds*. Boston: Houghton, 1964
G. W. PIERSON. *Tocqueville in America*. New York: Anchor, 1959
M. AND L. WHITE. *The Intellectual versus the City*. New York: Mentor, 1964
WM. COBBETT. *Rural Rides*. London: Reeves and Turner, 1908
ROBERT C. WOOD. *1400 Governments*. New York: Anchor, 1964
ROBERT C. WOOD. *Suburbia*. Boston: Houghton, 1958
J. T. ADAMS. *The Founding of New England*. Boston: Little Brown, 1949
T. E. HULME. *Further Speculations*. University of Nebraska, 1962
LEWIS MUMFORD. *The City in History*. New York: Harcourt, 1961
F. J. TURNER. *The Frontier in American History*. New York: Holt, 1964
GUSTAV KOBBÉ. *The New Jersey Coast and Pines*. Short Hills, 1889
WALT WHITMAN. *Complete Poetry and Selected Prose*. London: The Nonesuch Press
JOHN T. CUNNINGHAM. *The New Jersey Shore*. Rutgers, 1958
GEORGE MOSS, JR. *Nauvoo to the Hook*. Jervey Close, 1964
AUGUST HECKSCHER. *The Individual and the Mass*. New York: The Twentieth Century Fund, 1965
CONSTANCE McL. GREEN. *Washington, Village and Capital*, Vol. 1; and *Capital City*, Vol. 2. Princeton University Press, 1962-63

A Guide to the Architecture of Washington, D.C. New York: Praeger, 1965

PAMPHLETS

Wetlands of the United States. Department of Interior. Fish and Wildlife Service. Circular 39

Waterfowl Tomorrow. Department of Interior. Fish and Wildlife Service.

The Poverty of Abundance. New York: Planned Parenthood League

Sidney Goldstein and Kurt Mayer. *Metropolitanization and Population Change in Rhode Island.* Providence, 1961

Nathan Wetten and A. Green. *Ethnic Group Relations in a Rural Area of Connecticut.* Storrs: University of Connecticut, 1943

PROJECT REPORTS AND NEWSLETTERS OF

Rhode Island Statewide Planning Program
Hudson River Valley Commission
Connecticut General Life Insurance Company
Columbia
Penjerdel
Regional Plan Association
Reston
Wallace-McHarg Associates
Open Space Action Commitee
The Sierra Club

MAGAZINES AND PERIODICALS

Architectural Forum. August/September, 1964
Past and Present. December, 1964
Maritimes. Summer, 1965
New England Construction. August 2, 1965
Scientific American. September, 1965
Harpers. November, 1964
Annals of the American Academy of Political Science. March, 1964
Connection. June, 1965
New Republic. 1965–66
Look. January 30, 1962
Architectural Record. February, 1965; March, 1965
Regional Plan News. December, 1965
Life. December 24, 1965
Pequot Conservationist. January, 1966
International Science and Technology. October, 1965

NEWSPAPERS

Worcester *Evening Gazette*
Providence *Journal*

New London *Day*
Hartford *Courant*
Meriden *Morning Record*
Newtown *Bee*
Stonington *Compass*
The New York Times
New York *Herald-Tribune*
Bergen County *Record*
Hunterdon County *Democrat*
Philadelphia *Sunday Bulletin*
Baltimore *Sun*
Washington *Post*
Washington *Star*

Index

Princeton

Philadelphia

Baltimore

Washington